THE
DU MAURIERS

JUST AS
THEY WERE

Anne Hall

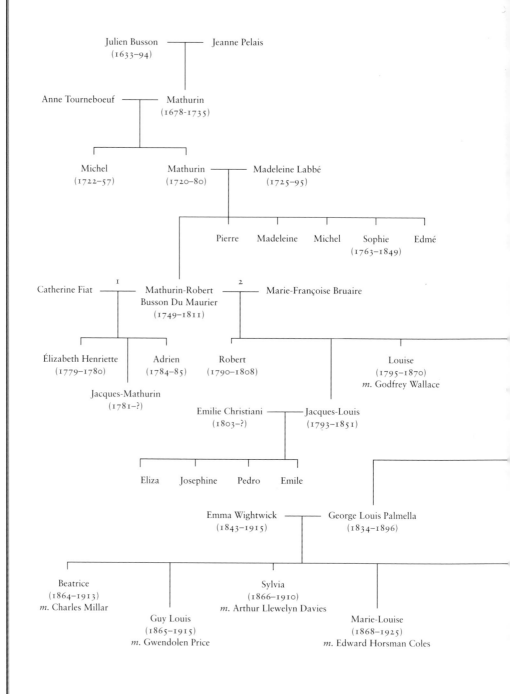

Julien Busson — Jeanne Pelais
(1633–94)

Anne Tourneboeuf — Mathurin
(1678-1735)

Michel   Mathurin — Madeleine Labbé
(1722–57)   (1720–80)   (1725–95)

Pierre   Madeleine   Michel   Sophie   Edmé
(1763-1849)

Catherine Fiat —1— Mathurin-Robert —2— Marie-Françoise Bruaire
                   Busson Du Maurier
                   (1749–1811)

Élizabeth Henriette   Adrien   Robert   Louise
(1779–1780)   (1784–85)   (1790–1808)   (1795–1870)
                                                m. Godfrey Wallace

Jacques-Mathurin
(1781–?)

Emilie Christiani — Jacques-Louis
(1803–?)   (1793–1851)

Eliza   Josephine   Pedro   Emile

Emma Wightwick — George Louis Palmella
(1843–1915)   (1834–1896)

Beatrice   Sylvia
(1864–1913)   (1866–1910)
m. Charles Millar   m. Arthur Llewelyn Davies

        Guy Louis   Marie-Louise
        (1865–1915)   (1868–1925)
        m. Gwendolen Price   m. Edward Horsman Coles

THE
DU MAURIER
FAMILY

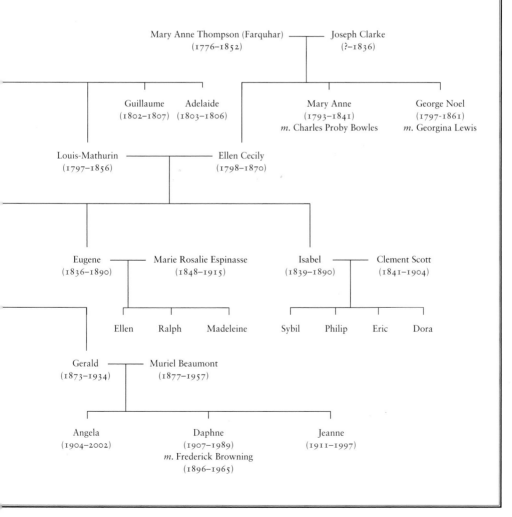

Mary Anne Thompson (Farquhar) ——— Joseph Clarke
(1776–1852)   (?–1836)

Guillaume   Adelaide
(1802–1807)   (1803–1806)

Mary Anne
(1793–1841)
m. Charles Proby Bowles

George Noel
(1797-1861)
m. Georgina Lewis

Louis-Mathurin ——— Ellen Cecily
(1797–1856)   (1798–1870)

Eugene ——— Marie Rosalie Espinasse
(1836–1890)   (1848–1915)

Isabel ——— Clement Scott
(1839–1890)   (1841–1904)

Ellen   Ralph   Madeleine

Sybil   Philip   Eric   Dora

Gerald ——— Muriel Beaumont
(1873–1934)   (1877–1957)

Angela
(1904–2002)

Daphne
(1907–1989)
m. Frederick Browning
(1896–1965)

Jeanne
(1911–1997)

Published in 2018 by Unicorn,
an imprint of Unicorn Publishing Group LLP
101 Wardour Street
London
W1F 0UG

www.unicornpublishing.org

ISBN 978-1-911604-09-9

Designed by Ocky Murray
Printed in Hong Kong for Latitude Press

CONTENTS

INTRODUCTION

*We ... like to see what our sires and grandsires were
like, and our grand-dams when they were young. Our
descendants will probably like to see us – just as we are.*
George Du Maurier, 'The Illustrating of Books. From the Serious
Artist's Point of View' II, *The Magazine of Art*, September 1890

Daphne Du Maurier traced her quest to discover her French ancestors'
story to 'sometime long after the [Second World] War' when, because she
was married and had more room in her house than her sisters, her late
father's furniture was shipped to her in Cornwall.[1]

Gerald Du Maurier's belongings included a shabby leather case containing 'the family Luck': a crystal tumbler engraved with the fleur-de-lys
and bearing the arms of King Louis XV.

Daphne remembered the Luck from her childhood, when it was taken
out of its case and displayed on special occasions. According to family
tradition, the Du Mauriers' émigré ancestor, a gentleman glass-blower,
had made the tumbler at the family glassworks in Anjou, now destroyed.
Gerald inherited the glass from his father George, the émigré's grandson,
and now it had come to George's granddaughter, Daphne.

When she then looked through George Du Maurier's bureau, which
she had also inherited, Daphne discovered an important clue to the
past: a ten-page letter headed 'Busson family', handwritten in French
by Sophie Duval née Busson, telling the story of her parents and her
brothers and sisters. Another hand had scored through some of the more

The crystal tumbler the Du Mauriers inherited from their French ancestor (left)

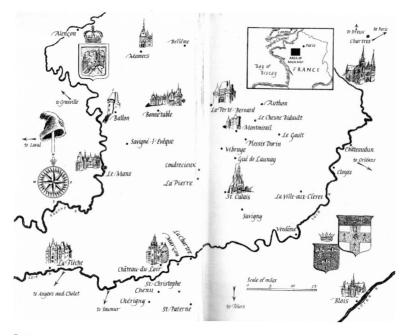

Endpapers of the Doubleday edition of *The Glass-Blowers*

interesting details concerning Sophie's eldest brother, the émigré. Daphne began piecing together the story of the black sheep of the Busson family, who immigrated to London during the French Revolution and added the suffix 'Du Maurier' to his surname. She ended up making several trips to central-western France to verify the information given in the letter and to try to find out more.

Accompanied by her younger sister Jeanne and by Jeanne's companion Noël Welch, Daphne made the first of these trips in October 1955. She and her friend Ronald Armstrong, a retired diplomat with a fluent command of French, also spent a few days carrying out research in Tours.

Daphne found the villages and former sites of glass factories that were mentioned in Sophie's letter, including the modest Le Maurier farmhouse on the estate of Chérigny in Chenu where her émigré ancestor was born. She also visited the château Du Maurier in La Fontaine-Saint-Martin, which had once belonged to the Aubéry Du Maurier family. The current owner was away at the time but they corresponded and Daphne learned he was a former president of the Maine Historical and Archaeological Society. Subsequent to her visit, he had published an article on the Du Mauriers' descent from glass-blowers in Sarthe, specifying that their suffix came from the Maurier farmhouse at Chérigny rather than from his château, about 30 km away.[2]

After her trip Daphne wrote to her friend Oriel Malet that 'I simply adored it, and adored all my part of the country, Sarthe and the Loir-et-Cher, and I found all the places of my forebears, birth and death certificates as well, and the proper real Maurier and everything, which was so exciting. Jeanne and Noël were very nice to be with....'[3]

When, several years later, she began writing *The Glass-Blowers*, Daphne decided to open it with a prologue. Sophie Duval meets her English nephew, informs him that his late father was an 'incorrigible farceur' and that Le Maurier was only a farmhouse, gives the crystal tumbler to her great-nephew George and promises to send him an account of family history.[4] Daphne explained the structure of her novel in a letter to Oriel,

> I shall make it be told by my old Gt.gt.gt.-Aunt person, to her nephew (my great-grandfather), who had been born in London during the Revolution, and came back to France, wanting to know about his family, and his father etc. (all this is true!). He gets a shock when he finds out that they were all for the new régime, and not aristocrats at all! This will happen in a sort of *avant-propos* [foreword], and the first chapter will be the old aunt talking, as though to a nephew, as she tells the whole story of what they were and so on.[5]

Daphne had discovered Sophie's letter, and she endorsed Sophie's demystification of family history by making her the narrator of this fleshed-out version of the Bussons' story.

Just one uncertainty remained: George Du Maurier had inherited both the crystal tumbler and his great-aunt Sophie's bowdlerised letter. He had even annotated the margins of the letter, proudly indicating his relationship to the French ancestors named, and signing his additions.

More problematically, he had also written a novel based partly on French family history, whose tone was anything but demystificatory. Daphne commented to Oriel:

> One terribly wants to get at the *truth*. Which is why I want to know so desperately *how* my Bussons lived, instead of being content to Gondal [imagine] them. It must be something to do with the age we live in. Imagination, yes, but so that you use it to *perceive* the past, and relive it.
>
> I have been looking into my grandfather's *Peter Ibbetson* again, and it's queer how he had these same feelings about forebears that I have

– an almost agonized interest – and how part of his dream in the book was to *become* them in the past, and how they became *him* in the future. I can't think why he did not go out to Sarthe and find out about them *truly*, instead of Gondaling them, for they are there, in embryo, in *Peter Ibbetson*, but he has Gondalled them wrong – making them aristocrats instead of bourgeois – I s'pose a natural Victorian reluctance to be a bit honky![6]

Daphne was entirely right to sense that her grandfather shared her 'almost agonized interest' in their forebears, and that the main ones are indeed 'there, in embryo,' in his first novel *Peter Ibbetson*.

However, on at least the two occasions that he relates in *The Martian*, the last of his three semi-autobiographical novels, George Du Maurier had in fact gone 'out to Sarthe and [found] out about [his forebears] *truly*'. When he was about thirteen he spent his summer holiday with his great-aunt Sophie, in the last years of her life, and had every opportunity to conclude that she, her son and his family were bourgeois, not aristocrats. As an adult in the 1870s, he also made a second trip to Sarthe.

In *Ibbetson*, George Du Maurier made his fictional alter ego's ancestors aristocrats instead of bourgeois because his purpose was to explore the psychosexual underpinnings of the aristocratic fantasy that he perceived as common to both branches of his family tree: the maternal English branch as well as the paternal French one. Where Daphne Du Maurier unmasked her French forefather as an 'incorrigible farceur', in *Ibbetson* George Du Maurier took the opposite approach and magnified the family trait of *folie des grandeurs* to an extreme.[7]

In the manner of a dream, George's hero's so-called pedigree consists in a wildly impossible conflation of a handful of borrowings from Sophie Duval's historically accurate letter, with geographical, historical and literary references to unrelated aristocratic figures. Significantly, Peter and his female alter ego Mary only discover the pedigree – and their kinship – in the novel's final section, which takes place after Peter has been sentenced to death for parricide, and in the climax of his and Mary's joint 'true dream'.[8]

The last page of *Peter Ibbetson* alerts the reader that the 'voluminous and hastily penned reminiscences' that make up the novel were written 'in the cipher [Peter and Mary] invented together in [their] dream'.[9] George Du Maurier signals that his novel must be unravelled, translated and put in order – in a word, deciphered – before it is possible to glimpse its hidden meaning and, in particular, his interpretation of family history.

In the course of her career Daphne Du Maurier wrote four family histories: *Gerald: A Portrait* (1934), *The Du Mauriers* (1937), *Mary Anne* (1954) and *The Glass-Blowers* (1963). *Peter Ibbetson*'s cast of characters already included the principal protagonists of *The Du Mauriers*, *Mary Anne* and *The Glass-Blowers*, and in more than embryonic form. Yet, because George Du Maurier wrote his first novel in a cipher, these figures are disguised to the extent that readers – including Daphne – have not identified them, nor have the biographers working in Daphne's wake. The historian who wants to get at the *truth*, as Daphne Du Maurier put it, to portray the Du Mauriers just as they were, in George Du Maurier's phrase, must therefore revisit the five generations that span from the émigré to Daphne, comparing their representations in various periods and from various points of view.

My book tells the Du Mauriers' story from the beginning, adding new information and also attempting to remove some of the veneer that has accumulated. Chapter One summarises what researchers have discovered about Mathurin-Robert Busson, who immigrated to London in 1789 and added the suffix 'Du Maurier', subsequent to his portrayal in *The Glass-Blowers*. Leaving his second wife and their six young children in London, he returned to France in the last years of his life and died there.

Chapter Two focuses on the émigré's three surviving children, who also returned to Europe at the Restoration. Mathurin-Robert's oldest son Jacques-Louis settled in Hamburg, while his daughter Louise and his younger son Louis-Mathurin, a talented singer and aspiring inventor, both married in Paris: their spouses came from highly colourful British families who had their own reasons for living in France. Considerable new historical information has come to light since Daphne's *The Du Mauriers*, *Mary Anne* and *The Glass-Blowers*, and Paul Berry's *By Royal Appointment: A Biography of Mary Ann* [sic] *Clarke, Mistress of the Duke of York* (1970).

In the context of Daphne Du Maurier's writings on her grandfather and Leonee Ormond's biography (1969), I devote the third and longest chapter to George Du Maurier's life. My chapter pays close attention to his portrayal of his early years in Passy in *Ibbetson* and *The Martian*, his Quartier Latin year in *Trilby*, his subsequent stays in Belgium and Germany, and his definitive return to London in *The Martian*; and also to the autobiographical aspects of his weekly *Punch* cartoons.

Two biographers have focused on Gerald Du Maurier: Daphne in *Gerald: A Portrait* and 'The Matinée Idol' (1973), and James Harding in *Gerald Du Maurier: The Last Actor-Manager* (1989). Gerald also figures in the memoirs of his daughters Angela and Daphne – *It's Only the Sister* (1951), *Old Maids Remember* (1965) and *Growing Pains: The Shaping of a Writer* (1977) – as well as in the memoirs of many of the actors who worked with him. Although Gerald was not a writer, he occupied a pivotal position between two authors of family history novels – his father and his daughter – and I will attempt to determine what he did and did not transmit.

Thanks to a variety of sources, not only her own memoir *Growing Pains*, but also *Letters from Menabilly* (1993) edited by her friend Oriel Malet, her biography by Margaret Forster (1993) and Jane Dunn's *Daphne Du Maurier and her Sisters* (2013), Daphne's story is by far the most familiar to readers today. Chapter Five begins after Gerald Du Maurier's death in 1934 and discusses the four volumes of family history his daughter went on to write.

Finally, Chapter Six returns to *Ibbetson* to decipher George Du Maurier's hidden interpretation of family history and then briefly considers the extent to which *Trilby* and *The Martian* express the same underlying fantasy.

CHAPTER ONE

MATHURIN-ROBERT BUSSON, THE FIRST DU MAURIER

*This young man had a charming appearance. He had
blond hair, blue eyes, an elegant turn of mind and he had
been raised with great care. His life was stormy
and somewhat adventurous.*

Sophie Duval, extract from her letter headed 'Busson family'[10]

The Du Mauriers were originally called Busson, a fairly common surname in central-western France. Their forefather, Mathurin-Robert
Busson, was born on 7 September 1749 in the village of Chenu – also
called Saint-Martin-de-Chenu – in the province of Anjou (the village is
at the southern extremity of what is now the Department of Sarthe).
Mathurin-Robert's mother, Madeleine Labbé, was the daughter of a
huissier royal (bailiff) from the neighbouring village of Saint-Christo-
phe-en-Touraine, now known as Saint-Christophe-sur-le-Nais.[11]

A century after Mathurin-Robert's birth, in the last years of her life,
his younger sister Sophie wrote two letters on family history for the benefit of her brother's English descendants. In one of them she devoted
an affectionate but frustratingly brief footnote to a description of their
mother: 'She was a superb woman, hardy, with a masculine character.
She was nicknamed *la reine de Hongrie* [the queen of Hungary].'[12]

Despite what Daphne Du Maurier wrote in *The Glass-Blowers*,
Madeleine Labbé's husband, the glass-blower Mathurin Busson,
would not have been a childhood acquaintance.[13] Sophie's letters fail
to mention her father's birthplace, which was the same as her own:
the village of Coudrecieux in Maine (also now in Sarthe), 30 km east
of Le Mans and 50 km north of Chenu. Their Busson ancestors had

lived there since at least the time of the first parish registers in the sixteenth century.

Mathurin Busson and Madeleine Labbé

Mathurin, born in 1720, and his brother Michel, born in 1722, lost their mother, the former Anne Tournebœuf, in early childhood. Their father, Mathurin senior, was a journeyman hemp weaver who died just as the marquis du Luart – the Lord of Coudrecieux – received royal authorisation to create a glass factory on his estate of La Pierre (literally, the stone). The name of the estate and glass factory was said to refer to a megalith nearby.

The glass factory would employ the Busson brothers and many others. The boys' grandfather, Julien Busson III, had been a master carpenter. After the younger Mathurin learned the trade of glass-blowing in the first years of La Pierre, his employer Henri de Cherbon – the *gentilhomme verrier* (gentleman glass-blower) who leased the foundry – sent him, in succession, to the three other similar operations that he directed in his native Anjou.

Mathurin Busson went first to the Vaujours glass factory in the defunct village of Chouzé-le-Sec (now part of the town of Château-la-Vallière) and then on to the newly founded Chérigny glass factory in Chenu. Mathurin married Madeleine Labbé in 1747 in Saint-Christophe; their marriage contract states that the bride received 100 livres from her parents (her inheritance from her late mother) for her bridal gown; the groom brought 800 livres (including 500 *louis d'or*).[14]

The Bussons lived on the estate of Chérigny in the farmhouse Le Maurier, not far from the foundry. Their first child was named Mathurin after his father and grandfather, and Robert after his godfather Robert Brossard, a master glass-blower; his godmother was Madeleine Labbé's sister, Anne.

The modest farmhouse Le Maurier – which is still part of the Chérigny estate, a short walk from the *pigeonnier* (dovecote), the foundry and the château – is the source of the suffix that Mathurin-Robert Busson would add to his surname after immigrating to England in the Revolutionary period, and that his English descendants would make famous. In 1752 Mathurin-Robert's brother, Pierre, was also born at Le Maurier.

In *The Glass-Blowers*, Daphne Du Maurier described Mathurin-Robert's dominant personality trait as *folie des grandeurs*, and imagined it had its origin in his petting and fondling by the young marquise de Cherbon at the château de Chérigny.[15] In fact, Henri de Cherbon was not a

Le Maurier, a farmhouse on the estate of Chérigny. The glass-factory
can be seen to the left of the château

marquis, and the young M. and Mme de Cherbon – Henri's nephew and
his wife – were not living at Chérigny in this period.

However, Robert Brossard, Mathurin Busson's associate and
Mathurin-Robert's godfather, was himself the grandson of a *gentilhomme verrier*, and he may have had some influence on his godson. Brossard's father, a glass merchant in Le Mans, also called Robert Brossard,

From inside the glass-factory, a view of Chérigny's dovecote

was the illegitimate son of Robert de Brossard, sieur de l'Aire du Bois, and his servant, of La Lande-sur-Eure in the Perche region.

The Brossards were one of the four most prominent French families of *gentilshommes verriers*, and said to descend from a royal mistress. In the last years of his life Robert Brossard directed a glass factory in Apremont-sur-Allier in the Berry region, where he remarried and restored the particle to his name.

Returning to the Bussons, from the farmhouse Le Maurier on the estate of Chérigny the family travelled about 30 km further south to the original Cherbon glass factory in Continvoir; Mathurin's brother Michel, a glass engraver, joined them from Coudrecieux. The two brothers and their respective families then relocated to Vaujours, where Mathurin and Madeleine's first daughter was born, and named for her mother.

In 1756 the Busson brothers left Henri de Cherbon's employ, to lease the La Brûlonnerie glass factory, over 70 km northeast of Vaujours near the village of Busloup, in the Vendômois region. The brothers took over the management of the foundry from Étienne de Menou, a Protestant *gentilhomme verrier* who let La Brûlonnerie because he knew he was dying. Mathurin Busson's third son, Michel, was born in Busloup and shortly thereafter his brother Michel, the glass engraver, died there.[16]

Mathurin-Robert was eleven in 1760, when his father and two associates – Louis Demeré from Château-la-Vallière and Eloy LeRiche from La Ville-aux-Clercs, near Busloup – signed a nine-year lease of the La Pierre castle and glass factory in Coudrecieux – where Mathurin Busson had been born and where he first learned his trade.

One can only imagine the reactions of Mathurin Busson's relatives and friends when, at the age of forty, he returned to his place of birth and resided in the château as master of the glass factory, for he was not a nobleman but simply the son of a journeyman weaver and the grandson of a master carpenter. Perhaps growing up at the château de La Pierre played a role in his eldest son's *folie des grandeurs*.

The Bussons' two youngest children, their daughters Sophie and Edmé, were born in Coudrecieux. By the end of the lease Mathurin Busson's two associates had died. He signed a second nine-year lease, so that he and his family spent a total of eighteen years there.

During his last years at La Pierre, Mathurin Busson put his eldest son in charge of the Montmirail glass factory in the village of Le Plessis-Dorin, about 20 km north of Coudrecieux.

Sophie Duval's account of her brother's early years

The only first-hand account of Mathurin-Robert describes his life in the years leading up to the Revolution. For his sister Sophie survived her siblings and, when she was in her eighties, met one of her 'English' nephews: Mathurin-Robert's son Louis-Mathurin, the father of George Du Maurier. In what would appear to be an expression of his own *folie des grandeurs*, Louis-Mathurin scored through certain passages of Sophie's letters; these have been placed in brackets here.

After describing her brother in the passage excerpted as epigraph above, Sophie began her anecdotes concerning him as follows, referring to herself in the third person:

Without his father's knowledge, Mathurin-Robert had joined the Arquebusiers, an officers' corps that only served at the château for three months a year. Thus his father believed he was at the glass factory whilst he was actually performing his service for the King.

Having travelled to Paris with his daughter Sophie, today the widow of M. Duval, M. Busson the father stopped to talk to one of his merchants in the rue St-Honoré. All of a sudden a young officer appeared

Charcoal drawing of the château de La Pierre, before its reconstruction
in the nineteenth century

who, upon seeing M. Busson, made a pirouette, jumped over a stream
and distanced himself rapidly. M. Busson, who had noticed him, was
completely dumbfounded and said to his interlocutor: 'If I did not
know that my son was at the Montmirail glass factory, I would think I
had recognised him in the person of the officer you just saw flee.'

It was indeed he, and Mlle Sophie Busson, the only one who was
in his confidence, had actually recognised him, but she took pains not
to enlighten her father regarding the conduct of the brother whom she
loved so well and whom she had so many reasons to love, since it was
to him alone that she owed the [knowledge she had acquired in gram-
mar, geography, history, music, etc.]

The day of the premiere of *The Marriage of Figaro*, the eldest Busson brother wanted his dear sister Sophie, who was due to leave Paris
the following day, to attend the play. He took her to the theatre, and

when he could not find a seat for her, he caught a glimpse of the Duke of Orleans alone in his box. Without communicating his idea to his sister, he approached the prince's box, knocked on the door and made a Masonic sign. He explained his predicament to the Duke of Orleans and asked for a seat.[17]

The prince presented his hand to Mlle Sophie and invited them both into his box. The curtain went up; the play began and ended without Mlle Sophie seeing or hearing anything, she was speechless at finding herself next to a person wearing a large blue ribbon, whom she took for the King, [and amidst great ladies in panniers and flounces.][18]

One day the eldest Busson brother gave a ball for the ladies of Chartres that cost him eighteen hundred francs; he made himself pass for an ambassador of Morocco. [Where did he take the money to provide for this expense and others? In the product of the cases of glassware that he sent to the Paris merchants.]

M. Busson's first wife was a very pretty *Parisienne* who brought him a dowry of one hundred thousand francs. He took the Rougemont glass factory, in the Department of Loir-et-Cher, [where he spent money madly and went through his wife's dowry in a period of eleven months.][19]

Daphne Du Maurier expanded upon these amusing anecdotes in *The Glass-Blowers*: they contributed to her convincing depiction of Mathurin-Robert's *folie des grandeurs*.

Nonetheless, Sophie's account contained a few inaccuracies; after all she was over eighty when she recorded her memories of events that occurred in her youth. Mathurin-Robert married his first wife Catherine Fiat, the daughter of a Parisian silk merchant, in Saint-Sauveur church in Paris on 21 July 1777. Their marriage contract mentions a dowry of 10,000 – not 100,000 – francs.

The glass factory Mathurin-Robert acquired shortly before his marriage was not Rougemont but La Brûlonnerie in the Vendômois, which his father had leased from 1756 to 1760. He used his wife's dowry to make the necessary improvements. In particular, Mathurin-Robert built a dam that still survives, although the site of the former glass factory is completely overgrown by forest. In 1800, Mathurin-Robert's youngest brother Michel and youngest sister Edmé would use their inheritance from their mother to repurchase the rights to the La Brûlonnerie glass factory. They relocated it to the grounds of the nearby château de Rougemont; this probably explains Sophie's reference to the latter.

George Du Maurier apparently associated the Rougemont glass

factory, located in the village of St-Jean-Froidmentel, with a local leg-end.[20] Montigny-le-Gannelon, a more ancient castle, is situated on a bluff high above the Loir River, a few kilometres upstream. The Lord of Montigny is said to have returned from the Crusades to discover his wife was attempting to drown eight of her children, born during his absence, in the Loir. After rescuing the children, the lord punished his wife by ducking her in the Loir. On emerging from the river, the Lady of Montigny said 'Froidmentel' – suggesting *froid manteau* (cold cloak) – giving their name to the twin villages of St-Jean-Froidmentel and St-Claude-Froidmentel.

From the provinces to Paris

In March 1778, Mathurin-Robert Busson bought a boutique in Paris in the Palais-Royal with an evocative name – *Le Lustre Royal* – that sold objects made of crystal such as mirrors, chandeliers and jewellery. The same month he sold the La Brûlonnerie glass factory to the business associates Pierre Busson – his younger brother – and a M. Rouillon – the former owner of *Le Lustre Royal*.

Eleven months later, in February 1779, the Parisian merchant repur-chased *Le Lustre Royal* and rented La Brûlonnerie back to Mathurin-Rob-ert, leaving him the option of buying it back within the next two years, if he had the means. At this point the young glassmaker had probably exhausted his wife's dowry, since he sublet the glass factory to a M. Caumont, a Paris-ian upholsterer and *valet du Roi* (valet to the king) and his associates.

In this same period Mathurin-Robert accepted a position at a glass factory in the village of Villeneuve-St-Georges, now one of the eastern suburbs of Paris. His daughter Élizabeth-Henriette was baptised there in September 1779. In March of the following year, Mathurin-Robert made the mistake that would eventually lead to his incarceration at the Prison de la Force.

He bought the Villeneuve-St-Georges glass factory from its owner, pay-ing 6,000 livres and mortgaging the La Brûlonnerie glass factory to guar-antee the remainder of the purchase price. In so doing Mathurin-Robert forgot – or perhaps chose to overlook – the fact that he no longer owned La Brûlonnerie.

Mathurin-Robert's young daughter died in April, followed in June 1780 by his father, Mathurin Busson. Each of M. Busson's six children received just over 12,000 livres from the estate, however Mathurin-Rob-ert had already been given his share when he married. Mathurin Busson's widow, the former Madeleine Labbé, stayed on at the Montmirail glass factory for several years after his death and managed it on behalf of her three youngest children, who were still minors. She then returned to her native Touraine.

In her letter Sophie mentioned two other business associates of Mathurin-Robert in this period: they would appear to be Achille-Henri Cannet, a merchant from Amiens, and Vincent-Léon Cagnon, who had begun directing the La Pierre glass factory in Coudrecieux in 1780. Jacques-Mathurin, the only child from Mathurin-Robert's first marriage to reach adulthood, was born in Paris on 17 April 1781.

In the course of her research in France, Daphne Du Maurier came across a letter from Mathurin-Robert to M. de Montaran, *Intendant de Commerce*, in which he summarised his professional activities. Referring to himself in the third person, Mathurin-Robert wrote:

> The sieur Busson has the honour of informing you that, as the first Frenchman to have acquired the art of engraving crystal and to have formed the first glass foundries that existed in Paris in the years 1779 to 1780 and 1781, he has experienced various misfortunes caused by the enormous expenses of his associates of whom he has been the victim.
>
> Through the efforts he has made to repair his losses, in 1783 he obtained permission to establish a furnace in Versailles and was then informed of the competing intentions of the *Manufacture de la Reine* [Queen's Manufactory] in Saint-Cloud, where he preferred to accept a position as first engraver.[21]

As Sophie related in her letter, she visited her brother during his years in Paris and on 27 April 1784 they attended the premiere of Beaumarchais's *Marriage of Figaro*.

In August of the same year Mathurin-Robert and his wife had another son, born in Sèvres, outside Paris. He survived for only a little more than a year and when he died in October, his father had been interned at the Prison de la Force for three months. Mathurin-Robert was freed after serving nine months when his wife promised to pay 12,000 livres.

By the time the prisoner was released, his former employers had moved their manufacture to Le Creusot in Burgundy. Mathurin-Robert explained his predicament in the letter cited above:

> Since this establishment has deprived the capital of its proximity, the aforesaid Sieur Busson begs for your powerful protection, Monseigneur, so that your permission will allow him to establish at least one

furnace in one of the *faubourgs* of Paris, in order to satisfy the still pressing demands that are made to him daily by chemists, physicians, mathematicians, apothecaries, opticians, and generally all lovers of experiments leading to discoveries that are interesting for society.

The aforesaid Sieur Busson, known for possessing from father to son and by practice every skill in the art of glass-blowing, has a shop at Number 255 Palais-Royal, and his laboratory on the rue Traversière where he continues to train pupils. In this position he dares to hope, Monseigneur, for your beneficence, in which case he will not delay to make use of all of his professional experience in this small establishment which will return to him the means to raise his large family and be useful to the views and the wisdom of government, always disposed to protect industry and to augment the resources of its citizens.[22]

Mathurin-Robert's reference to his large family suggests he and his wife had other surviving children in addition to Jacques-Mathurin. Sophie Busson evokes this period in another passage from her letter:

[Later M. Busson set up a superb glass shop in the rue St-Honoré. It was there that he] lost his wife who died [from indigestion] after giving birth.

The Revolution having arrived, he followed the example of the nobility and the clergy and immigrated to England, leaving his son with his maternal relatives.

Mathurin-Robert left for England sometime after 5 December 1789, for on this date he signed a notarised act giving his address as Palais-Royal.

Before leaving France, Mathurin-Robert remarried. According to the document cited below, the ceremony took place in May 1789 at the Parisian church of St-Roch on the rue St-Honoré. Mathurin-Robert's second wife, the former Marie-Françoise Bruaire, accompanied him to London.

The émigré life in London

London did not have enough Catholic churches to accommodate the émigrés, and Marie-Françoise Busson's first child, Robert, born on 28 February 1790, was baptised on 10 November at the Bavarian embassy chapel, now Our Lady of the Assumption and St Gregory, in Soho. Another son, Jacques-Louis, was born on 18 September 1792 but he was not baptised until he was twelve, as will be mentioned in the following chapter. Robert and Jacques-Louis's sister, Louise, born on 18 February 1795, was also baptised in the embassy chapel on 15 June.

The British government provided financial relief to the émigrés from 1794, and the Busson family – Robert, Marie-Françoise and their three children – appear in the Treasury Department records from April 1795.[23] By the time the Bussons' fourth child, Louis-Mathurin – the Du Mauriers' forefather – was born on 17 November 1797, the émigrés had begun to have their own chapels. Louis-Mathurin was baptised on 21 November at the French chapel on Conway Street, Fitzroy Square.

The baptism was recorded by J. Carissan, an émigré priest from Noyal-sur-Seiche in the diocese of Rennes, and witnessed by Carron the younger, also a priest, as well as the godparents and the father, who signed 'Busson Du Maurier'. Louis-Mathurin's godfather was Jean-Louis Caruel, a hosier and toy-man according to insurance records, originally from the Ardennes and who had married in Paris in 1786. When Caruel died in 1818, his address was given as Cleveland Street, Fitzroy Square.

The author of *The French Exiles, 1789–1815* provides the following information about the Abbé Carron:

> Born at Rennes in 1760, Guy-Toussaint-Julien Carron de la Carrière became a member of the Order of St Vincent de Paul. In 1792 he was imprisoned and deported with a convoy of two hundred and fifty other priests, landing with them in Jersey where he immediately resumed the work for which he had become distinguished in Rennes, beginning by founding a chapel and a school for orphan children.
>
> When he had to leave Jersey in 1796 the Abbé Carron came to London, settling first in Fitzroy Square, where he founded another chapel and a seminary for aspirants to Holy Orders. He also organised religious instruction for the children in the neighbourhood.
>
> Leaving these foundations to other hands to carry on, the Abbé Carron moved to Somers Town, where there was already a small chapel and where he found ample scope for his religious and charitable zeal, earning the gratitude of the émigrés for his selfless devotion to their interest and the admiration of the English, many of whom associated themselves with his work.[24]

The baptismal register describes Louis-Mathurin as follows:

> ... the son of Mathurin-Robert Busson Du Maurier, gentleman glass-blower, age fifty-two, born in the parish of Chenu, diocese of Angers, province of Anjou in France, and of Marie-Françoise Bruaire, age thirty-one, born in the parish of Dourdan, diocese of Orléans, also in

France, and married in the church of Saint-Roch, city and diocese of
Paris, in the month of May 1789.

When his son Louis-Mathurin was born, Mathurin-Robert was not fif-
ty-two but rather forty-eight, and as mentioned above he was a master
glass-blower rather than a gentleman glass-blower. The entry cited above
may also contain other inaccuracies.

In 1962 Madeleine Fargeaud, the Sorbonne doctoral student Daphne
Du Maurier had hired to assist her in archival research, wrote to the novelist that she could find no trace of Mathurin-Robert's second marriage,
nor of his wife's birth in Dourdan:

> Just one mystery remains: not only is it certain that Mathurin-Robert
> did not marry Marie-Françoise Bruaire at St-Roch in May 1789 (other-
> wise the act would appear on the complete table of Parisian marriages
> that goes up to 1792) but, in addition ... Marie-Françoise Bruaire was
> not born in Dourdan. The surname Bruaire does not appear on any act
> in Dourdan between 1755 and 1778. It is rather disconcerting![25]

Over half a century after Daphne Du Maurier carried out her research,
mystery still surrounds the birth, marriage and death of Mathurin-Robert's second wife. This important figure in family history is apparently
destined to remain something of a question mark.

Refugee relief records for 1798 list Robert Busson, master glass-
blower, his wife Françoise and an English domestic living at 24 Cleveland Street, Fitzroy Square. In the signature column one reads 'At King's
Bench'.[26] Few records concerning prisoners in this period survive, but
Daphne Du Maurier's research uncovered an entry for Robert Busson
in the Discharge Book dated 1 December 1791.[27] Then, when his son
Louis-Mathurin was only a few months old, Mathurin-Robert served a
second prison term.

An entry in the Register concerns 'Mr Busson Dumorier':

> Committed 7 July 1798 for want of Bail upon a writ of Habeas Cor-
> pus directed to the Sheriff of Middlesex and by return it appears that
> on 28 June 1798 he was taken and under the said Sheriff's custody
> determined by virtue of a bill of Middlesex [illegible] before the King
> at Westminster on Tuesday next after the Morrow of All Souls to
> answer George Carter in a plea of trespass and also to his bill for
> £135 upon premises....[28]

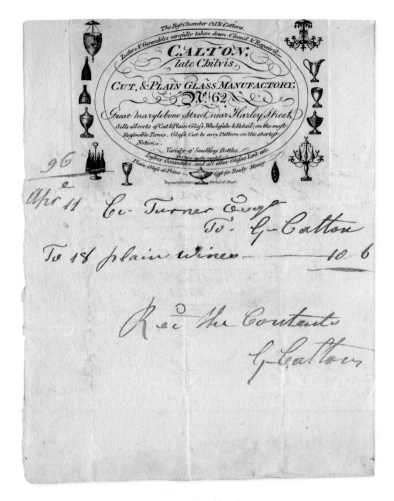

Trade card of George Calton, Cut & Plain Glass Manufactory

The prisoner was discharged on 7 February 1799.

It seems that 'George Carter' was in fact George Calton, the proprietor of a cut and plain glass manufactory at 62 Great Marylebone Street, which would suggest Busson may have continued to exercise his trade in London. Refugee relief records for 1799 give the Bussons' address as 14 Borough Road, St George's Fields in Southwark, very close to King's Bench prison.[29]

The author of *The French Exiles* paints a bleak picture of life in St George's Fields. Compared to the parish of St Marylebone, where the émigrés in the easiest circumstances lived, in this district 'the face of emigration was very different, sadder, more serious and more austere':

This was not the world of the Court but of the provinces, less frivo-lous and less gay, a living mosaic of French provincial life, made up of the lesser nobility of the robe and of the sword. It was composed of elderly officers and magistrates, of dowagers and widows, of young girls and venerable priests. Some of the émigrés lived with their *femmes de chambre* [chambermaids] and their menservants, of whom none received any wages but who still served their impoverished masters with devotion and affection.

In this unfashionable quarter lodgings were even cheaper than in Somers Town and away from the Court émigrés there were no social embarrassments to be feared, only the embarrassment of living. Sick-ness, misery and madness stalked the humble streets of St George's Fields, where people were sustained by pride in lieu of bread. In their wretched garrets their days were given up to melancholy reflection as each day brought news of a France which seemed to bear no resem-blance to the country of their birth and which was yet, in spite of all the horror it now inspired, so dear.[30]

From 1800 to 1802 the family's address is given as 7 William Street – now called Whitgift Street – in Lambeth.[31]

The baptismal records of the Bussons' two youngest children, Ade-laide and Guillaume, have not been found, but they were born after their father's stay in King's Bench.

Return to Tours
In 1803 the Bussons lived at 15 Mansfield Place – now called Holmes Road – in Kentish Town. The relief record is annotated with the obser-vation that on 16 July 1803 the husband was in France; he was removed from the relief list on 1 August.[32]

According to Sophie's notes on the Busson family,

M. Busson the elder took advantage of a truce to return to France, leaving his second wife and their children in London. He spent six months at Le Gué-de-l'Aunay with Madame Duval, his sister Sophie. War broke out once again between France and England. He took the course of going to Tours to found a *maison d'éducation* [boarding school]. He formed an association with his brother [Pierre] Busson Du Charme and died several years later, leaving regrets in Tours where he was greatly esteemed.

After marrying, Pierre purchased a notary's office in Le Mans and Sophie's letter summarises his story as follows:

> He became a revolutionary, and in his republican probity and pride, he sacrificed his income to reimburse to his clients the sums that the Vendeans [royalist insurgents] had taken from them. He raised his children according to the ideology of Rousseau and did not educate them. One daughter only was brought up in the care of her uncle, M. Busson senior [Mathurin-Robert]. This young person, full of talent, died in the *maison d'éducation* her uncle had founded.[33]

Out of an excess of revolutionary zeal, Pierre was eventually imprisoned twice in Le Mans, leaving his wife and children in pitiful circumstances.

Two weeks after Pierre was finally acquitted, his mother died in her native St-Christophe-en-Touraine, and he and his pregnant wife and their family left Le Mans to return to his mother's village. The Bussons' last two children were born there, bringing the total number of their children to twelve, although only a few survived to adulthood. The poetic names of the three youngest – Martagon (martagon lily), Pivoine-Belle de Nuit (peony-nightshade) and Sarrazin (buckwheat) – were borrowed from the revolutionary calendar.

Taking advantage of a new law, Pierre and his wife divorced, and he went on to become a schoolteacher in Sargé and then in Pezou, two villages in the vicinity of Vendôme. Pierre's ex-wife was still living with

1803 entry concerning the Bussons in the refugee relief register

him and he eventually lost his position due to complaints about their disorderly conduct. When Mathurin-Robert returned to France, his brother Pierre, after initially reacting in a rather hostile manner, must have been more than ready to collaborate in a new educational venture in Tours.

It is possible to pinpoint the approximate date of Mathurin-Robert's return, because on 24 October 1803 Pierre and his sisters filed a legal claim against their eldest brother. Madeleine had married Jacques-Michel Talbert, a glove merchant, and lived in Blois, and Sophie was the wife of François Duval, the son of an ironmaster. After Mme Busson died in Touraine, François Duval and his brother-in-law Michel Busson managed the Montmirail glass factory and led revolutionary activities in their district. When the goods of the clergy were sold, the Duvals bought and eventually relocated to a ruined abbey outside Vibraye, Sarthe (where young George Du Maurier visited them).

Edmé, the youngest Busson, had also divorced her husband, François Paumard, and from 1799 to 1803 she and her brother Michel bought the rights to the La Brûlonnerie glass factory which both their father and their brother Mathurin-Robert had managed in different periods, and transferred it to the nearby château de Rougemont.[34] The châtelain had emigrated at the Revolution and his vast domain was seized by the French state, subdivided and sold. The two Bussons lost almost all their money at Rougemont and Michel and his companion, who had had several illegitimate children, left the provinces to manage a wine bar in Paris.

According to the claim filed by Pierre, Madeleine, Sophie and Edmé, their brother Mathurin-Robert, 'a former master glass-blower and engraver who has resided in London, England since 1789', and who 'has been back in France for six or seven months', owed them 3,700 francs. Two years later, however, they withdrew the claim, noting in a letter that their brother's own financial needs were urgent.[35]

In *The Glass-Blowers*, Daphne Du Maurier imagined a failed reunion between Mathurin-Robert and Jacques-Mathurin, his son from his first marriage. It is not known whether this meeting actually occurred or what fate befell Jacques-Mathurin.

Whether the founder of the Du Maurier line intended to return to London or not, he left the six children from his second marriage – all under the age of fourteen and only three of whom would reach adulthood – to be raised by their mother. The record-keeper's annotation *le mari parti* (the husband has left) concisely articulates what would become a recurring motif in the lives of his descendants.

Mathurin-Robert Busson died on 2 June 1811 at 4 rue des Bons-Enfants in the centre of Tours, at the school he and his brother Pierre had founded. The two witnesses were unable to give the name of his parents or the date of his birth. Despite the fact that his wife Marie-Françoise was still living in London, Mathurin-Robert was described as 'widower of....'

CHAPTER TWO

THE WALLACES, THE CLARKES AND THE BUSSON DU MAURIERS

[Y]ou spent your childhood in England, as I did, and you grew up in France, even as myself. We may even have travelled here on the same boat!

Ellen Clarke to Louis-Mathurin Busson Du Maurier
in Daphne Du Maurier, *The Du Mauriers*

Only a handful of records survive concerning the existence of George Du Maurier's French grandmother Marie-Françoise and her six young children – Robert, Jacques-Louis, Louise, Louis-Mathurin, Adelaide and Guillaume – in London after her husband Mathurin-Robert returned to France in 1803.

In August 1806, three-year-old Adelaide Busson was buried at St Pancras parish church, followed in January 1807 by four-year-old Guillaume. (St Pancras Old Church and its cemetery are still standing, not far from the international railway station.) The French refugee records show that relief to Robert Busson ceased in the first half of July 1808, due to his death. Thus in the five years that followed Mathurin-Robert's departure, his oldest son, and youngest daughter and son had died.

On 6 April 1805, twelve-year-old Jacques-Louis was baptised at St Aloysius parish church in Clarendon Square. His godparents were Louis-Joseph-Marie Carluer, seigneur de Rumedon and knight of the royal and military order of Saint-Louis, and Marie-Louise-Laurence Ménard du Rocher, comtesse du Quengo. The comtesse, who was born in Santo-Domingo, married the Breton comte du Quengo in Jersey in 1792. In 1795 he participated in the disastrous royalist expedition to Quiberon and was executed by a firing squad.

Both the seigneur de Rumedon and the comtesse du Quengo played important roles at the Abbé Carron's boarding schools in Somers Town, where

> ... the instruction was relevant to the requirements of the elevated social class to which the children belonged, and was supposed to enable them to one day fill with distinction the positions entrusted to them in a regular government. The most educated of the émigrés offered their services to Abbé Carron. Suffice it to say that the educational supervisors in this singular establishment were all former knights of Saint-Louis.... They took a paternal interest in their pupils, spending study breaks with them, sleeping in their dormitories, and taking them out on their days off. It was the same in the girls' school....[36]

It is likely that Jacques-Louis, Louise and Louis-Mathurin – who respectively grew up to become a doctor of philology, the governess to the daughters of a Portuguese statesman, and an inventor – were all three educated in these schools. The émigré priests and aristocrats who taught at the schools may well have been the ones who instilled in the three young Bussons their firm but mistaken belief in their absent father's noble Breton origins.

The last record of the Bussons' presence in London dates from August 1811. Fourteen-year-old Louis Busson – George Du Maurier's father Louis-Mathurin – was confirmed at St Aloysius. The émigrés began returning to France at the second Restoration of the monarchy in 1815; from January 1816 Louis-Mathurin's sister Louise received a pension of 200 francs annually from the French king, payable every trimester.

In a brief fragment George Du Maurier described his Aunt Louise as 'a most beautiful and accomplished woman'.[37] In *Peter Ibbetson* the novelist characterised his fictional alter ego's father's family as 'Catholics of the blackest and Legitimists of the whitest dye – and as poor as church rats'.[38] The Legitimists opposed the French Revolution and the constitutional monarchy under Louis XVIII, and hoped to restore the *ancien régime*. Rather surprisingly for the daughter of such a family, after arriving in Restoration Paris Louise Busson married what has come to be called a Regency rake.

According to Daphne Du Maurier's semi-fictional account in *The Du Mauriers*, Louise married Godfrey Wallace, *secrétaire*, born in Craigie, county of Ayr in Scotland, the son of Sir Thomas Wallace, Baronet, and Rosina Raisne, on 14 April 1831 at the reformed church in Paris.

Immediately after the wedding Wallace learns his bride is penniless and disappears, leaving her to pay for the hotel. Louise has no news of her husband until July, when he writes to tell her he has been arrested at Calais for swindling and spousal abandonment. Later that month he writes again to say he has been released at her instigation and with her money, and is about to embark for England. Finally she receives a letter from the East India Company informing her that Wallace died in India in September 1833.

In reality the wedding took place fourteen years earlier, on 14 April 1817. The signature *v[euv]e* (widow) *Busson* on the register indicates that Louise's mother, the former Marie-Françoise Bruaire was present. The bridegroom's full profession is given as *Secrétaire à l'État-Major de l'Armée Anglaise d'occupation* (Secretary to the Headquarters of the English Army of Occupation).

Sir Thomas Wallace, Louise's father-in-law

The identity of the bridegroom's mother, Rosina Raisne, is a complete mystery, but certain aspects of the life of the groom's father, Sir Thomas Wallace (1750–1835) – born Thomas Dunlop-Wallace – are well documented. According to his obituary in the *Dumfries Times*:

> Sir Thomas conjoined in his person the representation of two families, both amongst the oldest, and one of them, ... the most honourable in all Scotland. He was the eldest son of General Dunlop, of Dunlop, which property has been in the hereditary possession of the family, for more than five hundred years, and by his mother, the well-known patroness of Burns, in whose poems and letters her virtues are consecrated to all time; he was the lineal descendant of the Wallaces of Craigie....

The Wallaces of Craigie claimed descent from the thirteenth-century Scottish hero Sir William Wallace.

Thomas Dunlop-Wallace enrolled as a lieutenant in the army in 1778 and served with two of his brothers in the Duke of Hamilton's regiment; two of their sisters would marry French royalist refugees. After the death of Sir Thomas Wallace of Craigie, his maternal grandfather, Thomas legally changed his name from Dunlop-Wallace to Wallace-Dunlop, in order to inherit his grandfather's titles and possessions. Rosina Raisne is said to have been the third of Sir Thomas's four wives.

An October 1788 article in *The Universal Magazine of Knowledge and Pleasure* provides an account of Sir Thomas's marital situation up to that date:

> Sir Thomas Wallace, the husband of the celebrated Lady Wallace [his first wife], having been divorced by her ladyship for infidelity to the marriage bed, by a process peculiar to the Commissary Court of Edinburgh, in the year 1783 paid his addresses to Mrs [Arabella] Bronsdon, the widow of a wealthy citizen of London. Sir Thomas's person and address were irresistible, for the widow, not at all dismayed with the numberless breaches of the conjugal vow, which had been proved against the baronet, gave him her hand and her heart, but prudently retained the greatest part of her fortune. Previous to this period, Sir Thomas had contracted debts to the amount of £50,000. His creditors seized upon his estates in Scotland, which were sold under the authority of the Court of Session, and Sir Thomas then left his native country with an intention never to return.
>
> With Mrs Bronsdon (now Lady Wallace) Sir Thomas lived in the utmost harmony for two years after their marriage, which happened in September 1783; but his affairs rendering a trip to the continent necessary, he left his lady and went to France, where he has ever since resided.
>
> In September 1787, the lady brought an action before the Commissaries of Edinburgh, setting forth her sufferings from the wanderings of a cruel husband, and stating particularly, that in the course of January and February 1787, Sir Thomas had been guilty of sundry acts of adultery in the Villa of Monthuy, near Montreuil, in France, and in the Hotel de la Cour kept by Francis Varenne, and concluding to have the marriage dissolved and annulled 'as if Sir Thomas were naturally dead'. The Commissaries entertained the action, and allowed the plaintiff to prove the infidelity of her husband. Here much difficulty occurred; the witnesses were not amenable to the laws of Scotland, and a petition was presented, praying the Commissaries 'to entreat the magistrates of Montreuil to recommend to Mary Michaux, Elizabeth Poisson, and Caroline Bersole, to come to this country to give evidence in the process of divorce respecting the acts of adultery alleged to have been committed by Sir Thomas Wallace'.[39]

When a court action was brought against Sir Thomas in 1792 for an unpaid bill from the period when he was living with his second wife Arabella, she could not be examined as a witness. For, according to a newspaper report, Sir Thomas's second 'divorce' was actually a separation 'a mensa et thoro [from bed and board], as nothing short of an act of Parliament could make the marriage void....'

Since Sir Thomas never divorced Dame Arabella Hamilton Dunlop-Wallace and she lived until 1808, he was almost certainly never married to Rosina Raisne, whose son married Louise Busson in 1817. He resided on the continent and after his first marriage ended there is no record of a son born in Scotland. Indeed, other than 'Godfrey' Wallace's marriage to Louise and the somewhat dubious record of baptism he presented at the time, there is no record of a son called Godfrey born to Sir Thomas: it may well have been an assumed forename.

In addition to John Alexander Dunlop-Wallace, Sir Thomas's only surviving child from his first marriage, he had a daughter Agnes Elizabeth, supposedly born in 1789, although her birthplace and her mother's name are unknown. Agnes Elizabeth Wallace's own illegitimate son Richard Wallace would inherit great wealth from the 4th Marquess of Hertford, said to be his father. In 1835 Hertford purchased the château de Bagatelle in the Bois de Boulogne, rebuilt for the comte d'Artois by the neo-classical architect Bélanger. Hertford lived there for many years and on his death his 'assistant' Richard Wallace – thought to be his son – inherited it. The works of art Hertford acquired formed the basis of the Wallace Collection in London.

In *Peter Ibbetson* George Du Maurier borrowed *Parva sed Apta* (small but fit) – the golden legend inscribed on the château de Bagatelle – for the Passy dwelling of Peter's childhood friend and female alter ego Mary. In their joint 'true dream' Peter and Mary meet every night – and ultimately discover their kinship – in *Magna sed Apta* (large but fit) 'for so we had called the new home and palace of art [Mary] had added on to *Parva sed Apta*, the home of her childhood'.[40]

A George Wallace, son of Sir Thomas and the mysterious Rosina, was baptised on 26 June 1792 at St Marylebone, Westminster, and said to have been born a few weeks earlier. Louise Wallace had a copy of her husband's baptism, dated the month before their wedding and certified by the British Consul General in Paris, stating that Godfrey George was born on 11 July 1793 and baptised the same day in Ayr, to Sir Thomas and 'Lady Raisne'.[41] A Rosina Charlotte Elizabeth Brown, the daughter of a Mrs Brown living with Sir Thomas Wallace, was baptised in 1796 at Imber in Wiltshire. Sir Thomas's household furniture was sold at Imber the same year and, from July 1798 to February 1800 he was with his Fencible Infantry in Guernsey.

After separating from his second wife and moving to France, Sir Thomas Wallace was a prisoner of war in Verdun from 1803 to 1814. Anne Catherine Thirion, a native of Verdun and forty years his junior, gave birth to their son Gustavus in 1806; on returning to England Sir Thomas married Anne Catherine, and she and her son were also baptised there.

Anne Wallace, the illegitimate daughter of Sir Thomas and Anne Young, born in Surrey in 1797, was presumably living with her father. For in 1812, in Verdun, Sir Thomas's fifteen-year-old daughter Anne married Charles Turrell, another prisoner of war who went on to become a lieutenant in the Royal Navy and, putting his prisoner of war experience to good use, a professor of French at the Royal Navy School in Camberwell. At the time of her husband's death Anne Turrell resided in Brussels.

Wallace the Younger, Louise's husband

For military registration in 1801, George Thomas Wallace the Younger of Leicester Square in the County of Middlesex declared that 'to the best of his knowledge, information and belief he is above the age of fifteen

The château de Bagatelle in the Bois de Boulogne

years and under the age of twenty-two years and that he was born of
English parents subjects of the King of Great Britain at the house of Sir
Alexander Guilmore [Gilmour] Baronet at Wokingan [Wacquinghen] in
the Boulognois (in the province of Picardy) where his parents were upon
their travels'.[42] George Thomas Wallace was therefore older than the
George Wallace born to Sir Thomas and Rosina in London 1792, and
the 'Godfrey George' supposedly born in Ayr in 1793. It seems that it
was 'George Thomas Wallace', or perhaps more fully 'George Thomas
William Wallace' who, under the alias 'Godfrey Wallace', married Louise
Busson in 1817.

Wallace the Younger first appeared in the newspapers in 1808, when
the captain of a ship serving the East India Company brought an action
against the young army lieutenant for nonpayment of his return fare
from India in 1805. Wallace argued that he was not of age at the time,
however the jury found a verdict for the plaintiff.[43]

We have some further information about Wallace the Younger in the
years leading up to 1821, because in that year he published the *Memoirs of William Wallace, Esq. late of his Majesty's 15th Hussars; containing an explanation and vindication of his conduct and character: with
a detailed account of the persecutions he underwent in France, and his
unjust imprisonment for almost three years in that country: an exposé
of the state of the French police: and an appendix, comprising the correspondence of the author and others with the British ambassador, on the
subject of his unlawful confinement: and other documents.*

The nineteenth-century author James Grant discussed Wallace's memoir in an article entitled 'Story of a Hussar of the Regency'. He states
at the opening that Wallace's life was 'one of the most extraordinary
and wasted, miserable and wandering, lives that ever existed....'[44] The
memoir itself is full of self-pity and, ultimately to a contemporary reader,
rather comical.

Wallace says very little on the topic of his early years:

It is unnecessary to begin my history from my infancy – it will be
enough to say, that my friends furnished me with a most liberal education, that spared no pains to implant in my mind the strictest principles
of honour and rectitude. Nothing was omitted to make me worthy of
the name I bore, and to fit me for the honourable profession to which
I was destined.... At the age of fourteen I commenced my career as a
soldier; and, in 1802, embarked to serve in India.

Injured in the Mahratta war, Wallace returned to England at the age of eighteen: 'My mind, habituated to oriental splendour and profusion, new to the world, and naturally warm, impetuous, and enterprising, was exposed to seduction, and I readily fell into the commission of every folly that was unmixed with dishonour or crime.'[45]

In the midst of this 'dissipation', Wallace was appointed to the 15th Hussars, one of the most expensive regiments, commanded by the Duke of Cumberland, and soon thereafter 'engaged to marry one of the richest heiresses in the kingdom'. He encumbered himself 'with horses, carriages, dogs, and every extravagant and useless appendage of fashionable life'. He was drawn into 'numerous *intrigues d'amour*' (love intrigues) and fought frequent duels.[46]

Wallace hoped to return to service anywhere but the East Indies, but found himself 'gazetted in the 17th Light Dragoons, *then* under orders for the East Indies'. Astonished and mortified, he presented a memorial to the Commander-in-Chief, the Duke of York: '... while awaiting the issue, I was led, by the evil fortune that has ever since pursued me, to an acquaintance with the celebrated Mary Anne Clarke'.[47]

I will return to George Du Maurier's maternal grandmother Mary Anne Clarke in greater detail below, noting here that before Wallace met her she

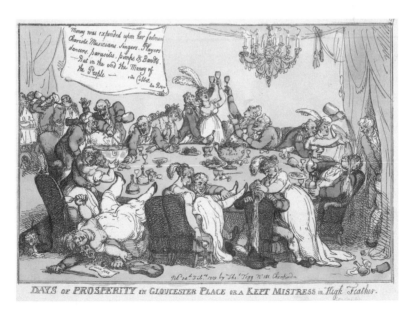

A Rowlandson caricature of Mrs Clarke and the Duke of York (both standing, in the centre). The punch bowl contains a bishop: a type of punch and also one of the Duke's titles

had left her husband, Joseph Clarke, had begun to pass for a widow and had risen to become the mistress of Frederick, Duke of York. After the relationship ended Mrs Clarke testified against her former protector in a House of Commons inquiry into the sale of military commissions. He was (temporarily) removed from office, and at the time she met Wallace, Mrs Clarke planned to blackmail the Duke by threatening to publish his letters.

According to Wallace:

> This lady admitted me to her peculiar confidence, and intrusted me with a curious correspondence, which she represented to have passed between her former liberal protector, his Royal Highness the Duke of York, and Colonel McMahon, of a nature highly serviceable to her in the measures she was about to adopt against him.[48]

Colonel McMahon was the secretary and keeper of the purse of the Prince of Wales, and he also enjoyed the confidence of the Prince's brothers.

Indiscreetly, Wallace mentioned these letters to several friends, leading to strenuous efforts by certain people in power to recover them. He suggests that his refusal to surrender the letters may have brought the displeasure of the very people whose interference he was soliciting regarding his military assignment. At a dinner with the Duke of York's brother, the Duke of Sussex, Wallace was induced to drink heavily; Lord Falkland then persuaded him to destroy the letters and accompanied him home to see that it was done. 'The whole merit of their destruction' is therefore ascribed to Falkland.

Wallace was wounded when a horse fell back on him. He addressed another memorial to the Commander-in-Chief, only to find his resignation reported in the Gazette. He joined the army in Portugal as a volunteer and engaged in daily skirmishes but when his 'Indian malady' returned, his friends advised him to return to England.

However, as Wallace sensed that his creditors there would expose him to more serious warfare than he had left, he retired to Scotland, where rest and leisure proved more unfavourable to his recovery than business and fatigue, so that his illness increased. On finding an arrangement with his creditors, Wallace returned to London, only to fall victim 'to the graceful, lovely, and fascinating Mrs Bartram, "the public care" of all the fashionable rakes in town'.[49] Wallace's mistress accompanied him back to Scotland but he began to find the affair debasing; 'In this state of debasement, the news of the Treaty of Paris reached me.'

The treaty that ended the war between France and the Sixth Coalition led to the liberation of Sir Thomas Wallace. As his son explained, '[m]y father, whom I had not seen since my childhood, had been detained with the other English, who, at the recommencement of the war, happened to be in France'.[50]

Sir Thomas's liberation prompted Wallace the Younger to dispose of Mrs Bartram and fly to his parent, 'whose affectionate reception of me compensated for all the ills that I had suffered'. To escape Mrs Bartram he spent four months in Paris but returned to England when he learned his father was dangerously ill. There, reports of Wallace's extravagance in Paris led his creditors to attack him, and at the age of twenty-five he was consigned to the King's Bench prison for debt. In order to be released from prison, he availed himself of the Insolvent Act.

Wallace concludes this chapter of his *Memoirs* with the melodramatic observation that 'if I could have foreseen other ills that awaited me on the recovery of my freedom, I would have consented to imprisonment for life, or suffered even death itself, rather than have accepted it'. The first ill that awaited Wallace was what could be called the Bradburne affair after Charles Bradburne, 'a sugar baker of the city'.[51]

At a masked ball Wallace attended at the Argyll Rooms in late January 1816, a lady fainted and when her mask was removed, he recognised Mrs Bartram, his former mistress. He and his friends accompanied her to her house, 'where a mad night of champagne and deep play [ensued], and the losses of Wallace [were] enormous'.[52]

Charles Bradburne was in the party and he lost so much that he shot himself; a newspaper article attributed the responsibility for the suicide to Captain Wallace and Mr Andrews. They proceeded to the nearest seaport and departed for Calais.

As James Grant put it, 'now began the most extraordinary portion of [Wallace's] misfortunes and adventures'.[53] Although neither Louise Busson nor a marriage is mentioned anywhere in Wallace's *Memoirs*, the dates suggest that their wedding took place in the midst of these misfortunes.

From Calais, Wallace and Andrews went to a hotel on the rue de la Paix in Paris but the maître d'hôtel – a M. Claude Marcel – insisted they would find better service and accommodation at another establishment in the rue de Richelieu. A quarrel with a fellow English resident convinced Wallace to change hotels but by this time his companion Andrews was in debt to Marcel and departed for Madrid. Wallace stayed on in Paris until late September, when he decided to return to England via Brussels. There he found English friends who took his side in the Bradburne affair and he was even elected into a Belgian club. After a few months in Brussels,

Wallace resolved to depart for England but the friend who proposed to travel with him needed pass through Paris before embarking. According to Wallace, they reached Paris in May 1817.

Could he then, under the assumed name of 'Godfrey' Wallace and the assumed profession of secretary to the headquarters of the English army of occupation, have married Louise Busson in Paris on 14 April 1817? In his *Memoirs* Wallace reported that, a few years earlier in Lisbon, he had been – falsely, he claims – accused of 'personating Colonel Burgh, an aide-de-camp to Sir Arthur Wellesley, and, in that usurped character, conducting myself in the most improper manner'.[54] During the occupation Wallace's older half-brother, John Alexander, commanded the 14th British Brigade of the Allied Army; possibly Wallace the Younger sought to profit from this family connection.

Returning to Wallace's narrative, after arriving in Paris in May, he received letters obliging him to return to England and proceeded to Boulogne-sur-Mer, where he was arrested at the instigation of Marcel for a pretended debt of 4,000 francs. Wallace engaged an advocate and an attorney to contest the allegation, which was brought before the *Tribunal de Première Instance Civile* in Boulogne a month later. Wallace was cleared and awarded damages; he reproduces extracts from the judgement in his favour, dated 1 August 1817, in the appendix to his *Memoirs*.

Wallace soon discovered that his adventures with Marcel and the French judicial system had only just begun. When leaving the debtors' prison he was arrested on the charge of having stolen three towels and a shoe-brush from Marcel's hotel eighteen months earlier, and was conducted to the Prison de la Force in Paris. The charges were dropped but he was then charged with forgery and returned to La Force. Apparently there had been some confusion over his name and he was accused of swindling. Wallace was acquitted but then landed in the prison of Ste Pélagie, whose horrendous conditions make him long for La Force. He spent eighteen more months in prison on the charge of having assassinated 'an English general at Valenciennes, and two bankers at Paris'.[55] An English friend of Wallace's managed to bribe Marcel to consent to Wallace's liberation and he was finally released on 6 October 1819.

Wallace's *Memoirs* end with a copy of the letter he received from his father, written after he had read the manuscript of the book. The letter's last paragraph, dated 22 December 1819, is as follows:

As to the French business, the ambassador's letters, joined to the other documents now before me, are quite sufficient, not only fully to exculpate you, but even to reflect much credit upon your conduct, which was firm, manly, cool, and irreproachable, through the whole of a most painful, unjust and infamous trial. This matter you may be proud of; it can never hurt you: it doubtless has very much injured your health; but you have an excellent constitution; and you know how happy we shall be to see you here, where you can have good society, and every amusement the country can afford; and where every attention will be paid to your comfort, and the recovery of your health; and I hope, in a short time, to see you restored to perfect happiness.

Despite the hopeful ending of the *Memoirs*, in March 1823 Captain Wallace was involved in a fracas in Offley's Burton Ale Rooms in Covent Garden. He was charged with assaulting the Right Hon. Charles Barry Bingham, Baron Clanmorris, with whom he was slightly intimate. After insulting Clanmorris, Wallace struck him twice with a walking cane, causing the former to hit him with a large candlestick. According to the *Morning Post*, 'Capt. Wallace complained that it was the foul and groundless aspersions thrown on his character, by Lord Clanmorris, which had induced him to call him out; his rank was not so high as his Lordship's, but his family was as noble, and in the army, he might safely say, he was a more distinguished officer.'[56]

In January 1828 Wallace again appeared in the newspapers:

Joanna Murphy, a young Irish widow, and Mary Linch, her servant, were charged with assaulting Lawrence Isaac Nathan, a sheriff's officer, and Thomas Ward, his assistant. – Mr Nathan stated, that having a warrant under the Sheriff of Middlesex to execute upon the person of Captain William Wallace Dunlop, he and Ward proceeded on Tuesday night to one of the Moscow cottages in Bayswater, of which Mrs Murphy says she is the occupier. They knocked at the door: 'Who is there?' said some female, and the officers made no answer. Presently the defendant Linch carefully opened the door to the extent of two or three inches. The officers introduced a thick stick to prevent her from again shutting it, and endeavoured to force an entrance. Mrs Murphy cried, 'Thieves, murder, thieves!' The Captain called out for a hatchet, a carving knife, and a poker, swearing – 'So help me G-d, the first man who enters I'll cleave his skull, even if I am hanged at Tyburn afterwards.' 'It's of no use to make resistance, Captain,' said the assistant; 'we must have you.' 'Never from this house alive,' replied the Captain; 'I have a carving knife, it's a jolly good one, don't you hear it?' – and at the same time rubbing it against something as if to sharpen it – 'and the first man who lays his hand upon me, it shall go through him.' The officers saw Mrs Murphy put a hatchet and a poker into the hands of the Captain: Linch threw water upon them; and afterwards the lady and her servant came out of the house and drove, or rather dragged the officers from the place. – The charge was not denied. Mr Rawlinson ordered the defendants to find bail.

Burial records for the parish of St John the Evangelist in Westminster show that William Wallace Dunlop died in London in September 1835, a few weeks before his father's death in Dumfriesshire.

It may well be that it was after marrying and after Wallace's imprisonment that Louise taught at a *maison d'éducation* on the rue Neuve-Saint-Étienne in Paris. Between approximately 1810 and 1821 a congregation called *l'Ordre de Notre-Dame de la Miséricorde* had a girls' boarding school at 6 rue Neuve-Saint-Étienne, before it moved to new quarters on the rue Sainte-Geneviève. Daphne Du Maurier suggests that it was at a *maison d'éducation* at this address that Louise met Ellen, the younger daughter of the notorious Mary Anne Clarke.

Mrs Clarke and her daughters in England

The first half of Mrs Clarke's life was described in her book *The Authentic and Impartial Life of Mrs Mary Anne Clarke*, and repeated with variations in numerous contemporary accounts. More recently, her story was researched and retold in Daphne Du Maurier's semi-fictional *Mary Anne* (1954), in Paul Berry's *By Royal Appointment: A Biography of Mary Ann* [sic] *Clarke, Mistress of the Duke of York* (1970), and in a chapter of Derek Winterbottom's *Grand Old Duke of York* (2016).

Mary Anne Thompson was of very humble London origins. After her father's death, her mother remarried a Mr Farquhar, a journeyman printer who trained Mary Anne as a compositor. While still a minor she eloped with Joseph Clarke, a stonemason. In the following years she gave birth to three children who would grow to adulthood – Mary Anne, George Noel and Ellen Cecily – and then left her husband to become what her friend Elizabeth Taylor in her own memoir called 'a loose fish, an enterprising adventuress in the field of gallantry'.

Mrs Clarke eventually became the mistress of the Duke of York and lived with him at Gloucester Place from 1803 to 1806. In this period she contracted huge debts, her wayward husband reappeared and finally the Duke left her. In 1809 she appeared before the House of Commons

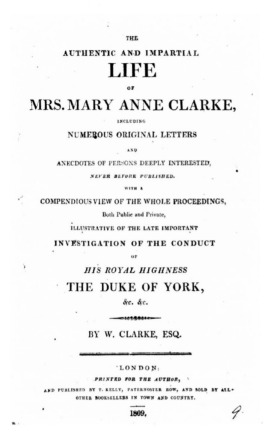

Frontispiece of *The Authentic and Impartial Life of Mrs Mary Anne Clarke* (left), and a portrait of the subject that featured in the first edition (above)

twelve times to testify against her former protector in their inquiry into the sale of military commissions. She gradually won over her audience; one of her bons mots made it into the *1811 Dictionary of the Vulgar Tongue*. When asked how, after her separation from the Duke, she managed to send him a letter, she replied 'By this Ambassador of Morocco' – designating a ladies' shoemaker in Bond Street. (In a curious coincidence, in his youth Mathurin-Robert Busson had disguised himself as an ambassador of Morocco at a masked ball in Chartres, as mentioned in Chapter One.)

As a result of the inquiry the Duke of York resigned his position as commander in chief, although he was subsequently reinstated. Mrs Clarke eventually agreed to return the Duke's letters and burn 18,000 copies of her memoirs in exchange for £7,000 and an annuity of £400 that would pass to her daughters after her death. These events brought her into the public eye, and she was one of the most caricatured Britons of the period. In 1810 she published a second work entitled *The Rival Princes*, in which she accused the Duke of Kent of having plotted against his brother, her former paramour. A few years later Mrs Clarke was found guilty of libelling the Chancellor of the Irish Exchequer and imprisoned for nine months in the Marshalsea Prison.

Biographer Paul Berry writes that after Mrs Clarke's release from prison in November 1814, 'she was swallowed up once more by the obscurity from which she had so unexpectedly emerged'.[57] In fact, Mrs Clarke remained something of a celebrity. Thanks to British newspapers and French judicial archives, it is possible to trace her whereabouts and activities in the years leading up to her younger daughter's marriage to Louis-Mathurin Busson Du Maurier.

On 11 November 1814 Mary Anne was already in Brighton, 'with the avowed intention of sailing in the *Neptune* packet, tomorrow, for Dieppe'. Yet it seems she may not have crossed the Channel until August 1815. The young Henry Hart Milman, a future dean of St Paul's Cathedral, happened to sail on the same boat. In a letter to his sister, Milman gave a somewhat uncharitable description of his fellow passenger:

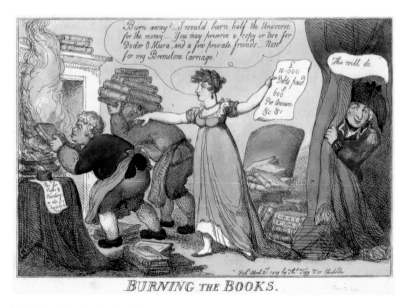

Rowlandson, 'Burning the Books'

I had a most prosperous journey; found a vessel ready to sail, got on board at eight o'clock in the evening, and was in Dieppe before eight the next morning; but the ship not being able to come into the harbour, I could not get my luggage till two, which gave me plenty of time to reconnoitre the particularly and notoriously thick ankles of the Dieppese ladies. One of my companions in the vessel was Mary Anne Clarke, 'my darling', in the last stage apparently of consumption, without any remains of beauty, of which, I believe, she never had a great share, but excessively amusing. I did not find out who she was till just before we parted company.[58]

In October 1815, Mary Anne and her daughters were in Margate: she appeared 'in a new and remarkably light and elegant barouche landau, drawn by four bay blood horses: in the vehicle were her two daughters, dressed in all the paraphernalia of modern fashion; outriders in elegant liveries completed the *set-out*'.[59]

Perhaps it was this article that attracted the attention of Mary Anne's creditors. For in the same month one of them learned of her residence, and had her twenty-three year old daughter, also called 'Mary Anne Clarke', arrested. It is noted that 'The mother escaped and is now in France.' Later in October,

A silly young man, who will soon possess £50,000, accidentally saw Mary Anne Clarke (the girl who was lately arrested by mistake for her well-known mother), at a library at Broadstairs, and fancied he had fallen desperately in love with her; so much so, that he declared, at the first interview with the mother, that he should die, if he did not possess her ere Christmas. He professed honourable intentions, and with the consent of a *third party*, he commenced his suit. When all matters were in a train of forwardness, the capricious youth suddenly absented himself. On inquiry, a discovery, fatal to the hopes of Miss Clarke, took place. Mr M. eloped on Thursday last with a handsome girl he accidentally saw at St Peter's.[60]

In late 1816 Mrs Clarke was in London, where she 'came to give information against a servant that had robbed her. She appeared in good health, very lively, was dressed in a cloth pelisse, a dark blue silk bonnet, with a profusion of the most beautiful artificial flowers, and a white lace veil.'[61] In July 1817 Mrs Clarke, 'attended by her daughters, *honoured* the Birmingham Theatre with her presence'.[62]

In November of the same year, a newspaper report announced that 'a wealthy Baronet will shortly lead Miss Clarke, daughter of the celebrated Mary Anne Clarke, to the hymeneal temple, at Leamington Spa'.[63] Once again the anticipated marriage did not take place and in August 1818 Mrs Clarke and her family departed from Brighton on board a packet for Le Havre. In September 1818 Mrs Clarke and her daughters landed at Portsmouth, from the Isle of Wight, on their way to London. For the next five years Mrs Clarke and her activities were absent from the British newspapers. In this period, she apparently lived in Paris and Tours.

The Burke-Clarke affair

In January 1822 Sir John Ignatius Burke, hereditary baronet of Glinsk in the kingdom of Ireland and a papal marquis, currently residing in France, wrote to the French Minister of the Interior to complain of persecution by Mrs Clarke and her allies.[64]

Over the next few months a correspondence ensued between, on the one hand, Burke and his ally the comte de Courchamps – a shady figure of the Empire and Restoration who is best known today for having forged *The Memoirs of the Marquise de Créquy*, and who is also said to have written the letters signed by Sir John – and on the other, French authorities including the Prefect of the Department of Indre-et-Loire and the Minister of the Interior. These letters offer new information concerning Mary Anne's existence during her first years in France.

In late winter 1819, Sir John and his wife were dining in Paris with the duke of Luxemburg, the count of Durfort and other friends, when a letter from Mrs Clarke was brought to him. Referring to himself in the third person, Sir John wrote: 'He suspected, not without motives, that this letter contained either injurious reproaches or *propositions* that were no less injurious, and he returned the said letter to Mrs Clarke's envoy without opening it.'

A short time thereafter a sieur de Fouchécour challenged Sir John to a duel on behalf of Mrs Clarke; he responded that he did not want to go because of the motive alleged by the assailant. A friend of Sir John's spoke to Fouchécour, who told him among other things that he was a Life Guard and that he would take revenge on Sir John. Some time later a stranger attacked Sir John in the rue de la Paix. Sir John lodged a complaint with the police and discovered his assailant was none other than the sieur de Fouchécour, who was in fact no longer a Life Guard and who had been expelled from an infantry regiment for misconduct. A few months after these events Sir John received another challenge to a duel, this time from England.

Burke's challenger was a Mr Best, well known for both his poor conduct and his skill at fencing. In 1804 Captain Thomas Best had killed his former friend Thomas Pitt, 2nd Baron Camelford – termed 'the half-mad lord' by his biographer – in a duel over a woman, which took place behind Holland House in London.[65]

At the end of the same year Captain Best married Lady Emily Stratford. (Their son, John Stratford Best, would become a friend and business associate of Mrs Clarke's son George.) A few years after his marriage, Captain Best was imprisoned for debt and his wife left him for another man. In 1812, during Best's imprisonment, a Mr Agg was convicted of libel for a biography of Best in a magazine called *Town Talk*. The captain, born in Barbados, was said to have spent his youth 'flogging and torturing negroes', to have 'wantonly killed Lord Camelford, an amiable nobleman' and is described as the *cher ami* of Mrs Clarke.

Best's challenge accused Sir John of having slandered him, Mrs Clarke and her daughters, one of whom had supposedly been Best's mistress. The baronet responded that these were lies and a machination by *la dame Clarke*; he would not bother going to England to explain himself.

Sir John then arrived in Tours, where he planned to spend the winter – presumably the winter of 1820–21 – with his wife, children, equipages and entire household. Soon after his arrival he attended a dinner with many Englishmen, including Mrs Clarke's son George, a cavalry officer, and a Mr Luttrell, an infantry officer, who had arrived from India. Mrs Clarke was also residing in Tours at the time.

At the dinner George Clarke insulted the Irishman but because Sir John did not want to measure himself against such a man, various consorts and proponents who frequented the Clarkes' residence in Tours presented themselves as alternates. Burke finally agreed to face Luttrell – presumably Lieutenant Thomas Luttrell, who had served in India with the 47th Regiment of Foot.

After gendarmes managed to separate the two men, Lady Burke became ill and was so frightened that her husband had to take her back to Paris to consult her usual doctor. She suffered a miscarriage and her state was alarming. Nonetheless, Sir John had to return to Tours for his children and he suspected that Mrs Clarke would put further obstacles in his path.

Sir John evokes the testimony of M. de Commaille, the owner of the house in the rue du Faubourg-St-Honoré where Mrs Clarke had previously stayed in Paris, adjoining the British embassy.[66] Mrs Clarke's landlord claimed she had her intimates threaten him and challenge him to duels whenever he asked her to pay rent, and added that she ended up removing her furniture at night, through the garden that gave onto the Champs-Élysées.

Sir John, or the person who was writing for him, concluded that one could easily judge who this woman was and who Sir John Burke was by inquiring of the British ambassador, the Dukes of La Châtre and Luxemburg, etc. He asked for the Minister's protection from Mrs Clarke's supporters, to facilitate his return to Tours for his children.

A few weeks later the prefect responded to the minister. He tended to agree that Sir John provoked Clarke and Luttrell, and mentioned that the latter intended to marry one of Mrs Clarke's daughters. The English residents of Tours – a community of about 1,200 at the time – praised Luttrell's conduct in the negotiations with Sir John and blamed the latter for having involved his friend, M. de Courchamps, in the affair.

George Clarke made an express trip to Paris – without the passport he had been obliged to leave at the Préfecture in Tours – in an unsuccessful effort to solicit an interview with the British ambassador.

Gradually the attention of the authorities shifted from Sir John Burke and Mrs Clarke to Burke's French ally, the comte de Courchamps. In early March the prefect warned Mrs Clarke to refrain her friends from any zeal that could compromise her case. She persisted in affirming that she has nothing to do with Sir John and added that she intended to leave Tours the following month to return to England.

Mary Anne was next found in the British papers in August 1824: 'The celebrated Mrs Mary Anne Clarke, who has been residing in Brighton for the last two or three months, has just left. While there, she occupied a house on the Grand Parade.'[67] In September 1826 it was noted that Mary Anne visited Brighton and then returned to Dieppe, 'where she has been residing for some years'.[68]

Louis-Mathurin Busson Du Maurier in Paris

Between his confirmation in Somers Town in 1811 and his marriage at the British ambassador's residence in Paris in 1827, only a few traces of Louis-Mathurin have been found. Both are dated 1821 and they suggest he was quite well connected in Restoration Paris.

On 15 February 1821, Louis Busson presented himself at the École royale de musique et de déclamation, as the Paris Conservatory was then called. The register includes the following evaluation: 'The aspirant has a good beginning in solfeggio. His voice is not strong and a bit throaty, but it may improve with work.'[69]

Described as the son of a gentleman glass-blower, Louis Busson brought with him a letter from M. Pacini – presumably the composer, conductor and musical editor Antonio Pacini, born in Naples in 1778, who came to Paris in 1804. Pacini's compositions include a romance called *Portrait charmant* (Charming Portrait), which Peter Ibbetson's adoptive father performs on the guitar in one of George Du Maurier's illustrations.

In an autobiographical fragment, George Du Maurier recalled: 'There was ... a peculiar refinement and courtliness in [Louis-Mathurin's] accent, partly inherited, partly assimilated from association with such artists as Mlle Mars who had given him many lessons in *dire la romance*.'[70] The Conservatory gives Busson's address as rue d'Angoulême-St-Honoré (now part of the rue La Boétie) and notes he was employed by the count de Stacpoole of the rue du Faubourg-St-Honoré.

In *Irish and Other Memories*, a descendant of the first Count writes that his ancestor had purchased this large house with extensive grounds in 1817. The author characterises his great-grandfather and grandfather as follows:

> My great-grandfather, born in 1736 in Cork, was High Sheriff for Clare in 1763, and returned to the Catholic faith of his fathers in 1778.... He had a residence in Grosvenor Place, London, where he constantly entertained the exiled French King Louis XVIII, and on the restoration of the latter after the defeat of Napoleon, was rewarded by titles and honours, and persuaded to establish himself and his family in Paris, where he died in 1824.
>
> His successor and only child, Richard, who was educated at Rugby, was a very munificent man. Later in life, while visiting Rome when Leo XII was appealing to the faithful for various restorations, such as the rebuilding of St Paul's and one of the bridges over the Tiber, my grandfather contributed generously, and the Pope conferred various honours on him, making him a Marquis (1826) and subsequently Duke (1881) and also a Knight of the Order of Christ.[71]

Since the first count was over eighty at the time he employed Louis-Mathurin, perhaps it was the munificence of his son Richard that led to a papal honour for Mathurin-Robert's youngest surviving son.

On 25 August 1821 Louis-Mathurin Busson Du Maurier became a Knight of the Illustrious Order of the Golden Spur and Palatinate Count, sponsored by Jacques Auguste Vie de Cesarini, Commander of the Order of St John of Jerusalem. Duke Salvatore Sforza-Cesarini conferred the honour. Louis-Mathurin's belief that he descended from the aristocratic Busson family of Brittany – the Du Maurier archives contain a parchment headed *Maison de Busson Originaire de Bretagne* (House of Busson originally from Brittany) with a hand-painted coat of arms, bearing the stamp *Archives Généalogiques de l'Ordre de St Jean de Jérusalem (Malte)* (Genealogical Archives of the Order of St John of Jerusalem) – probably also played a role. As mentioned in the Introduction, Louis-Mathurin later saw fit to bowdlerise his Aunt Sophie's letter – the only authentic document on his father's origins.

The Order of the Golden Spur was an ancient papal order of knighthood and once a very prestigious one, but by the nineteenth century titles were given very liberally and even sold, leading Pope Gregory XVI to drastically reform the order and change its name in 1841. In this same period the caricaturist Honoré Daumier depicted a knight of the golden spur in one of a series of lithographs satirising the 'Bohemians of Paris'. The drawing's legend reads as follows:

> The so-called former Colonel of the Papal Guard, later aide-de-camp to the Prince of Monaco, awaiting as a prize for his services a distinguished post in the Government! ... he would, however, willingly accept a tobacconist's shop or a position as an inspector of [street] sweeping; besides he is a gallant man like all knights of his order, for a trifle demanding satisfaction from five-year-old children, perfectly making excuses from the moment you look at him in the face.

If George Du Maurier's portrait of his hero's father in *Ibbetson* is accurate, Louis-Mathurin's attitude toward his origins was inconsistent:

> By the strangest inconsistency my dear father, a genuine republican at heart (for all his fancied loyalty to the white lily of the Bourbons), a would-be scientist, who in reality was far more impressed by a clever and industrious French mechanic than by a prince (and would, I think, have preferred the former's friendship and society), yet took both a pleasure and a pride in his quaint old parchments and obscure quarterings.[72]

A little house in the Champs-Élysées

On 24 December 1827 – just over a decade after his sister Louise's marriage – Louis-Mathurin married Ellen Cecilia Clarke at the British

Peter's father sings 'When in death I shall calm recline,/ Oh take my heart to my mistress dear!/ Tell her it lived upon smiles and wine/ Of the brightest hue while it lingered here!' (Thomas Moore, 'The Legacy')

A parody of 'The Legacy' (probably known to Du Maurier) goes: 'When in jail I shall calm recline,/ Bear my best coat to some pawnbroker near,/ Show him how stylish the gilt buttons shine,/ And ask him a price that is not too dear' (probably also by Thomas Moore)

Embassy Chapel in Paris. Little is known of the first six years of Lou-is-Mathurin and Ellen's life together, other than that she suffered more than one miscarriage before the birth of their son George. Ellen played the harp, and in *Ibbetson* George Du Maurier portrayed his musical par-ents as M. and Mme Pasquier de la Marière.

At the end of October 1833 the Busson Du Mauriers bought the 'lit-tle house in the Champs-Élysées' where George was born on 6 March 1834.[73] After mentioning the house, Du Maurier went on to explain to an interviewer that as an adult he could only remember the pine trees that used to be on the Champs-Élysées. This is unfortunate because the little house has a distinguished history.

At the time of the purchase, the Busson Du Mauriers' address was 6 rue des Bouchers, Barrière de l'Étoile (part of the current rue Chalgrin, just west of the Arc de Triomphe). The notary provides a precise description of their new house, its garden and dependencies:

> … two square pavilions, to the right and left of the entry gate, a small building adjoining the left-hand pavilion, the main building facing the entry gate, consisting in one underground floor, a ground floor, and a first floor *en mansarde* above; a courtyard before the said main building and open terrain to the right and the left serving as a passageway to the garden which is at the back of the property.[74]

The origin of the property dated back to 1792, when Charles-Maurice Talleyrand-Périgord, ex-*député* of the *Assemblée Nationale*, wished to have an *hôtel* built for himself.[75]

He bought a terrain that had belonged to the fief of the count of Artois, located on the Champs-Élysées between the rue d'Angoulême-St-Honoré (the current rue La Boétie) and the rue Neuve-de-Berri. He commissioned it from François-Joseph Bélanger – the architect of the château de Bagatelle in the Bois de Boulogne (pictured on page 31).

According to the author of a book on Bélanger:

> On 10 July 1815, prince Talleyrand ceded his property, which was situated at No. 20 of the avenue de Neuilly, to Alexandre-Daniel de Talleyrand-Périgord, baron Talleyrand, prefect of the Loiret department, for the sum of 20,000 francs. The new owner then resold it, on 15 July 1819, to Casimir-François Meyer and Jean-Sébastien Vaume. The former property of prince Talleyrand, an area of 2,466 metres, was divided between the two buyers and the house Bélanger had designed was demolished.

Vaume built a new house on his portion of the land. On 21 August 1828, Marguerite-Félicité Berlot, Vaume's widow, sold the property for 40,000 francs to Stanislas-Romain Petit, who then sold it for the same price to Joseph Bergmiller, from whom the Busson Du Mauriers acquired it, for 41,000 francs, on 31 October 1833.

Jacques-Louis and the Hamburg Du Mauriers

Jacques-Louis, the older brother of Louise and Louis-Mathurin, married Emilie Sabine Maria Christiani, born in Göttingen to Christian Christiani, a former bookkeeper who became a lecturer in French and English at the University of Göttingen, and his wife.

Jacques-Louis and Emilie lived in Hamburg, and between 1832 and 1838 their four children – Eliza, Josephine, Pedro and Emil (who died at the age of nine) – were born there. Pedro's godparents were the Portuguese aristocrats the Palmellas, who employed Louise Wallace.

From 1835 the Hamburg Address Book describes J.-L. Busson Du Maurier as a doctor of philology. There are a few traces of his existence in the 1840s. Louise Wallace saved the letter she received from her older brother in 1842. In apologising for his silence, Jacques-Louis displayed his erudition when he combined references to the Gospel, Dr Johnson, the Prince de Polignac, the supposed Breton motto of the Bussons, and Hercules. He carried on to complain of the Hamburg climate, schools, governesses and interruptions, and thanked heaven his children were 'good' and 'open'.

Hamburg's Staats- und Universitäts-Bibliothek holds a brief note from Jacques-Louis in French, dated 1845: 'I have the honour of begging His Excellency M. von Struve to agree to grant me an interview of a few minutes on the subject of a proposition, which could be agreed to by the Ministers of His Majesty the Emperor.'[76] Possibly the proposition Jacques-Louis wished to discuss was related to the pamphlet he published two years later, in German and at his own expense. It was entitled *How can the wealthy classes, as well as the particularly poor classes, protect themselves against the constant increase of the cost of living? Statutes of a Hamburg-formed supply society: 'Unity and Strength'.*[77]

Jacques-Louis died in Hamburg in 1851, and his younger daughter Josephine also died there in 1863, at the age of twenty-eight. In 1874 Jacques-Louis's surviving son Pedro applied for a tradesman's license and was required by the High Senate of Hamburg to defend his aristocratic surname: was he really a Busson Du Maurier, or merely a simple Busson? In response he produced a copy of his father's baptism and his own, and stated that he was currently the only Busson Du Maurier living in Germany, since two of his siblings had died and his surviving sister was living in London, where she went by the name 'Eliza de Busson'.

Louis-Mathurin's letters to Louise Wallace in Portugal

It is not clear when or how Louise met the Portuguese aristocrat Eugenia Francisca Telles Da Gama, who married the Portuguese diplomat and statesman Pedro de Sousa Holstein (1781–1850) – the future Duke of Palmella – in Lisbon in 1810, when she was twelve. Among non-specialists, he is sometimes still remembered for his relationship with Mme de Staël in 1805–06 and for having informed Napoleon at an international conference in 1808 that the Portuguese would not consent to becoming Spanish.

George Du Maurier wrote in a fragment that his Aunt Louise was 'an old school friend and sister émigrée in bygone times of the Duchess'.[78] The remark seems to imply that Eugenia had been raised in London, as had Louise. George also suggested that Louise's husband was 'a poor relation of the Duchess', but it has not been possible to find a connection between the Telles Da Gama family and the Wallaces. Between 1812 and 1841 the Palmellas had fifteen children. According to a work on the Duchess's family, after giving birth to eleven children, she lived quietly in Passy while her husband's travels took him to Brazil, and their twelfth child was born in Paris in 1830.[79] It was possibly in this period that she first employed Louise as governess to her six surviving daughters, aged from two to seventeen at the time.

By 1834 Louise had accompanied the Palmellas to Portugal and she remained with them until the Duchess's death in 1848. Beginning a few months after George's birth in March 1834 and over the next twenty years, forty letters from Louis-Mathurin to his sister Louise Wallace survive.[80] On Christmas day 1834 Louis-Mathurin wrote a long letter to Louise. Louis-Mathurin was alone in Paris on account of his brother-in-law's business and his own, but hoped he would soon be able to join Ellen and young George, in England, with Ellen's mother and sister. Only a year had passed since the Busson Du Mauriers bought their little house in the Champs-Élysées and already Louis-Mathurin was trying to let or sell it, and planned to sell most of the furniture.

In his autobiographic interview, George discreetly characterised his father as 'a man of scientific tastes'. In one of his letters, Louis-Mathurin referred to a project he was about to undertake with George Clarke, Ellen's brother: 'passing a contract with any government for clearing any sea port or river'. He mentioned having laid out the project in a previous letter and seemed to hope his sister would seek financial support from the Duke of Palmella.

In 1838 Louis-Mathurin joined with Captain Matthew Henry Willock to obtain a ten-year patent to supply an artificial combustible, called 'Uppekkauma-Neon', which he described as follows:

> ... composed according to the resources offered by localities, the intended usage, and the quality of the peat, ground or mud, of nitre, sulfate, linseed and other oily substances; nuts and kernels of different types; pitch, coke, peat and other clays and muds, substances

containing a high degree of vegetal matter, all kinds of green plants, excrement, all sorts of animal matter. The whole is mixed together, pressed into bricks and dried in the sun and air if possible, or by artificial means if necessary.[81]

In January 1839 Louis-Mathurin was granted a six-month patent 'for improvements in the construction of springs for carriages'. He also invented a safety lamp – its sudden explosion leads to Peter's father's death in *Ibbetson* – and published a proposal in English and French to replace passports with medallions.

Louis-Mathurin apparently continued a business partnership with his friend Captain Willock. When in 1844 a second British protectorate over the Mosquito Kingdom – now part of Nicaragua – was declared, Willock, who had travelled there, received the title 'Protector General of the Indian Subjects of the Mosquito Kingdom'. Several Prussian investors also became involved, leading eventually to a complex international dispute over land rights that caused Louis-Mathurin to spend the winter of 1848–9 in Berlin.

Ellen Du Maurier's brother-in-law, a rascal named Charles Proby Bowles

In a letter written in Brussels, Louis-Mathurin announced his plan to go to Sardinia 'to follow a rascal of an Englishman for a large sum of money which he has defrauded and run away with and is gone to pass the winter in those quarters where I shall join him soon after Ellen's *accouchement* [confinement]'. He added that

> The name of the man I am going to Italy after for 300,000 [francs] is Bowles – and for his rascalities has been put up on the blackboard in the Stock Exchange in London for defrauding the stockbrokers there of 30,000 pounds. My claim is for money defrauded in Paris. He ruined one poor stockbroker in Paris who out of despair shot his brains out and left a widow and three children in poverty and despair. This Bowles is in fact one of the greatest villains on earth.
>
> One half of the three hundred thousand francs belong to me....[82]

In May 1836 Louis-Mathurin was in Paris on the way to Italy: 'it is my intention to take the steamer at Marseilles and go to Naples (where my debtor is) by sea'. He hoped to be back home within two months.

The outcome of Louis-Mathurin's expedition is not known, but it is possible to shed some light on the chequered career of Charles Proby

Bowles. Ellen's older sister Mary Anne presumably married Charles Proby Bowles sometime between his November 1829 letter published in *The Dublin Morning Register*, asserting he was divorced from his first wife and had not clandestinely remarried, and the birth of their son in January 1831, although no record of the marriage has been found. Like Wallace, Bowles was a former soldier, and something of a rake. He seems to have been born around 1785.

According to the *Peninsula Roll Call* Bowles was an ensign, then a lieutenant in the 83rd Regiment of Foot from 1808 and he served in the peninsula from 1809 to 1813. He was severely wounded in the storming of Badajoz and granted a temporary pension of £100 per annum. In 1826 he purchased a captaincy in the 26th Regiment of Foot.

In Dublin in 1813 Bowles had married Catherine Davis, a widow; they went on to have a daughter and two sons in approximately 1816, 1818 and 1819. Bowles and his first wife Catherine then separated and eventually, as will be mentioned below, divorced.

In February 1825 Bowles was in Pisa according to a breach of promise case.[83] The plaintiff was Charlotte Augusta Daniel, the convent-educated daughter of a retired British army officer and his Italian wife, aged eighteen when she met Bowles. In April the couple eloped to England, where Charlotte discovered her suitor was in fact already married. Her family took her from Kensington back to Italy, where she gave birth to Bowles's daughter. The jury returned a verdict for the plaintiff with damages of £1,500.

In November 1829, Bowles's name appears in *The Dublin Morning Register* under the heading 'Reward of Ten Pounds':

> To any person who will communicate the present abode of Captain Charles Probey [sic] Bowles, late a Captain in his Majesty's 26th Regiment, and late of the Combe, Dublin; also who shall give an account of the individual the said Captain Bowles has clandestinely married within these few years. A reward also of five pounds will be given to any person who may communicate the dwelling of Captain Bowles's two children, both the grandchildren to the late Samuel Hanley, of the town of Galway, and County Galway. The said grandchildren are in stature tall of their age, a young lady 13 years of age, of auburn hair, hazel eyes, and remarkably fair in colour; the brother of the said Miss Louise Hanley Bowles, is of a dark colour, chestnut colour hair, hazel eyes, and ten years of age. Both these children had been secreted in London and on the continent by Captain Bowles; and as all letters and

communications cannot find them, in consequence of a sum of money left to these children by a relative, it becomes necessary to ascertain their dwelling and existence, a circumstance which causes this public inquiry to be made; and under the above reasons it is hoped, that if this reaches high life, that the bosom of exalted personages, too noble to receive remuneration, will speedily, by some inquiry, hasten the discovery of these little children, which deed of compassion must receive a much higher reward than that which could be presented. All communications, franked or post-paid, will be received at the Hibernian Government Stock Bank House, Marlborough Street, Dublin, directed to C[atherine] Hanley Bowles.[84]

Ten days later Bowles wrote the following reply to the Editor of the paper:

Having seen an advertisement in your paper of the 13th instant, by C[atherine] Hanley Bowles, offering a reward of 1ol. to any person who would procure her my present address, and that of my children; and also falsely asserting that I am clandestinely married: I beg your immediate insertion of this letter, stating that I am at present residing in Paris, rue Neuve de la Ferme des Mathurins, No. 30, where I superintend the education of my children, and in the exercise of parental authority I forbid them holding any intercourse with the aforesaid Catherine Bowles, their mother, from whom I obtained a divorce in the Prerogative Court of Dublin, in the month of April, 1825, on the grounds of adultery committed by her.[85]

Bowles had moved to Paris and on 26 December 1829, for 10,500 francs, had bought all the furniture of the château de Puteaux – located just across the Seine from the Bois de Boulogne – from William Sinnott, another Irishman living in France.

Three months later, what would become the lengthy case of Proby-Bowles versus Goldsmith began in the French courts. Bowles had deposited over 227,000 francs in the bank of Orr and Goldsmith and had a remaining balance of 114,000 francs. The bank invested the money according to his verbal instructions and lost over 90,000 francs, which they then requested from him. Bowles maintained that, on the contrary, the bank owed him approximately 100,000 francs. Eventually both the *Tribunal de Commerce* and the *Cour Royale de Paris* ordered Bowles to pay the bank the 90,000 francs plus interest.

On 12 January 1831 Alfred Arthur Loraine Bowles, the son of Charles

Proby Bowles and Mary Anne Clarke (Ellen Du Maurier's sister) was born, and baptised a few months later in the parish of Christchurch. Alfred's brother, Charles Hubert Noel, was christened at Newchurch on the Isle of Wight on 4 July 1832. Between 1832 and 1835, Bowles owned the estate of Old Park on the Isle of Wight.[86]

Bowles was present when Louise Catherine, his daughter by his first wife, married John Edward Venables Vernon Esq. in Brussels in August 1836. Their marriage settlement, dated 1839, signed Dublin's Clontarf Castle and its lands – which had previously belonged to the Venables Vernons – over to Bowles and Louise's two brothers for ninety-nine years.[87] In the same year Louise's younger brother, John Edwin, entered the Military Service of the East India Company.

It is not known if Louis-Mathurin ever recovered the money Bowles owed him, but it seems unlikely.

Louis-Mathurin's last years

In the last few years of his life Louis-Mathurin's letters to his sister express concern for his children, as well as their late brother's children:

> Eliza called on us about a fortnight ago – she is quite blooming and will not take an appointment at less than 70 pounds a year. There was one to be had at 40 pounds a year but she would not go after it. She is fond of money and knows how to take care of her own. Josephine is with a family in Prussia and the Mother had an appointment in Hamburg or somewhere near there. Pedro comes to England next year....[88]

Louis-Mathurin worried that his younger son Eugene was not an officer but a mere 'common soldier', and as for his elder son:

> Kicky has had nothing to do since he returned from the country, *c'est peu encourageant – mais il n'y a pas de quoi se désespérer – Espérons donc mieux* [it is not very encouraging, but there is no reason to despair – Let us therefore hope] – If I can, I will soon send him to Paris for a fortnight to learn a new process of instantaneous photography whereby I think he could make a good bit of money. He will be delighted to go and see you [Louise was living in Versailles] – you are a great favourite with him – indeed if things took the turn I might fairly expect I would pay a visit also.[89]

Louis-Mathurin did pay another visit to Paris, for when the first

Exposition Universelle was held in the summer of 1855, he won a medal of honour in the field of the art of mines and metallurgy, 'as the inventor of a remarkable process for the carbonisation of peat':

> The novel feature in this process consists in the intimate intermixture of coal dust from pit banks, etc., with powdered peat, by the aid of a machine, and by which means the inventor obtains a coke, or fuel of which the specific gravity, although a little less than that of the best Newcastle coal-coke is such as to offer the consistency required to render it fit for all purposes where coke (pure coal) is used, whilst it is applicable to many uses for which that is with difficulty employed.[90]

Louis-Mathurin's last letter to his sister in Versailles appears to have been written from Paris, sometime in the early autumn of 1855. He was feeling ill and may not have been able to go out to meet her the next day, but explained how to get from Versailles to the exhibition.

Louis-Mathurin died at home in Clerkenwell on 8 June 1856. George recalls: 'My poor father ... died – in my arms – as he was singing one of count de Segur's drinking songs. He left this world almost with music on his lips.'[91]

CHAPTER THREE

GEORGE DU MAURIER, 'THE PASSY NIGHTINGALE'

*I became the enfant-prodige [child prodigy] of Passy, the
Passy nightingale, before my parents suspected anything,
and was forgiven for being half-English, wearing the tall
hat, large shirt collar, and short jacket of an English boy.*

George Du Maurier, autobiographical fragment

In an autobiographical interview, George Du Maurier gives the following
description of his birthplace:

> ... I was born in Paris, on March 6, 1834, in a little house in the
> Champs-Élysées. It bore the number 80. It was afterwards sold by my
> father, and has since been pulled down. I often look at the spot when
> I am in Paris and am walking down the Champs-Élysées, and what
> I most regret at such times are the pine trees which in my childhood
> used to be there – very different from the miserable, stumpy avenue of
> today. It is a disillusion which comes upon me with equal force at each
> new visit, for I remember the trees, and the trees only.[92]

About a year later young George and his parents joined his maternal
grandmother Mary Anne Clarke, and his maternal aunt Mary Anne
Bowles and her two sons, Alfred and Charlie, at Rother House, Rotherfield, Sussex. (In *Peter Ibbetson* Alfred and Charlie Bowles appear briefly
as Peter's cousins Alfred and Charlie Plunkett.) George Louis Palmella
was christened there in April, after his maternal uncle George Clarke, his
father Louis-Mathurin, and the Palmellas, the Portuguese family who
employed his paternal aunt Louise Wallace.

In October 1835, for reasons that are not entirely clear, the Busson Du Mauriers were living in Laeken (now part of Brussels), and Ellen was expecting another baby. Alexander Eugene was born in Laeken on 9 February 1836 (and also named after two of the Palmellas). Daphne Du Maurier wrote that the Du Mauriers moved to Brussels because Palmella was the ambassador there, but in fact the poet and politician Almeida Garrett was Portugal's diplomatic representative in Belgium from 1834 to 1836, and he did not have a secretary.[93]

George Du Maurier mentioned a memory from this period in his auto-biographical interview:

> I remember with peculiar vividness a Belgian man-servant of ours, called Francis. I used to ask him to take me in his arms and to carry me downstairs to look at some beautiful birds. I used to think that these were real birds each time that I looked at them, although, in fact, they were but painted on the panes, and I had been told so.[94]

From Marylebone to Boulogne-sur-Mer

George recalled in his interview that '[w]e stayed three years in Belgium, and when I was five years old I went with my parents to London, where my father took a house – the house which a year later was taken by Charles Dickens – 1 Devonshire Terrace, Marylebone Road'.[95] The Du Mauriers' last child, Georgina Isabella, was born at this address on 2 March 1839.

In an 1884 letter to Henry James, George mentioned his 'sweet recollections' of the six months his family spent in Dover in 1840:

> ... I was a little English boy there, with a delightful circle of parents, uncles, cousins, aunts and a grandmother – all dead, alas! and my first love, a lovely creature, Miss Ellen Glascock, whose papa (Admiral Glascock) was for a time the rival of Captain Marryat and wrote tales of the sea, she was some 15 years my senior (21 and I, 6), but oh how I loved her – we used all to congregate on a little wooden pier at the northern extremity of the town, and have a lovely time.... If dear Ellen Glascock is alive, she is just 65 years of age. I shouldn't know her if I met her – even on that pier.[96]

Captain William Nugent Glascock's daughter, Ellen Letitia, was born in 1826, making her only about eight years older than George Du Maurier, not fifteen.

As an adult Ellen Glascock achieved something of a reputation as an amateur composer, who 'associated the more striking of our national occasions with as characteristic music'. Her works included 'The Star of the East Waltz', dedicated to Florence Nightingale, 'The Queen of Greece Waltzes', 'The Sea Serpent Polka', 'The Louis Napoleon Polka', and 'India: The People's Polka'. *The Ladies' Companion* described her compositions as 'refined but simple, and original without attempting eccentric individuality'.[97] Ellen married in 1859 and died in Kensington in 1865.

From London, the Du Mauriers moved on to Boulogne-sur-Mer. In George's words,

> We only stayed a year in Devonshire Terrace, for my father grew very poor. He was a man of scientific tastes, and lost his money in inventions which never came to anything. So we had to wander forth again, and this time we went to Boulogne, and there we lived in a beautiful house on the top of the Grande Rue. I had sunny hours there, and was very happy.[98]

Ellen Du Maurier's mother, sister and nephews were also living in Boulogne. Here George began his studies. According to one of his father's letters,

> He has an Irish professor who goes to his house every day to teach him Latin, cyphering and writing – his mamma teaching him geography, English and history in which he is rather advanced and he sometimes teaches his cousin who is two years and a half older than himself. As to master Eugene his taste for learning has not yet shown itself. He far prefers riding a pony or a donkey than learning a column of spelling – but he seems inclined to learn drawing and I shall soon give them both a drawing master.[99]

The Du Mauriers' Boulogne hours were not all sunny, as Ellen's sister Mary Anne Bowles died there in June 1841.

George Du Maurier recalled the period of his aunt's funeral in a letter to his mother, on the occasion of his honeymoon in Boulogne in 1863. He returns to the Pont de Brigue,

> … about three miles from Boulogne – if you recollect uncle [George Clarke] took Alfred and Charlie and me there for two or 3 days, during

the funeral, and while Alfred fished Charlie and I made sand pies near a little watermill and my uncle laid himself down and cried as I very well perceived but I could not understand why. I made a mud pie there on Saturday (just 2 and 20 years after) of which I send you a small fragment. Though I had not much affection for any of them, all but Charlie, it made me sad to think they are all gone.[100]

The 1841 Boulogne-sur-Mer census listed the Busson Du Mauriers and their three children at an address on the Grande Rue. Young Alfred and Charlie Bowles lived in a household on the rue Basse des Tintelleries headed by 'Mary Chamberts, *rentière* [annuitant]', a widow – possibly an assumed name of their maternal grandmother Mary Anne Clarke.

Passy-lès-Paris

Du Maurier related in his interview:

> From Boulogne we went to Paris, to live in an apartment on the first floor of the house No. 108 in the Champs-Élysées. The house still stands, but the ground floor is now a café, and the first floor is part of it. I feel sorry when I look up at the windows from which my dear mother's face used to watch for my return from school, and see waiters bustling about and my home invaded.[101]

In 1842, on George's eighth birthday, Louis-Mathurin wrote to his sister 'that my children and their little mamma are all well; the eldest and master Eugene also go to school at Passy where I believe I told you that Ellen is stopping'. Revealing a certain anti-French sentiment, despite the fact that he himself was French on both sides, Louis-Mathurin asked Louise,

> Did you know the house which the Palmellas had at a part of Passy called La Muette? If you did you will perhaps recollect a house at the entrance of the avenue which leads to it, on the right hand side – This is the house which I am about taking for Ellen, and which I should already have taken, if I could have done as I had liked. Whether I shall be able to manage it I am not certain but I will do everything in my power for my family would be very comfortable there and then Ellen would be quiet about her boys as she could see them in the playground of the school and they would only have to cross the street backwards and forwards and not be exposed to dirty sights etc. – which is continually the case in the *beau pays de France* [beautiful country of France]. Of course they do not

board and sleep at school, though it is a very good reputed school and great attention is paid to the morals and religion of the children, still I would rather they never went to school at all than be at a French school entirely – I like Passy for my family pretty well.[102]

Louis-Mathurin took the house he liked; many years later in a letter to his wife George described returning to look 'at the outside of the house where I lived from 8 to 11, and which is to me the dearest of all these Passy dwellings. What my luck to find *"Maison à Louer"* [House to Let]! I have never put foot in it since we déménagéd [moved house] 22 years ago!'[103]

Until its annexation to Paris in 1860, as part of the sixteenth arrondissement, Passy was a sleepy village known mainly for its mineral springs. After a brief stay at an unknown address on the rue de la Tour, the Busson Du Mauriers resided at 31 rue de la Pompe, Passy between 1842 and 1845. It is this location that features in *Peter Ibbetson*. An 1851 newspaper advertised for sale or rent a pretty house with a beautiful garden, a henhouse, a stable, sheds and other outbuildings at number 31 bis.

The Du Mauriers' street took its name from the pump that furnished water to the nearby château de la Muette, a former royal domain. The far end of their avenue off the rue de la Pompe led to what Peter Ibbetson describes as a 'large private park that seemed to belong to nobody'; it had probably once been part of the château's grounds.[104] After the Revolution, the estate was divided into two parts and the château's central wing, connecting two pavilions, destroyed: 'The right wing, that closest to Passy, had four windows and a small side garden. It was thus called "La Petite Muette"; the left side, with five windows and a more spacious garden, retained the name "La Muette".' La Petite Muette 'passed through several hands until it was purchased for the newly formed Auteuil Railroad': a source of despair for George and his hero.[105]

The wealthy piano-maker Sébastien Érard bought La Muette in 1820 and restored and expanded it; at his death in 1831 his heir rented the property for a time. From 1835 Jules Guérin, a prominent surgeon, superintended a children's orthopaedic institution there. An American doctor gave an account of his 1839 visit to La Muette that confirms *Peter Ibbetson*'s description of its author's childhood playground:

... I spent the greater part of a fine day in ranging over the numerous buildings and apartments of the fine old château, now converted to

"O NIGHTINGALE!"

Peter's father's 'nightingale' voice lulls him to sleep

other purposes, and its beautiful grounds of forty acres, ornamented with every variety of tree and shrub, and tastefully laid out with gravelled walks, gardens, lawns, all furnished with every species of rural luxury calculated to please the fancy or benefit the health of those who, from choice or necessity, may seek such an asylum.[106]

A *maison de santé* (nursing home) was close by the Du Mauriers' house. In 1847 the Parisian newspaper *La Presse* advertised Dr Tirat de Malemort's *maison de santé et de convalescence* for patients over age ten suffering from chest complaints at 31 rue de la Pompe: 'Beautiful site, garden and park. Gymnastics, riding.'

Admirers of the nightingale
An unpublished autobiographical fragment by George Du Maurier centred on his musical awakening, which took place during this period. After describing his mother's playing on the harp and his father's voice – 'He *was* the nightingale' –, George wrote that

... of all the sounds of that time, the sound of sounds, *the* sound, was that which suddenly burst from my throat on one April morning and changed the world for me. It seems to me now that after a long hard winter, the spring came along in a single night, and that with it the warmth and fullness of my throat was loosened and something melted away therein which had kept my melodious little soul in bondage. I would rush off to the park and warble all the songs I knew, which means all the songs I had ever heard, and every day I warbled better and louder and sweeter, and the gift soon found other admirers than I.[107]

The first admirers George recalls were tenants of the *maison de santé*.

In *Ibbetson* they are described as 'four or five gentlemen who had tried to invade France, with a certain grim Pretender at their head, and a tame eagle as a symbol of empire to rally round'. Peter calls them 'Colonel Voisil, le Major Duquesnois, le Capitaine Audenis, [and] le Docteur Lombal'.[108] Three of these names are recognisable as Colonel Voisin, Lieutenant Aladenize, and Docteur Lombard, who were among the fifty participants in Louis-Napoleon's unsuccessful Boulogne expedition of 1840.

According to Du Maurier's autobiographical fragment, the 'Napoleonic officers never seemed to tire of my warblings ... ; among these was a Major Duquesne, an old man with a large grey moustache, a long green coat, and the most simple childlike courtly manners.'[109] Major Florent Joseph Duquesne, born in 1788 and retired in 1842 from the Fourth Regiment of Hussards (and apparently not one of the Boulogne conspirators, despite what Du Maurier implies), may well have been the inspiration for 'le Major Duquesnois'. The autobiographical fragment continues:

> In return for my strains, Major Duquesne used to tell me long fairy tales, which he probably invented as we walked along, and which never came to a point, so that the delights of anticipation never came to an end and I used to sing to him songs of Béranger, especially one: *Parlez-nous de lui, grand'mère,/ Grand'mère, parlez-nous de lui....* [Speak to us of him, grandmother,/ Grandmother, speak to us of him].
>
> I believe '*lui*' was the great Napoleon but I was innocent of any party feeling and only thought of the tune.

The boys' school opposite the Du Mauriers' house was the Pension de Pellieux: here, too, the young nightingale's voice attracted attention. The headmaster, Louis-Benjamin-Léopold de Pellieux – called 'Monsieur

Philibert' in the autobiographical fragment – came from a conservative Catholic family. At the Revolution his father, an army officer, had emigrated and married in Hamburg.

George recalled that one day he stole in amongst 'the vocal boys' at the Pension who were being trained to sing a religious melody with the refrain *Stabat Mater dolorosa*.[110] 'My pipe rose triumphant over the other pipes, and as soon as we had finished the singing master beckoned me to him' and asked the boy his name, age, and where he lived:

> He and Monsieur le Curé held a consultation, and the result was that Monsieur Philibert, the headmaster, called on my mother, with a very warm request that I should be allowed to take part in the coming fête and sing the solo parts – this request was denied and reasons given which apparently satisfied Monsieur Philibert. But I used to sing to Monsieur le Curé and to Monsieur Philibert; and to Madame Philibert, who gave me sweets; and I was made to sing to a wet nurse who was nourishing a young Isidore Philibert, and on whom my strains according to Madame Philibert produced the most beneficial effect...

On another occasion,

> The music master, Monsieur Philibert, and Monsieur le Curé asked me to sing *Francs Lurons* [a bacchanalian air] in my father's style, but when I came to *Partout où mes yeux verront femme jolie* [Wherever my eyes see a pretty woman], Monsieur le Curé checked me – conscious of having made a terrible mistake and blushing ingenuously, I changed my tune and sang *Stabat Mater* with such sad and chastened emotion that Monsieur le Curé took a pinch of snuff and gave me a kiss.

For a brief period Du Maurier was a day scholar at the Pension de Pellieux.[111] In *Ibbetson* the boys' school opposite Peter's home is M. Jules Saindou's *maison d'éducation*; he mentions its 'gymnastic fixtures in the playground, M. Saindou's pride'.[112]

The Passy nightingale's final musical memory from this period concerned an impromptu visit by the Duke and Duchess of Palmella and their daughters. Du Maurier described his aunt's employer as 'a great Catholic and a stupendous swell':

> My mother was out and we young people had to do the honours until she returned, and after we had exhausted the guinea pigs and white

mice, I bethought me of singing to them – I shall never forget the Duke and Duchess's enthusiasm as long as I live – when my mother returned, they could talk of nothing else – they wanted to adopt me, to have me Romanised on the spot, to pay for the most gorgeous musical education, to ungodfather my poor brother and godfather me instead – my mother was as inexorable as fate and would not even allow me to go back with them to Paris for a week; they supplicated and promised in vain, and drove away in a huff; and with them drove away, as I often feel with painful regret, the greatest chance in life I ever had. For their wealth and influence were boundless and their kindness, generosity and fidelity to their friends were proverbial among those who knew them.[113]

When Ellen Du Maurier was a child, her mother had negotiated to receive an annuity from the British royal family. Then, as an adult, she had to tolerate her husband's largely unsuccessful attempts to find wealthy patrons for his scientific pursuits. Although Ellen and Louis-Mathurin were agnostics, she allowed their second son, named after the Palmellas, to be raised as a Catholic. In this context Mrs Du Maurier's reluctance to also 'loan' George to the Palmellas, even for a week, is perhaps understandable.

The Institution Froussard, and a summer holiday in Sarthe

From 1847 to 1851 George and Eugene were boarders at the Institution Froussard on the avenue de Saint-Cloud, called the 'Institution F. Brossard' in *The Martian* where George fondly recalls the Froussard father and son, and includes their portraits. Baptiste Froussard, the father, left his mark in French history.

Froussard was born in Grenoble in 1792 to a family of modest origins. In secondary school he befriended his fellow pupil Jean-François Champollion, who went on to become the renowned Egyptologist. When Froussard married Rose Césarine Champollion, Jean-François, the 'first cousin of the bride's father' as stated in the parish register, was one of the guests. In 1819, in association with Froussard's older brother, Froussard and Champollion founded the École Latine in Montfleury near Grenoble.[114] Due to the political climate the École Latine only lasted for three years; after it closed Baptiste Froussard was called to Paris where the liberal grenoblois banker and statesman Casimir Perier hired him to tutor his sons. Froussard went on to direct the École normale primaire in Versailles and then the Prytanée (military academy) in Ménars, near Blois.

When his administrative responsibilities conflicted with his democratic ideas, he resigned from the latter.

It was then that Froussard founded a flourishing institution in Passy, which he eventually – in the years George Du Maurier attended – turned over to his son Melchior. As George's narrator puts it: 'the headmaster was a famous republican, and after February '48 was elected a *représent-ant du peuple* [representative of the people] for the Dauphiné, and sat in the Chamber of Deputies'.[115]

Several of the letters Louis-Mathurin sent to Louise Wallace in the 1840s mentioned their father's sister – 'dear aunt Duval' – who was still living in Sarthe at the time. The Duvals' daughter had married a Dr Rosiau, and they were also living in Paris. In Paris the Busson Du Mauriers met the Rosiaus and probably also Mme Duval. (In the prologue to *The Glass-Blowers*, Daphne Du Maurier would imagine their meeting.) It was in this period that, for the benefit of her English relatives, Mme Duval wrote the letter on Busson family history that would eventually prompt George's and then Daphne's genealogical research, as we saw in the Introduction.

The Martian contains George Du Maurier's thinly disguised account of his visit to his father's Duval relatives, renamed the 'Lafertés'. (The Duvals' home near Vibraye, Sarthe, was about 15 km from the town of La Ferté-Bernard.) The episode might be of limited anecdotal interest, were it not for the longstanding confusion over what George knew versus what he imagined about his family's French origins.

In *The Martian*, Laferté is a schoolfellow of Barty Josselin, the hero of the novel, and Robert Maurice, the narrator. He invites them to spend the summer holiday with his family:

> The Lafertés lived in the Department of La Sarthe, in a delightful country-house, with a large garden sloping down to a transparent stream, which had willows and alders and poplars all along both its banks, and a beautiful country beyond.
>
> Outside the grounds (where there were the old brick walls, all overgrown with peaches and pears and apricots, of some forgotten mediaeval convent) was a large farm; and close by, a watermill that never stopped.
>
> A road, with thick hedgerows on either side, led to a small and very pretty town called La Tremblaye, three miles off....
>
> [M. Laferté] seldom moved from his country home, which was called 'Le Gué des Aulnes', except to go shooting in the forest....[116]

The 'very pretty town called "La Tremblaye"' is Vibraye, and 'Le Gué des Aulnes' is the hamlet called Le Gué de l'Aunay, where 'some forgotten mediaeval convent' – the Abbaye Saint-Laurent – had been located. When church lands were seized by the state and sold after the Revolution, Louis-Mathurin's aunt Duval and her husband, an iron-master and former revolutionary, bought the ruins of the abbey and began building a house there.

The Martian includes a drawing of a character based on the Duvals' oldest son François – the first cousin of George Du Maurier's father – who was the mayor of Vibraye for many years: 'M. Laferté was a man of about fifty – *entre les deux âges* [middle-aged]; a retired *maître de forges*, or iron-master, or else the son of one – I forget which. He had a charming wife and two pretty little daughters, Jeanne et [sic] Marie, aged fourteen and twelve.'

Barty's singing and other accomplishments impress the Lafertés, M. Laferté in particular: 'two or three times a day would Barty receive some costly token of this queer old giant's affection, till he got quite unhappy about it. He feared he was despoiling the House of Laferté of all its treasures in silver and gold....'[117]

George's evocation of M. Laferté's mother – based on Sophie Duval née Busson – is particularly important:

His old mother, who was of good family and eighty years of age, lived in a quite humble cottage in a small street in La Tremblaye, with two little peasant girls to wait on her; and the La Tremblayes, with whom M. Laferté was not on speaking terms, were always coming into the village to see her and bring her fruit and flowers and game. She was a most accomplished old lady, and an excellent musician, and had known Monsieur de Lafayette.

We breakfasted with her when we alighted from the diligence at six in the morning; and she took such a fancy to Barty that her own grandson was almost forgotten. He sang to her, and she sang to him, and showed him autograph letters of Lafayette, and a lock of her hair when she was seventeen, and old-fashioned miniatures of her father and mother, Monsieur and Madame de something I've quite forgotten.[118]

'Monsieur and Madame de something I've quite forgotten' – the parents of this 'accomplished old lady' who had 'two little peasant girls to wait on her' and who was on such good terms with the local aristocrats – were Mathurin Busson and his wife Madeleine, George's great-grandparents.

By the time he wrote his novels in the last years of his life, Du Maurier ought to have concluded from his great-aunt Sophie Duval's letter on family history – if not from his conversations with her when he was an adolescent – that her parents were simple Bussons without an aristocratic particle or a suffix to their surname. Chapter Six explores the intricate cipher in which George enveloped family history in his first novel.

In late September M. Laferté took his guests 'to make a tour of provincial visits *en famille*':

> We put up at the country houses of friends and relations of the Lafertés; and visited old historical castles and mediaeval ruins – Châteaudun and others – and fished in beautiful pellucid tributaries of the Loire – shot over *des chiens anglais* [English dogs] – danced half the night with charming people – wandered in lovely parks and woods, and beautiful old formal gardens with fishponds, terraces, statues, marble fountains; *charmilles, pelouses, quinconces* [arbors, lawns, quincunxes]; and all the flowers and all the fruits of France!
>
> If being made much of, and petted and patted and admired and wondered at, make up the sum of human bliss, Barty came in for as full a share of felicity during that festive week as should last an ordinary mortal for a twelvemonth. *Figaro quà, Figaro là*, from morning till night in three departments of France![119]

George's stay with his Duval relatives seems to have taken place in either 1848 or 1849, and Mme Duval died in Vibraye at the end of September 1849, at the age of eighty-five.

Return to London

Du Maurier related the end of his secondary studies in France to an interviewer:

> At the age of seventeen I went up for my *bachot*, my baccalaureate degree, at the Sorbonne, and was plucked for my written Latin version. It is true that my nose began to bleed during the examination, and that upset me, and, besides, the professor who was in charge of the room had got an idea into his head that I had smuggled a 'crib' in, and kept watching me so carefully that I got nervous and flurried. My poor mother was very vexed with me for my failure, for we were very poor at that time, and it was important that I should do well. My father was then in England, and shortly after my discomfiture he wrote for me to

join him there. We had not informed him of my failure, and I felt very
miserable as I crossed, because I thought that he would be very angry
with me. He met me at the landing at London Bridge, and, at the sight
of my utterly woebegone face, guessed the truth, and burst out into a
roar of laughter. I think that this roar of laughter gave me the greatest
pleasure I ever experienced in all my life.[120]

The 1851 census has Louis-Mathurin and George at 54 Princes Street,
St Andrew's parish, Lambeth. By September the rest of the family had
joined them and they had moved to 44 Wharton Street, Pentonville.

Both George and Eugene were enrolled at University College. George's
friend Tom Armstrong, a painter who studied with him in Paris and who
went on to become director for art at the South Kensington Museum,
recalled in his 'Reminiscences of Du Maurier': 'In one of his books [*The
Martian*] there is an account of the hero going out street-singing with a
guitar, and meeting with much pecuniary success. This was founded on
fact, and happened when he was a student at University College, or when
he was supposed to be in practice as an analytical chemist.'[121]

A newspaper profile of Du Maurier also mentions his musical aspira-
tions in this period:

> Inheriting a beautiful tenor voice from his father, and a love of music
> from his mother, also an accomplished musician, it is probable that he
> would have made himself celebrated in the world of song had he been
> regularly educated for that career; but his parents, jealous of any occupa-
> tion or diversion which appeared likely to interfere with his developing
> into a second Faraday, the aim of their hopes, systematically snubbed
> and ridiculed their son's vocal efforts. However, nothing daunted, he
> insisted on singing, and finally he did sing, attaining proficiency by con-
> stant practice, unknown to his parents, wherever opportunity afforded.
> His father, shortly before his death, relented in his persecution; for, com-
> ing by accident upon a sketch which his son had made, representing him-
> self bowing low to an applauding audience with Beethoven's 'Adelaida'
> in his hand, he was so intensely amused by it, that he consented to give
> his son a few lessons in what the French call *dire la romance*.[122]

Both anecdotes concerning Louis-Mathurin cast him in a sympathetic
light.

In June 1852 Mary Anne Clarke died in Boulogne-sur-Mer. In *The
Du Mauriers*, Daphne Du Maurier imagined that Mrs Clarke's son,

daughter-in-law and grandson were with her. In fact her son George Clarke did not marry until May 1853, and there is no evidence that any member of her family was with her when she died. Mr Clarke's widow was – probably erroneously – said to be the daughter of the late Robert Farquhar Mackenzie and the former Ann Elizabeth Vernon, and to have been born in Oxford.

Emma Wightwick and 'Leah Gibson'

The 1851 census records George's future wife Emma Wightwick, age nine, scholar, at 21 Russell Grove, parish of St Mark's Kennington, Lambeth. She was staying with her maternal uncle, Reuben Fitch, described as a commercial traveller in oils and dry salting, and his wife.

In 1853 Emma seems to have been a pupil in Bedford Square, where she met George's sister Isabel. Isabel Du Maurier is called 'Ida' in *The Martian* and in the novel 'Ida, when about fourteen (1853), became a pupil at the junior school in the Ladies' College, 48 Bedford Square'. The novel portrays Emma Wightwick as Ida's friend 'Leah Gibson'.

Du Maurier described and illustrated the scene in which, accompanied by his sister, he first met Emma with two other girls, at the gates of the Foundling Hospital:

> The black-haired one was the youngest and the tallest – a fine, straight, bony child of twelve, with a flat back and square shoulders; she was very well dressed, and had nice brown boots with brown elastic sides on arched and straight-heeled slender feet, and white stockings on her long legs – a fashion in hose that has long gone out. She also wore a thick plait of black hair all down her back – another departed mode, and one not to be regretted, I think; and she swung her books round her as she talked, with easy movements, like a strong boy.[123]

Isabel recalled her brother's first meeting with Emma in the letter she wrote to her on her engagement. She identified the other girls as Helen and Annie Levy, two of the daughters of Joseph Moses Levy, the owner of a printing shop who was soon to buy the *Daily Telegraph*.

In *The Martian*, Du Maurier gave quite a detailed account of the 'Gibson' family, which, when applied to the Wightwicks, is for the most part accurate. Emma's father William was a linen warehouseman, born in Sevenoaks, Kent. He and his wife, the former Emma Jemima Fitch, lived at 42 Torrington Square in Bloomsbury. Mrs Wightwick's father John Fitch was a wealthy solicitor in Southwark, who died in 1842 leaving a good deal of property to his seven children.

The narrator of *The Martian* is particularly taken with Leah's mother: 'She was such an extremely pretty person, and so charmingly dressed, and had such winning, natural, genial manners, that I fell in love with her at first sight; she was also very playful and fond of romping; for she was young still, having married at seventeen.' Emma Jemima Fitch was indeed a minor – aged twenty however, not seventeen – when she married William Wightwick.

'Leah' does not resemble her own mother, 'Mrs Gibson', so much as her maternal grandmother:

> … Mrs Bletchley (who was present), was a Spanish Jewess – a most magnificent and beautiful old person in splendid attire, tall and straight, with white hair and thick black eyebrows, and large eyes as black as night.
>
> In Leah the high Sephardic Jewish type was more marked than in Mrs Gibson (who was not Jewish at all in aspect, and took after her father, the late Mr Bletchley).[124]

Here the novelist departed from biographical accuracy. Emma's maternal grandmother, Frances Fitch, née Smith, died in 1849 and therefore he would not have known her. Her place of birth and her parents' names are not known and her surname does not indicate a particular origin.

Regarding Emma's maternal origins, however, in annotating George Du Maurier's letters, Daphne commented that 'Emma had an uncle Reuben, which is perhaps significant'.[125] Emma's mother was also present as a witness at the Christ Church, Spitalfields wedding of Frederick Charles Fitch, another of her brothers, to Louise Rodrigues, the daughter of Isaac Rodrigues, a butcher residing in Norton Folgate. Years later Frederick Charles's daughter Julia, Emma Wightwick's first cousin, would be in her wedding party.

The characteristics the narrator admires in 'Leah' – her black hair, her height, her straight bearing – were supposedly inherited from her maternal grandmother. Recalling the heroines of *Peter Ibbetson* and *Trilby*, Leah's movements are said to be 'like a strong boy', and she also has 'a fine, bold, frank, deep voice, like a choir-boy's'.[126]

The narrator notes that Barty loves Byron and is 'faithful' to his Hebrew melodies. He concludes the passage about 'Leah' by quoting from 'She walks in beauty, like the night'. The poem was originally published as one of Byron's Hebrew melodies, and set to music – to a Sephardic tune – by Isaac Nathan.

The Britannia Gold and Copper Mining Company

In his autobiographic interview, George explained:

> My father ... put me as a pupil at the Birkbeck Chemical Laboratory of
> University College, where I studied chemistry under Dr Williamson. I
> am afraid that I was a most unsatisfactory pupil, for I took no interest
> at all in the work, and spent all my time in drawing caricatures....
>
> I remained at the Birkbeck Laboratory for two years, that is to say till
> 1854, when my father, who was still convinced that I had a great future
> before me in the pursuit of science, set me up on my account in a chem-
> ical laboratory in [Barge] Yard, Bucklersbury, in the city. The house is
> still there; I saw it a few days ago. It was a fine laboratory, for my father
> being a poor man naturally fitted it up in the most expensive style, with
> all sort of instruments. In the midst of my brightly polished apparatus
> here I sat, and in the long intervals between business drew and drew.[127]

Du Maurier's uncle, George Clarke, sent some early business. In 1853,
fifty-six-year-old Captain Clarke, retired from the military, had married
nineteen-year-old Emma Georgiana Lewis, known as Georgie. Their son,
Robert Fulke Noel, was born a few months after the wedding and the following year, Captain Clarke began to manage the Milford Haven estate
of Colonel Robert Fulke Murray Greville, with whom he had served in
the 17th Lancers.

Du Maurier's next and apparently last employment as a chemist came
in July and August 1854. In the midst of gold fever, the Britannia Gold
and Copper Mining Company in North Molton, Devon (which also had
an office at Barge Yard) hired him to confirm that their mine contained
significant amounts of gold. According to his own account he charmed
the miners, and for a time the members of the board of directors but lost
his job when he told them the mine contained 'no more gold than is to
be found in traces everywhere'.[128]

All three of Du Maurier's fictional alter egos frequent the British
Museum in their youth. Armstrong situates his friend's period of drawing from the antique just after his short stint as an analytical chemist.[129]

When George and Eugene Du Maurier were nine and seven respectively, their father had written to his sister that '[t]he youngest, who is
quite a childish giddy boy, fond of play, hates reading except to find
out the description of the pictures in the books, a perfect *Sans Souci*
[without a care], is, according to the master, a perfect genius for drawing'. However, he added, Eugene 'is a "Devil may care" chap like his

father – good-hearted, kind, affectionate and disinterested, but careless and without the least pride and ambition of any sort'.[130]

Eugene does not seem to have found a vocation during his studies at University College. He returned to France and in June 1854 joined the 8th regiment of *chasseurs à cheval* (light cavalry) of the Imperial Army. An official document described him as having blond hair and eyebrows, brown eyes, a wide forehead, a well-formed nose, an average mouth, measuring 1.68 m and being somewhat heavy. He spent the next fourteen years in the army and received a medal for his service in the Franco-Mexican War. Many of his colourful letters to his Aunt Louise, his mother, his brother and, later, his wife, survive. He still had a talent for drawing and his letters sometimes include his sketches.

Louis-Mathurin Du Maurier died in Clerkenwell on 8 June 1856. Eugene was with his regiment in Châlons-sur-Marne (now Châlons-en-Champagne) and at the time he learned his father was seriously ill his Aunt Louise was visiting him there. She suggested he travel to London. He wrote home saying he could be there in two days, reminding his brother that he had not seen any of his immediate family for two and a half years. A long silence followed the news and George's next letter informed his brother of their father's death. Eugene recommended having a priest announce the news to Aunt Louise, who had returned to Versailles: 'Never contradict what I am going to tell my aunt, which is that my father died with the consolation of the *Catholic* religion.'[131]

Paris and the Quartier Latin

Louis-Mathurin's death cleared the way for his widow Ellen and their older son, using the income that had come to them from the late Mrs Clarke, to return to Paris. As Du Maurier explained to his interviewer,

> ... at the age of twenty-two I returned to Paris and went to live with my mother in the rue Paradis-Poissonnière. We were very poor, and very dull and dismal it was. However, it was not long before I entered upon what was the best time of my life. That is when, having decided to follow art as a profession, I entered Gleyre's studio to study drawing and painting. Those were my joyous Quartier Latin days, spent in the charming society of Poynter, Whistler, Armstrong, Lamont, and others. I have described Gleyre's studio in *Trilby*.[132]

The identification of these 'others' – in particular the originals, if there were any, of Trilby and Svengali – has proved a challenge to biographers.

In answer to a question from Tom Lamont, who was present for his friend's interview by the American journalist Edward Marshall, Du Maurier said Svengali's only 'real-life prototype' in the Quartier Latin was 'a poor Englishman, not too clean, but a wonderful pianist'. The pianist came in one day to find George bathing in a big wine tub. '"What are you doing that for?" he asked. "To get clean," I replied. "And how did you get dirty?" he queried, innocently. I think that was the only bit of real life that I introduced into the character.'[133]

'Ye Societie of our Ladye in the Fieldes', a sketch Du Maurier made in the period, shows, in addition to himself and the four artists named above, Alecco Ionides, called 'the Greek' in the novel, a somewhat younger man who was studying in Paris, and a musician called Sotiri. Armstrong's reminiscences of Du Maurier and Whistler were published posthumously, as were the memories of Luke Ionides, who had visited his younger brother Alecco in Paris and remained friendly with 'the Paris gang' in London. On the question of whether or not the composer Sotiri could have inspired Svengali, the two sources disagree.

Tom Armstrong wrote: 'There was nothing in him to suggest Svengali, for he was a mild-mannered sort of man, little given to assert his views about music, and he never showed any symptoms of being a mesmerist.'[134] However, Luke Ionides claimed that 'Svengali was taken from a Greek student in Paris, who was extremely ugly but an able musician and who had an idea that all women fell in love with him. He claimed to have mesmeric power but we had no proof of it.'[135] It has not been possible to find any trace of Miltiade A. Sotiri beyond three musical compositions and a law thesis: two waltzes for piano, *Souvenirs d'Athènes* and *Ismaïlieh*; a polka called *Terpsichore*; and a thesis entitled *Des privilèges sur les immeubles*. The notice for the thesis states that Sotiri was born in Alexandria, Egypt.

In an article on his experiences at Gleyre's in 1859, Du Maurier's friend Valentine Cameron Prinsep identified the original of the character Mimi la Salope, as someone whom he saw in another atelier, known as the Atelier Suisse:

> I recollect there was ... a female model, 'la petite Sara', who is mentioned in *Trilby* under the name of 'Mimi la Salope'. She had a very sweet voice, and while she was sitting would warble charmingly songs of what Du Maurier called '*tout ce qu'il y a de plus canaille*' [of the most daring kind].[136]

It is also possible to identify another member of Trilby's entourage. For '[a]t the time [*Trilby*] begins, this small waif and stray was *en pension* with *le père Martin*, the rag-picker, and his wife, the dealer in bric-à-brac and inexpensive old masters'.[137] *Le père Martin* was the epithet of Pierre-Firmin Martin (1817–91), originally a saddle-maker and occasional actor who married a seamstress and became a second-hand merchant specialising in the sale of paintings by members of the Barbizon school, and later, the impressionists. Adolphe-Félix Cals painted portraits of *le père* and *la mère Martin*; the picture dealer is also portrayed as *le père Malgras* in Zola's novel *L'Œuvre* (1886).

Turning to Trilby herself, it is difficult to determine the extent to which she is based on a particular person. Du Maurier gave different answers to two different American journalists in interviews published only a few months apart. To John D. Barry, the novelist asserted categorically that the character Trilby 'was wholly imaginary'.[138] However, when Edward Marshall, in the interview already cited, asked if Trilby had an original in real life, George replied:

Oh, yes; half a dozen in a way, but none literally. I tried to imagine what women whom I knew well would have done had they been born as Trilby was, grown up as she did, and lived as she did, and from this vague basis I built her. Ellen Terry was one of the women from whom I drew much of the good in Trilby's nature.

If, as Du Maurier suggested, Trilby was 'in a way' based on half a dozen women he knew well, of whom (the non-Parisian) Ellen Terry was one, there is also a possible Parisian source.

Both Armstrong and Ionides identified the same figure as having Trilby-like characteristics. In their 1908 biography of Whistler, the Pennells quote the following written statement by Luke Ionides:

[Whistler] was a great favourite among us all, and also among the grisettes we used to meet at the gardens where dancing went on. I remember one especially – they called her the *tigresse*. She seemed madly in love with Jimmie [Whistler] and would not allow any other woman to talk to him when she was present. She sat to him several times with her curly hair down her back. She had a good voice, and I often thought she had suggested Trilby to Du Maurier.[139]

According to the Pennells, this grisette, called Héloïse, was the model for Whistler's 'Fumette'; she is said on one occasion to have torn up his drawings in a rage. In his *Memories*, published in 1925, Ionides once again mentions 'a little grisette with fair hair who was desperately in love with Jimmy [Whistler]. They called her *la petite lionne* [the little lioness] and she used to sit to most of those men'.[140] Héloïse modelled for at least five of Whistler's etchings; most of them are dated after Du Maurier left Paris for Belgium. They are entitled 'Au Sixième' (1857), 'Fumette' (1858), 'Fumette's Bent Head' (1859), 'Fumette, Standing' (1859), and 'Venus' (1859). Armstrong also evoked 'Fumette' in his 'Reminiscences of Whistler':

Among the early etchings by Whistler, in the set of twelve, if I am not mistaken, there is one of a seated figure of a girl, with long hair hanging loose about her shoulders and with a basket in her lap. This was done from Héloïse, a girl-model well known in the Quartier [Latin]. She was a remarkable person, not pretty in feature, and sallow in complexion, but with good eyes and a sympathetic sort of face. As this was long before the fashion came in for women and children to wear their hair hanging loose, and not in plaits down their backs, Héloïse attracted the notice of passers-by almost as much as Whistler did when he was wearing 'more Americano', his summer suit of white duck, with the jaunty little flat-crowned Yankee hat. She used to go about bareheaded and carrying a little basket containing the crochet work she was in the habit of doing, and a volume of Alfred de Musset's poems. This little pose added to the interest excited by her flowing locks and her large eyes. She was a chatterbox, and at times regaled us with songs, rather spoken than sung, for she had not much voice or power of musical expression. She used to sing:–

Voulez-vous savoir, savoir, [Do you want to know, to know,]
Comment les artistes aiment? [How artists love?]
Ils aiment si artistement, [They love so artistically,]
Ils sont de si artistes gens. [They are such artistic people.]

Spoken:–

Qu'ils s'en vont tout en disant: [That as they leave they say:]
Voulez-vous venir chez moi, Mademoiselle? [Would you like to visit me, Miss?]
Et je ferai votre portrait. [And I will make your portrait.]

Refrain:–

Ramenez vos moutons, bergères, [Bring back your lambs, shepherdesses,]

'Fumette', Whistler's
etching of Héloïse

Sung:–

> *Ramenez vos moutons des champs.* [Bring back your lambs from
> the fields.]

In later couplets the amatory peculiarities of soldiers, lawyers, doctors,
and others were sung about. In this Héloïse were some slight sugges-
tions for the character of Trilby, but only in the basket of work and
in the book, and I know of no other female inhabitant of the Quartier
Latin who had any of the characteristics of Du Maurier's heroine. I am
very sorry and feel like an impostor, but really this Héloïse is as near as
I can get to the original of Trilby.[141]

Armstrong recalled Héloïse's song about 'the amatory peculiarities' of
men in various professions, and the name Du Maurier gave the heroine of
his Quartier Latin novel seems to refer to one 'peculiarity' in particular.

Héloïse, the prototype of Trilby?

In the French author Charles Nodier's Scottish tale 'Trilby, or the Imp of Argyll', from which Du Maurier ostensibly borrowed the name, Trilby is a male *feu follet* (will-o'-the-wisp).

'Trilby' is also a near-anagram of 'Litrebili' – the French nickname of Du Maurier's fictional alter ego Little Billee – and her Irish surname 'O'Ferrall' suggests his acquaintance Oscar Wilde (since 'feral' is synonymous with 'wild'). According to a late nineteenth-century slang dictionary 'trillbye' is an old term with the same meaning as 'double-barrelled': 'Said of a harlot working both before and behind.'[142]

Du Maurier's novel opens with Musset's well-known refrain about a grisette: *'Mimi Pinson est une blonde/ Une blonde que l'on connaît;/ Elle n'a qu'une robe au monde,/ Landérirette! et qu'un bonnet!'* (translated in the Appendix to *Trilby* as 'Mimi Pinson is a blonde,/ A blonde whom people know;/ She has but one dress in the world,/ Landérirette! and but one hat!'). Du Maurier used the Biblical phrase *Quia multum amavit* (Because she has loved much) – Christ's defence of Mary Magdalene – to describe his heroine's 'frailties'.

Swinburne published an apostrophe to 'prostituted France' with the same title in *Songs Before Sunrise* (1871), a volume of political poetry. Wilde's *Quia multum amavi* (Because I have loved much) (1881) is part of a series of poems addressed to a woman indifferent to the poet's love. In 1892 another acquaintance of Du Maurier's, the painter Simeon Solomon, used *Quia multum amavit* as the title for a drawing of Mary Magdalene.

In Du Maurier's novel, Trilby poses for Little Billee's studies of the girl in his painting 'The Pitcher Goes to the Well', and after the climactic Christmas dinner scene she accepts his twentieth proposal of marriage. This leads to the arrival and intervention of Little Billee's mother and uncle, and the sudden departure of Trilby and her 'little brother' or 'godson' Jeannot ('almost every one ... believed he was the child of Trilby').[143] In February, Little Billee's friends Taffy and the Laird learn that

> Trilby's little brother had died of scarlet fever and was buried, and Trilby had left her hiding-place the day after the funeral and had never come back, and this was a week ago. She and Jeannot had been living at a village called Vibraye, in la Sarthe, lodging with some poor people she knew – she washing and working with her needle till her brother fell ill.[144]

Then, on 'a fine, sunny, showery day in April ... a railway omnibus drew up at the *porte cochère* in the Place St Anatole des Arts, and carried away to the station of the Chemin de Fer du Nord Little Billee and his mother and sister, and all their belongings....'[145]

As it happens, the novelist himself knew some people in 'Vibraye, in la Sarthe'. As already mentioned, Vibraye was the town where his father's Duval cousins lived, and where he had spent the summer holiday ten years previously. In July 1858 and May 1860 respectively, Vibraye's civil registry recorded the deaths of two illegitimate children with a Paris address. Ernest Alphonse Théophile and Julie Léonide Alphonsine were listed as the children of Stéphanie Augustine Héloïse Trotin, without a profession. They were born to her in Paris in April 1858 and August 1859, as were six other illegitimate children, in 1853, 1854, 1855, 1857, 1861 and 1864. The civil registry for Paris prior to 1861 was destroyed and is only partially reconstituted, however for the children born in 1861 and 1864 the mother's profession is given as *brodeuse* (embroideress) and *tapissière* (upholstress) respectively.

When placed in the context of what is known of Du Maurier's year in the Latin Quarter, these records allow the double hypothesis that Héloïse Trotin, born in Paris in 1832 to a watchmaker and his first wife, may have been Whistler's model and also, the inspiration or one of the inspirations for Trilby. In 1840 Héloïse Trotin's mother had died in childbirth, as does Trilby's mother in the novel. At Christmas 1856 – at which no 'Trilby' was present, according to Armstrong – Mlle Trotin would have been expecting her second daughter, born 1 February 1857; her second son died while in the care of a nurse in Normandy on 5 April.

If Trilby was indeed based on Héloïse Trotin and if Du Maurier proposed to her as Little Billee does in the novel, Mrs Du Maurier could hardly have thought a grisette – what is more, one with illegitimate children – would be a suitable match for her son, particularly in light of her own 'colourful' origins. She would not have needed to travel from England to prevent the marriage, since she was living with her son at the time. An aborted union with this so-called 'tigress' or 'lioness' would explain the Du Mauriers' abrupt relocation to Antwerp, something of a grey area for memorialists and biographers, including George himself.

Before coming to Paris, Tom Armstrong had spent several months at the Royal Academy in Antwerp. He wrote that his experience 'led to Du Maurier going there later': 'living there was very cheap at the time and the instruction at the Academy gratuitous'.[146] But financial reasons alone do not seem sufficient to explain the move, particularly since Gleyre's instruction was also free.

Du Maurier fictionalised his stay in Belgium in his last novel, *The Martian*. The narrator writes that the hero Barty 'suddenly took it into his head to go to Antwerp; I don't know who influenced him in this direction, but I arranged to meet him there at the end of April....'[147] Daphne Du Maurier's version is that 'Kicky had become a little tired of the Gleyre tradition, and by the sound of it De Keyser's Academy seemed just the place for him. He discussed the idea with his mother, who showed no objection to a change of quarters.'[148]

Biographer Leonee Ormond concedes,

> There is no convincing reason to explain why Du Maurier suddenly left his congenial companions, a happy studio and a comfortable home to go to an unfamiliar city in a new country. He had, it is true, learned little about art at Gleyre's atelier, but it is difficult to believe that a sense of vocation alone drove him to Antwerp. There must have been more urgent reasons for his departure.

She also acknowledges that 'there may have been relationships in Paris which it will never be possible to trace'.[149]

One possibility is that Whistler's Parisian model and mistress Héloïse was surnamed Trotin, that, presumably before her relationship with Whistler, Du Maurier proposed to her, that his mother objected, that the resulting unpleasantness caused them to leave Paris abruptly, and that, decades later, Héloïse Trotin inspired Trilby. (It would put Whistler's threat of a libel suit, somewhat puzzling in view of the original version of *Trilby*'s relatively only mildly critical portrayal of a minor character based on the American painter, in a new light.)

There are admittedly significant differences between what is known of Whistler's Héloïse, the shadowy historical figure Héloïse Trotin, and Du Maurier's Trilby. For example, Whistler's model was small, Trilby tall; and Mlle Trotin was French on both sides, while Trilby is of Scottish and Irish origin. Finally, Whistler's model is said to have gone to South America with a musician and to have died there. Héloïse Trotin apparently left no trace in the two decades between the birth of her eighth child in 1864 and the marriage of her oldest son in 1884, which she attended (the civil registry lists her as residing in Vincennes). She died in Paris in 1888. Whether these discrepancies disqualify the identification, or are simply the result of Du Maurier's efforts to partially 'disguise' a character drawn from life, the reader must judge.

A 'dreary, deserted, dismal little Flemish town'

In the spring of 1857 – after less than a year of his 'happy Quartier Latin life' – Du Maurier left Gleyre's atelier for the Royal Academy of Fine Arts in Antwerp.

As noted above, *The Martian* contains a semi-fictional account of this period of the author's life. Like George, Barty

> ... became a pupil at the academy under De Keyser and Van Lerius, and worked harder than ever.
>
> He took a room nearly all window on a second floor in the Marché aux Œufs, just under the shadow of the gigantic spire which rings a fragment of melody every seven minutes and a half – and the whole tune at midnight, fortissimo.[150]

Barty befriends one 'Tescheles', an Englishman who had also previously studied under Gleyre. Tescheles was obviously inspired by the painter Felix Stone Moscheles (1833–1917), who, in the wake of *Trilby*'s tremendous success, penned a memoir entitled *In Bohemia with Du Maurier* (1897), illustrated with his friend's sketches from the period.

Du Maurier's new friend was the son of the composer Ignaz Moscheles and his wife Charlotte, whom her son described as a sort of cousin of Heinrich Heine's. The child's godfather was Felix Mendelssohn; the renowned composer was a former pupil and friend of Ignaz Moscheles. In 1858 Moscheles' parents and sister Clara visited him in Antwerp. Clara was a soprano, the goddaughter of Maria Malibran; Moscheles writes that 'Du Maurier and she were soon on a brotherly and sisterly footing, and they ever remained so.'[151]

Barty is 'happier than he had ever been in his life' in Antwerp, but 'a great horror' befalls him 'towards the end of summer': he loses sight in his left eye.[152] A doctor from Louvain recommends the seaside resort of Ostend or, since Ostend was expensive, Blankenberghe. Barty leaves Antwerp for Blankenberghe where, suggestively, '[h]is new life was soon to open....' He travels via Bruges where he 'slept at the "Fleur de Blé", and heard new chimes, and remembered his Longfellow'.[153]

In Blankenberghe, Barty is popular and has 'many droll adventures'. Yet the narrator concedes that when Barty is 'alone in his garret, with his seton-dressing and dry-cuppings, it was not so gay'.[154] His eye gets worse instead of better. In an implausible sequence, one afternoon, 'lolling in deep dejection', Barty suddenly recognises Lady Caroline Grey, the 'very devout' favourite sister of his late father. 'Lady Caroline meant to pass the winter at Malines, of all places in the world. The Archbishop was her friend, and she was friends also with one of two priests at the seminary there.'[155]

Malines also had the advantage of being near the eye-doctor in Louvain. Barty is an orphan, but in reality it was George's mother who accompanied him in Malines. Moscheles was a frequent visitor from nearby Antwerp; he wrote that 'Du Maurier's mother had come to live with him, his sister joining them for a short time, and the home in quiet old Malines soon became a sort of haven of rest.' Malines was the seat of an archbishopric and, as Moscheles noted, it 'boasts of a great many churches and of a very great many more priests'.[156]

The religious presence is clear from the description of Barty's lodgings: 'At the back of their house in the rue des Ursulines Blanches, Barty's bedroom window overlooked the playground of the convent "des Sœurs Rédemptoristines"; all noble ladies, most beautifully dressed in scarlet and ultramarine, with long snowy veils....'[157] The street name is invented but the description corresponds to an early twentieth-century map showing the rue de la Blanchisserie (Bleekstraat), with the *Petit Séminaire* and *Couvent des Sœurs Noires* on one side and the *Couvent des Rédemptoristines* on the other.

Barty becomes great friends with 'the aristocratic Father Louis', a young priest who teaches at the *Séminaire* and, eventually, dies a Cardinal. There were only three Belgian cardinals in the nineteenth century. If Du Maurier was indeed the friend of a future cardinal, the description can only correspond to Pierre-Lambert Goossens, who became a priest in 1850 and was named as a professor at the *Petit Séminaire* in 1851. Born in 1827, he outlived Du Maurier and died in 1906.

One happy event in Malines, Du Maurier recalled in *Social Pictorial Satire*, was the arrival of *Punch's Almanac*: 'To be an apparently hopeless invalid at Christmas-time in some dreary, deserted, dismal little Flemish town, and to receive *Punch's Almanac* (for 1858, let us say) from some good-natured friend in England – that is a thing not to be forgotten! I little dreamed then that I should come to London again, and meet John Leech and become his friend....'[158]

The narrator of *The Martian* observes discreetly that 'Barty also made one or two other friends in Malines'.[159] More to the point, Moscheles acknowledged in his memoir that '[i]n addition to these attractions

[churches and priests], there was, however, a factor of paramount interest to us'.[160] This other factor was female beauty: the two friends shared
an interest in seventeen-year-old Octavie L., 'the daughter of an organist who had held a good position at one of the principal churches in
Malines'. Mr L. had died and his widow had set up a tobacconist's store;
Moscheles and Du Maurier derived Octavie's nickname 'Carry' from
'Cigar'. Moscheles writes that 'to give a correct idea of her I need but say
her soul was steeped in the very essence of Trilbyism'.[161] (By 'Trilbyism',
Moscheles presumably meant 'Bohemianism'.)

Hypnotism was a frequent 'topic of conversation between Du Maurier and myself', wrote Moscheles. A sketch of Du Maurier's illustrates
the 'mesmeric séance' Moscheles once held in Mrs L.'s back parlour –
probably to amuse Carry. Apparently, Moscheles never tried to actually
hypnotise Carry. Still, he expressed confidence that it was with himself
and in Malines that 'Du Maurier was inoculated with the germs that
were eventually to develop into Trilbyism and Svengalism'.[162]

In *The Martian*, Barty begins to believe he has lost sight in his right eye,
consults a second doctor and concludes both Belgian doctors are incompe-
tent. He becomes suicidal and it is at this point that a supernatural being
called Martia first appears in the novel. She advises him to '[g]o to Düsseldorf, in Prussia. Close by, at a village called Riffrath, lives an old doctor,
Dr Hasenclever, who understands a deal about the human heart and something about the human body; and even a little about the human eye, for
he is a famous oculist'.[163] In his interview Du Maurier said simply, 'In the
spring of 1859 we heard of a great specialist who lived in Düsseldorf, and
we went to see him.'[164] The great specialist was Dr Friedrich Hermann de
Leuw (1792–1861), who practised in the village of Gräfrath.

Barty and his aunt leave Malines 'with a mixed feeling of elation and
regret' – elation because they 'had not been very happy there', but regret
because 'many people had been very kind; and the place, with all its
dreariness, had a strange, still charm, and was full of historic beauty and
romantic associations'.[165]

Gräfrath *alias* Riffrath

En route to Düsseldorf, Barty and his aunt meet Lady Jane Royce, who
is also going to consult the eye doctor, accompanied by her daughter, 'the
divine Julia'. Julia Royce stands in for Louisa Catherine Lewis, who was
in fact the oldest daughter of Leyson Orton Lewis, a widowed solicitor
from Carmarthenshire. In Düsseldorf, Du Maurier conducted a mild flir-
tation with Miss Lewis.

Barty's aunt rents a house 'in the Schadow Strasse, opposite Geissler's' (a restaurant known as the *Geislerisches Lokal*); Du Maurier enjoyed many concerts in the gardens there. Riffrath 'was about half-an-hour by train, and then half-an-hour's walk – an immensely prosperous village, which owed its prosperity to the famous doctor, who attracted patients from all parts of the globe, even from America'.[166]

After his first interview with the doctor, Barty attends a small party where everyone already seems to know all about him:

> It was the old London world over again, in little! the same tittle-tattle about well-known people, and nothing else – as if nothing else existed; a genial, easy-going, good-natured world, that he had so often found charming for a time, but in which he was never quite happy and had no proper place of his own, all through that fatal bar-sinister – *la barre de bâtardise*....[167]

"FOR EVER AND A DAY."

Du Maurier's drawing of Felix Moscheles, 'Carry' and himself

Margaret Raine, soon to marry the landscape painter Alfred William Hunt and become known as a novelist and translator, was in Gräfrath at the same time as Du Maurier, and also left a written account of the place.[168] According to her, the English had been going there for 'about sixteen years'. She specified that 'of late years there have generally been from 100 to 150 English at one time every summer'. Margaret Raine's comments on Gräfrath's 'little English colony' confirm Du Maurier's:

> ... when so many people were gathered together without any definite employment but washing their eyes at stated times and submitting them to inspection on certain days, their thoughts were necessarily much occupied with each other's affairs. All were in a fever to know who – and what – you were, and the social rank of all your relatives. We never could quite make up our minds whether it was better at once to give full information on this subject, or to throw down the relatives one by one for discussion and minute inspection, out all must come in time, for they had nothing else to talk about but eyes....[169]

In a May 1860 letter to his friend Louisa Margaret Fortescue, who had recently left Gräfrath with her much older husband, retired from the Indian Civil Service, Du Maurier wrote that he was part of 'a very intimate little circle'. In addition to George, his mother and sister, it included his friends Henry Molyneux Best and Tom Armstrong (recently arrived), as well as Mr Lewis and his two daughters: 'The elders, Mr Lewis and my mother indulge in boundless political speculations (arrosés de Walportsheimer [soaked in the local wine]) and reminiscences which to us appear fabulously antediluvian.'

George informed Mrs Fortescue that he and Armstrong intended to return to England soon: 'I cannot stay here doing no good whatsoever – and my health and eyes do not seem to require at present the constant interference of the Gräfrath powers.'[170] In The Martian, the dénouement comes about when Martia commands Barty to go from Düsseldorf to Gräfrath to see 'the divine Julia'. As Barty leaves Düsseldorf, the narrator inserts a flashback to London, where the Gibsons' financial situation has suffered. They have been forced to give up their carriage and their private house in Tavistock Square (in reality, Torrington Square) for Conduit Street (in reality, Grosvenor Street). As a consolation Mr Gibson sends his wife and daughter on a trip up the Rhine.

Between Düsseldorf and Gräfrath, the train stops at Neanderthal and Du Maurier's hero gets out to take a walk. He suddenly recalls the

Gibsons are due to arrive. When Barty first sees Leah, Schubert's famous song '*Du bist die Ruh', der Friede mild!*' ('You are my rest,/ My calm and peace') comes into his head, and he has soon made his choice between the two women.

After the Gibsons' arrival, Barty performs in the chorus of *Iphigenia* and observes Julia and Leah in the audience:

> ... it was impossible to say which of these two lovely women was the loveliest; probably most votes would have been for Julia, the fair-haired one, the *prima donna assoluta*, the soprano, the Rowena, who always gets the biggest salary and the most applause.
>
> The brunette, the contralto, the Rebecca, dazzles less, but touches the heart all the more deeply, perhaps; anyhow, Barty had no doubt as to which of the two voices was the voice for him.[171]

In addition to their contrasting hair colour and voices, another factor may also have played a role: Louisa Lewis was twelve years older than Emma Wightwick. In 1860 Louisa, born in 1829, was just over thirty while Emma, born in 1841, was not yet twenty.

During his years as an art student, Du Maurier's attitude toward the papal title his father had acquired on his return to France at the restoration of the monarchy had clearly evolved. Armstrong recalled that

> This title of Count was often a subject for banter among us. [Du Maurier's] grandfather [in reality, his father] had been made a Count by the Pope of those days, but his father never made any use of the title, and Du Maurier always spoke of it with his tongue in his cheek. Sometimes one of us would make him a bid for it, and I remember that a bottle of English gin, at that time a rare and precious liquor in Paris, was proposed as a suitable equivalent. But there were to be thrown in to boot the title deeds of a certain landed estate on the Mosquito shore which had been conceded to his father. These deeds and the Pope's patent of nobility were left, some years afterwards, at Malines in a box which was lost and never recovered, so it would have been better for him to have taken the bottle of gin.[172]

The patent of nobility must have been recovered from Malines because it still exists. Indeed, George's brother Eugene mentioned in a letter to his aunt Louise that George had in his possession 'two legal donations of the Pope':

> I received some time ago a letter from Kicky, asking if I could do the necessary *démarches* [steps] to have our title legalised. He has two legal donations of the Pope to papa. In one of your pastime hours you could go as far as the *ministère* [ministry] (I don't know which one) and enquire *munie des titres* [with the titles in hand]. It would be of great use to me.[173]

It is not known whether any of the Du Mauriers ever pursued the matter; if they did they would have learned that the French state does not recognise papal titles.

In the spring of 1860, George Du Maurier travelled from Düsseldorf to London with Tom Armstrong and the Wightwicks. He would return to the continent many times but only as a tourist.

The singsongs of Rotherhithe

According to an 1891 interview, the first drawing Du Maurier made for publication hung in his Hampstead studio:

> I did it ... in the year 1860 for a paper called the *British Lion*, but, unfortunately, the paper died before the appearance, though I got a guinea for it.
>
> ... It was a good joke, too, and one that Mr Whistler told me. The subject was a man asking a young lady if she was engaged for the next dance, and, on her replying 'Yes', exclaiming, 'Oh, well then, I may as well take your seat!'[174]

In the first drawing Du Maurier contributed to *Punch*, he represented himself as 'Dick Tinto', initiating the many literary pseudonyms he would adopt. Accompanied by figures based on Whistler and Lamont, he visited the studio of the photographer Herbert Watkins. In a letter to his mother, the cartoonist commented that the sketch was 'so badly engraved that I hardly recognised my drawing, none of the likenesses are preserved'.[175] The studio setting and the presence of Lamont and Whistler recall Du Maurier's year in Paris and anticipate *Trilby*.

George stayed for a time in Whistler's studio at 70 Newman Street. Armstrong was a visitor and referred in his memoir to 'the Bohemian life [Du Maurier] and Whistler were living then' (p. 151).[176] George informed his mother that 'I lead a very dissipated life as far as going out in the evening to people and all that....' He mentioned that Whistler

> ... is working hard & in secret down in Rotherhithe, among a beastly set of cads and every possible annoyance and misery, doing one of the greatest *chefs d'œuvres* [sic] [masterpieces] – no difficulty discourages him. I think that I am more *liked* than he though, and this 'Horgin' of mine, you know. He talks women over to him, and I sing them back again to me, and both are delighted at being cut out by the other – ah! this immoral world.[177]

Among the 'beastly ... cads' of Rotherhithe, Du Maurier and his musical 'Horgin' competed for women's attention with Whistler and his talk.

One such woman was Polly Levy, whose fiery gaze and enchanting voice Du Maurier mentioned in a letter to Armstrong.[178] It is possible to determine her identity because of the poignant note she sent to Whistler in 1896, from the Strand Union Workhouse in Edmonton where she would die in 1903. She recalls her friendship with George, their visits to Rotherhithe with Ionides and mentions her famous brother 'who used to delight all the frequenters at Covent Gardens' but who now 'takes no notice of me'. She states that she has enclosed a letter to Du Maurier asking him for assistance.[179]

According to census records Polly (recorded as both Mary and Miriam) Levy, born in the parish of St George in the East in 1831, was the third of the eight children of David Levy and his wife, the former Maria Franks. Polly's youngest brother was the renowned cornet player Jules Levy (1838–1903), who eventually immigrated to the United States.

When Du Maurier came to represent this period of his life in his novels, however, it is the 'cads' rather than the women who interest his alter egos Peter Ibbetson and Little Billee. Peter gets to know the 'slums at the east end of London' by heart: 'In addition to the charm of the mere slum, there was the eternal fascination of the seafaring element; of Jack ashore – a lovable creature who touches nothing but what he adorns it in his own peculiar fashion.'[180] In *Trilby*,

> ... it was also [Little Billee's] pleasure now and again to study London life at its lower den – the eastest end of all. Whitechapel, the Minories, the Docks, Ratcliffe Highway, Rotherhithe, soon got to know him well, and he found much to interest him and much to like among their denizens, and made as many friends there among ship-carpenters, excise-men, longshoremen, jack-tars, and what not, as in Bayswater and Belgravia (or Bloomsbury).
>
> He was especially fond of frequenting singsongs, or 'free-and-easies',

where good hard-working fellows met of an evening to relax and drink and sing....'[181]

Listing sentimental songs from Du Maurier's repertoire, Tom Armstrong wrote: 'I believe he sang some of these songs with great success at the ordinary of the public-house at Rotherhithe when Whistler was working there.'[182]

Engagement and 'the two voices'

Du Maurier wrote to his mother in May 1861, explaining that one day, on coming home from the opera, he had told Emma about his feelings for her and they 'came to the conclusion together that we had more or less liked each other for the last seven years and that now the affection having reached fever heat on both sides it was as well to calm it by a mutual explanation'.[183] Thus, within a year of their joint return from Düsseldorf, George and Emma were engaged.

Emma's parents agreed that the marriage could take place once the future bridegroom had £200 in the bank.[184] Du Maurier's letters detail his introductions to the editors of the *Cornhill*, *Once A Week*, *Punch* and other publications, and his negotiations with them over his illustrations and sometimes texts. 'Recollections of an English Goldmine', his first published narrative, appeared in *Once A Week* with two of his illustrations in September 1861.

By March 1862 the fiancés were growing tired of the long wait. In a letter to his mother, Du Maurier stated that 'if we don't get married soon, we shall have brain fever or something'. In April he wrote to his mother that one day, as he was sitting with Emma, 'I felt all my affection for her, you, Isabel, and my friends, cease as by enchantment; yet my powers of reasoning strange to say were by no means impaired; indeed [they were] remarkably clear and active.'[185]

His next letter conceded that 'the agony of mind was worse than anything I ever experienced from my eyes in Malines'.[186] To Tom Armstrong, Du Maurier wrote that 'I fell into the slough of despond'. To his mother:

It suddenly came across me that I was a thoroughly bad man who had by a marvel been sustained by good example until now, and that the original badness of my nature was just going to break out at last like a regular conflagration, and that the last year's virtue had been the crowning point of my goodness on earth – a temptation to break loose and indulge in every riotous excess, drink, opium, and the most shameless intrigues....

He added that his friends' kindness and Emma's devotion only make him worse. At the same time, he continued, '[o]nce married I am safe – so say my doctors'.[187]

Du Maurier habitually peppered his cartoons and writings with French words and phrases, and in a July 1862 letter to Tom Armstrong, he included a sketch entitled 'The Two Voices', depicting a confrontation between his French and English 'selves'. The French voice is the 'naughty' one, which torments the other voice 'till sleep forsakes my pillow' and whose very existence must be hidden from Emma. The English voice concludes the dialogue with the words 'I scorn thee, pig and trample thee under foot.'[188]

On his return to London, in the years leading up to his marriage, what were the temptations Du Maurier's French 'self' found so hard to resist? In a paragraph of the letter accompanying his sketch of 'The Two Voices' that begins in French and ends in English, he proclaims his very great disgust with the aristocratic world and asserts that if he had talent he could write volumes on one or two houses. He adds that he is privy to the confidences of both his artist friend Val Prinsep, whose parents housed the painter George Frederic Watts at Little Holland House, and Hamilton Aïdé, later described by Henry James as 'the Diane de Poitiers of our time': 'Val, for whom I have a great fondness, is great on the Sartoris faction. Little Captain Aïdé, who entertaineth, apparently, an immense affection for me, is most instructive on Little Holland House; everybody is the best of friends.' Du Maurier also comments that 'the Rossetti clique [is] awfully droll, full of the strangest and most childish irrepressible affectations; to give you an idea of their tone and minds would take a quire – who's right and who's wrong?'[189]

Decades after this letter, a passage of *The Martian* contains that 'quire' or something like it in its representation of the contrasting opinions of Barty Josselin, the hero and his old friend Robert Maurice, the narrator.[190] The author gives some of his attributes to each one and he also appears in his own name as another friend, who has edited and illustrated the novel.

After he arrives in London, Barty's acquaintances include a string of artists mentioned by name – Millais, Walker, Keene, Lawless, Du Maurier, Poynter, Holman Hunt, and F. Leighton – 'whose talk and example soon weaned [him] from a mixed and somewhat rowdy crew'. Like Peter

Ibbetson (but unlike George Du Maurier), Barty is a guardsman and his 'old brother officers' are also mentioned in a favourable light.

The narrator then contrasts these artists and officers with certain 'others':

But there were others he got to know, rickety, unwholesome geniuses, whose genius (such as it was) had allied itself to madness; and who were just as conceited about the madness as about the genius, and took more pains to cultivate it. It brought them a quicker kudos, and was so much more visible to the naked eye.

At first Barty was fascinated by the madness, and took the genius on trust, I suppose. They made much of him, painted him, wrote music and verses about him, raved about his Greekness, his beauty, his yellow hair, and his voice and what not, as if he had been a woman. He even stood that, he admired them so! or rather, this genius of theirs.

Du Maurier's sketch of a dialogue between his English and French voices

He introduced me to this little clique, who called themselves a
school, and each other 'master': 'the neo-priapists', or something of
that sort, and they worshipped the tuberose.

They disliked me at sight, and I them, and we did not dissemble!

The narrator makes his own position clear: 'Like Barty, I am fond of
men's society; but at least I like them to be unmistakably men of my own
sex, manly men, and clean; not little misshapen troglodytes with foul
minds and perverted passions....'

For good measure, the narrator then adds the following remark,
which a footnote attributes to the 'Editor': 'How encouraging it is to
think there are no such people now, and that the breed has been thoroughly stamped out!'

Taken as a whole, this passage of *The Martian* conveys the impression
that Du Maurier, in the very last years of his life, still found it necessary
to suppress an insistent 'French voice'.

An 'absolute domestic pelican'

Du Maurier's prospects and mood had improved by the time he visited his mother in Germany in August, and on his return to London he
persuaded Mr Wightwick to let him marry Emma in January. The wedding took place on 3 January 1863 with the Wightwicks' friend Douglas
Fisher as best man, due to the illness of Tom Armstrong.

George and Emma spent their honeymoon in Boulogne-sur-Mer;
while they were there they visited the graves of his grandmother and
aunt. Their new residence was '3 rooms second floor furnished and a
jolly studio in Great Russell St. just opposite the British Museum', a few
doors from the Burne-Joneses.[191]

Two of Du Maurier's English friends from Düsseldorf made marriages
of two very different kinds in the same period as his own. In late December his former roommate, the painter Lionel Henley, married Esther
Lydia Newman, a widow who had previously lived with Henley. George
expressed his disapproval in a letter to Tom Armstrong.

At the end of January, Du Maurier's former flirt, Louisa Lewis, married the barrister John Mirehouse – the brother-in-law of her uncle
Major-General Charles Algernon Lewis. Mirehouse died within a year
of the wedding; in a letter George noted that 'Louisa seems to be a not
inconsolable widow, with about 700 a year.'[192]

The Du Mauriers' first child, Beatrice Clara Isabel – called 'Trixy'
– was born on 1 January 1864; her godparents were Clara Bell, a

translator and the sister of Edward Poynter, Isabel Du Maurier and Tom Armstrong. Trixy's godfather was 'known in the family as Uncle Tom'.[193] George was illustrating Mrs Gaskell's works at the time and he and his family spent the summer holiday in Whitby – 'the most beautiful place I ever saw'. They became 'quite intimate' with the illustrator and *Punch* caricaturist John Leech and his family, whom Du Maurier had previously only met briefly.[194]

Leech had been ill in Whitby and he died at the end of October, at the age of forty-seven. George's talents were required and in December he was able to write to his mother that 'I am regularly on the staff of *Punch* and have taken Leech's place at that sacred dinner table on Wednesdays.'[195] For the next thirty years, Du Maurier published two cartoons each week in *Punch*, leading to a total of over 3,000 drawings.

Du Maurier's biographer, Leonee Ormond, devoted entire chapters to his cartoons on the aesthetic movement and his social cartoons; these have drawn the most critical attention. I shall focus here on a handful of cartoons that seem most directly to reflect his personal and family history.

Du Maurier had several drawings in the 1865 Almanac and informed his mother that 'they've been very much admired....'. He added that '[y]ou must look out for a ballad of mine which will appear I believe in next week's *Punch*, illustrated all down one side'.[196]

'*L'Onglay a Parry. Ballard* [sic]' (14 January 1865) is written in the anglicised French that Du Maurier occasionally used with members of his entourage who could understand it. It was the first of four interconnected, autobiographically-inspired strips published in *Punch* between 1865 and 1867, that represent the on-going exchange between the cartoonist's two cultures and the two 'voices' he felt he had within.

The ballad is 'sung' by a young Englishman who one morning is sad as he watches people strolling along the Parisian boulevards. Sipping coffee in a café, he smokes and dreams but finds ennui everywhere. He admires the elegant passers-by: a *député*; a *dame de qualité* going out without her husband; women of all sorts – actresses, women of the world, domestics and grisettes; dirty, ill-coiffed students; beautiful and ugly carriages; soldiers; and finally, on horseback, the imperial prince, his father and their suite.

Suddenly a father, his blond wife and a beautiful golden-haired girl – compatriots – pass in front of the Englishman. The daughter has an escort, a very distinguished *swell* (George uses the English word). The Englishman feels that the amorous couple, at whom everyone looks, are more beautiful than anyone else on the boulevard, and the aged parents

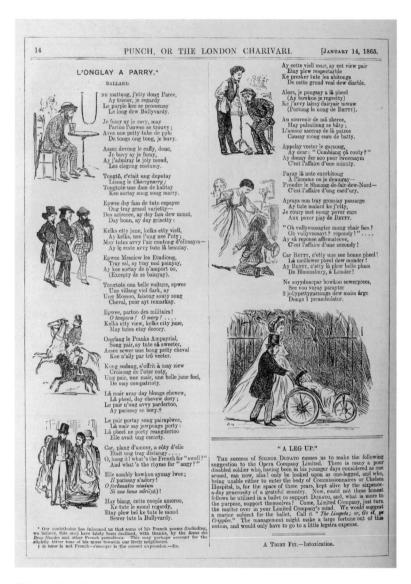

'L'Onglay a Parry' from *Punch*

are more respectable than almost all the inhabitants of the big, old, diabolical city. These thoughts lead him to regret Betty, the girl he has left behind. He quickly summons the waiter, pays the exorbitant sum, proceeds to the train station, and, still ill after a rough Channel crossing, runs to put his heart at Betty's feet. She immediately accepts his proposal

Scenes of the 'Tomtits'

of marriage and he decides Betty is the most beautiful woman in Bloomsbury. In conclusion, the poet admonishes the reader not to be surprised if
he sees two pretty little boys of the same age in a perambulator.

The ballad is a kind of comical reduction of Du Maurier's continental
experiences in 1856–60. It seems to suggest it was the respectable, largely
middle-class English community he and his mother frequented in Düsseldorf that led him to formalise his long-standing friendship with 'Betty of

Bloomsbury' – in reality, Emma of Torrington Square. Betty's distinctive feature is her height: she towers above her husband, even when he is wearing a top hat. As in 'The Two Voices', the cartoonist's English self evicts his French one; the Englishman is saved from the French by his marriage to 'Betty'.

The Du Mauriers' second child, Guy Louis, was born on 13 May 1865; he had for godparents his father's artist friends Val Prinsep and Henry Stacy Marks, and his mother's friend Ellen Levy. In a note to Ellen Du Maurier, the new father predicted that 'Trixy, from her hands and feet will be a large and tall woman, like her mother – Guy Louis, in spite of his gigantic proportions, will not depass [surpass] me.'[197]

That Betty's large size had a protective function becomes clear from a series of drawings that began in *Punch*'s Almanac for 1866 with an alternate version of an artist's meeting with his wife, and continued in the January numbers. Tom Tit is an artist whose features and profession are obviously modelled on the cartoonist. He invites the giants Chang and Anak to dine with him and his mother and sister. (Chang was Chinese and Joseph Brice, known as Anak, was French. Their respective heights were said to be over eight feet and over seven feet.) According to the legend: 'Tom Tit entertains Chang and Anak, and concludes, that next to being a giant oneself, the best thing is to be the husband of a giantess. Chance favours him in his travels. He meets a very fine girl and a very fierce bull. One saves him from the other – he loves, courts, and marries his beautiful preserver.'[198]

Mr Tomtit – in the second instalment, 'Tom Tit' becomes 'Mr Tomtit' – does not quite arrive at his wife's waist. Her instrument is the cello, which she holds like a viola; in Rotten Row she rides an elephant alongside her husband on horseback. Her large size allows her to lift him through a window when he forgets the latchkey; in her arms he is able to paint 'a big picture for the academy'. Mrs Tomtit's mother is also gigantic, as is the Tomtits' first child, Tommy; their second child, Cissy, 'takes after dear papa'. The legend of the final drawing reads as follows: 'But domestic happiness on so large (and so rapidly increasing) a scale as T.T.'s is too sacred for the gaze of the multitude. We draw the veil. Farewell for the present to the House of Tit.'[199]

The Du Mauriers' son-in-law, Charles Millar, described their marriage as follows:

All through his life Du Maurier owed much to his faithful and devoted wife, 'Pem' as he called her in the early years of their married life, who was an unfailing companion, always at hand and with no interests outside her home life. Placid in temperament, nothing ever seemed to move her strongly or to excite her. She literally waited on her 'Kiki' hand and foot, each and every day, and lived only for him and her children, whom she was inclined to spoil, generally laughing over their peccadilloes and never really scolding them.

'In the family,' he added, '[Mrs Du Maurier] was often called banteringly an "old cup of tea", which more or less described her.'[200]

George's five-part 'Legend of Camelot', parodying the Pre-Raphaelites, appeared in *Punch* in March 1866. In September, he and his family spent a holiday in Boulogne-sur-Mer with his *Punch* colleague Shirley Brooks. After their return the holiday appeared in another partially autobiographical series: the first drawing depicts 'Napoleon Titwillow, Esq., his Betty, the twins (Washington and Lucretia), and their respective nurses (Ann and Sarah) "ong root poor Bulloin-sewer-Mair".' As 'Betty and the Nursemaids are prostrate' due to a rough crossing, Titwillow attempts to look after the twins himself.[201]

In subsequent drawings, Frenchwomen carry the baggage and even offer to carry Mr T.; Mrs T. dislikes the communal bathing; and the 'indelicate' clothing of French fisherwomen shocks the nursemaids. On the final page, after sneaking away from the barber's, Mr T. runs into his wife with the twins and nursemaid. He manages to restore domestic peace by having his hair cut and his beard shaved.

In August the painter Edward Poynter, a member of the Paris gang, had married Agnes MacDonald, Burne-Jones's sister-in-law, and in September Tom Lamont, also part of the gang, married Mary Elizabeth Ranken. Lamont stood as godfather to the Du Mauriers' third child, Sylvia Jocelyn, born on 25 November 1866. Her sister Beatrice had been named after Thackeray's character, and Sylvia's name came from Mrs Gaskell's heroine. 'Jocelyn' was apparently one of Ellen Du Maurier's names, as we will see below.

'A Ballad of Blunders', Du Maurier's clever parody of Swinburne (that the poet himself appreciated) appeared in *Punch* in December. In August 1867 the cartoonist and his friend Emanuel Oscar Menahem Deutsch, a German-born Semitic scholar employed at the British Museum – later the tutor and friend of George Eliot – visited the Universal Exhibition in Paris. Du Maurier gave a detailed account in letters to Emma, who stayed at Ramsgate with the children.

They arrived on a Friday and dined at the Exhibition; on their way

'Titwillow for Tatwillow'

back to their hotel, George glimpsed the lights of Passy. This led him to embark his sleepy friend on a whirlwind tour of the Passy he remembered. The tour continued on Saturday with an unsuccessful attempt to locate Du Maurier's 'old schoolmaster and friend' Melchior Froussard. They also visited the rue Notre-Dame-des-Champs in the Latin Quarter where the Paris gang had their studio, and looked up George's Aunt

Louise, whom he had not seen since Malines, then living at 'a convent of young she-orphans' on the rue de Bayen (presumably the *Sœurs Auxiliatrices de l'Immaculée-Conception*).[202]

On Sunday the visitors returned to Passy and the Bois de Boulogne, where George discovered the Mare d'Auteuil 'ha[d] been brutally modernised and prettyfied'. The next day, after swimming at the Bains Deligny, they returned to the Exhibition to see picture galleries and the giants Chang and Chung. Finally, on their last full day in Paris, Du Maurier let Deutsch visit the Exhibition on his own while he returned to Passy, 'as the sensations I get by doing so are priceless and worth all the exhibitions in the world, including pictures'.[203] In the evening they attended a performance of Offenbach's *Grande-Duchesse de Gérolstein*. In the end George spent at least part of every day looking for his old haunts, because of the priceless sensations they brought him. One could hardly be further from the sadness and ennui experienced by 'l'Onglay a Parry'.

From mid-March to the end of July *Punch* had published an eighteen-part series on an Englishman's adventures at the Paris Exhibition, entitled *Peeps* [punning on 'Pepys'] *at Paris* by 'Peeper the Great' (in reality Du Maurier's *Punch* colleague, the comic writer F.C. Burnand). At one point a French editor challenges 'Peeper' to a duel for having slandered him. On returning to London, partially inspired by Burnand's series, the cartoonist fictionalised his own visit to the Exhibition in a series of drawings accompanied by two full pages of text. Curiously, it is the French reaction to Titwillow's recitation of his ballad *L'Onglay a Parry* that leads to a climactic duel.

In 'Mr and Mrs Titwillow. PPC' (i.e. *pour prendre congé*, 'to take leave'), the artist and his family have sprouted wings and taken flight over London's rooftops (31 August 1867). In 'Ramsgate Sands. – No. 1' they and their friend 'Uncle Pip' – inspired by Deutsch – have arrived at their destination and are bathing. Later in the same issue of *Punch* in 'Ramsgate Sands. – No. 2', however, 'Mr Pip has got slightly tired of the twins' and suggests spending a week in Paris (21 September 1867).

'Mr Titwillow in Paris' finds the two friends in a Parisian restaurant, where Pip is pulling an assailant off Titwillow: it is at this point that the first page of narrative intervenes. On arriving in Paris, Titwillow and Uncle Pip take a breakfast of several courses with wine and then, while waiting for the bus to the Exhibition, meet three French cavalry officers who are also aristocrats. They spend the day together visiting the fair and drinking in restaurants from various parts of the world, and eventually Titwillow decides to recite his ballad *L'Onglay a Parry* (28 September 1867).

Some of its lines '[stir] up the latent incompatibility of temper which has ever existed between the two countries': very possibly the lines stating the young English couple are more beautiful than anyone else on the boulevard, and that the woman's parents are more respectable than anyone in Paris. The soldiers challenge Titwillow to a duel: 'the French cavalry [has] been insulted, and nought but blood [can] efface the stain'. Pip wires for five bosom friends to come over from England. The penultimate drawing depicts the duel, and the second page of narrative explains that the five friends have arrived (5 October 1867). They all go to the Passy fortifications where Titwillow is to fight – and he wakes up in Ramsgate, where he has fallen asleep after an early dinner and dreamed he was in Paris (12 October 1867).

If the Parisian dream motif announces *Ibbetson*, Titwillow's imminent duel with a French count marks a new development in the contest between the cartoonist's 'two voices': one might say that the French voice threatens to fight back. The violent struggle is echoed in *Ibbetson* where the hero – born Pierre Pasquier de la Marière – murders the maternal 'uncle' who adopted him, changed his name and sought to make an English gentleman of him. Parricide is the necessary prerequisite to 'dreaming true' and to Peter's nightly meetings with his female alter ego and cousin Mary, by the Mare d'Auteuil in the Bois de Boulogne.

Towards the end of *Trilby* Svengali spits in Little Billee's face and Little Billee's friend Taffy smacks him, leading Svengali to challenge him to a duel (which never occurs). In *The Martian*, Barty's father Lord Runswick has been killed in a duel by a French lieutenant: 'they fought with swords, by the Mare aux Biches, in the Bois de Boulogne'.[204]

In addition to following Burnand's example with a Franco-British duel, Du Maurier's narrative employs several devices – already familiar to the readers of *Punch* – that he would re-use in *Ibbetson*, making it difficult for the uninitiated to decipher. Not only is French occasionally spelled 'Englishly' but English is also occasionally spelled 'Frenchly' (cf 'Mr de Titouilleau'). Foreign words and phrases are sometimes left untranslated or intentionally mistranslated. (For example, in the context of the narrative '*la morgue anglaise*' does not constitute an allusion to the 'ghastly building by the river-side', but rather to English arrogance or disdain.) Finally, Du Maurier uses pastiche, as when Titwillow comically modifies lines about a gladiator from *Childe Harold*.

In early 1868 the Du Mauriers moved to 12 Earl's Terrace in Kensington. In April George's sister Isabel married Clement Scott. The son of the vicar of Hoxton – who wrote for the *Morning Chronicle* and the

Saturday Review, and edited the *Christian Remembrancer* – Scott had been educated at Marlborough and had converted to Roman Catholicism. He was a clerk in the War Office until retirement, but his chief interest was the theatre and from 1871 he was the dramatic critic of the *Daily Telegraph*.

The Du Mauriers' fourth child and third daughter, Marie-Louise (or May), was born in Kensington in August. In 1869 they moved to Hampstead, where George, now a professional artist, would spend almost all of the rest of his life. Gerald Hubert Edward, born on 26 March 1873, was the youngest of George and Emma Du Maurier's five children and the only one born after their relocation to Hampstead.

What's in a name?

In February 1870 Du Maurier's mother died in Kensington, where she had lived since she left Germany in 1865. She had been christened Ellen Cecily Clarke and married, at the British Embassy in Paris, as Ellen Cecilia Clarke.

'Jocelyn' has only been found as one of Ellen Du Maurier's names on documents dating from after her death. Presumably her children placed the name on these documents; they also borrowed it for the next generation. George's second daughter was Sylvia Jocelyn; Eugene's younger daughter would be called Madeleine Marie Jocelyn (and her own daughter Marcelle Marie Jocelyn); and Isabel would give Jocelyn as a middle name to both her sons. (Eugene's three children's names all contain an echo of his mother's, since Madeleine Marie Jocelyn's siblings were called Ellen Marie Louise and Ralph Cecil.)

In the 26 February 1870 issue of *Punch*, Du Maurier published a four-part comic strip under the recurring *Punch* heading 'What's in a name?', subtitled 'Fancy studies of certain people writing "to the editor of the *Times*"'. Each of the drawings depicts a person with a common British surname – Mr Smith, Miss Robinson, Mr Jones and Mr Brown – writing to inform the editor that he or she has no connection to the identically-named person – the assailant, complainant against an amorous dragoon, swindler, or proponent of workhouse reform – who has recently been named in the *Times*.

Du Maurier reused the surname 'Robinson' a few months later in the 16 April cartoon 'Things they manage better in France. Scene – at a publisher's'. A Mr Robinson informs the publisher of 'an annual of the French *noblesse*' that 'I have reason to believe that on my mother's side I am distantly connected with the French aristocracy, and....' The publisher interrupts to say that if Robinson wishes to subscribe to the annual, he will of course be allowed to write anything he pleases 'about yourself and your distinguished French extraction'.[205]

On his father's side, Du Maurier was of wholly French extraction.

George Du Maurier's carte de visite, 1870s

He believed – or at least half-believed – 'Busson Du Maurier' to be an aristocratic surname, and he was also curious about his maternal ancestry. Ellen Du Maurier's maiden name – Clarke – is a very common one, however there is reason to question her paternity. The surname 'Jocelyn' is said to derive from the French 'Josselin' and the hero of *The Martian* is called 'Barty Josselin' after his unmarried mother Antoinette Josselin, 'the daughter of poor fisher-folk in Le Pollet, Dieppe'.[206]

In his last novel, Du Maurier used aspects of his own experience for both Barty, the hero, and Robert Maurice, the narrator. The author's uncle, George Clarke, had been a captain in the 17th Lancers; similarly Robert Maurice had an 'uncle Charles (Captain Blake, late 17th Lancers)'. In the novel the 'Blakes', of Irish ancestry, 'had aristocratic notions. It used to be rather an Irish failing in those days'. Later the narrator refers to 'those maternally ancestral Irish Blakes of Derrydown stirring within me', and again to 'some maternally ancestral Blake of Derrydown, who may have been a proper blackguard!'[207]

The conflation of 'Josselin', the surname of Barty's maternal ancestors, with the Irish heritage of the Blakes, Robert Maurice's maternal ancestors, points to the Anglo-Irish Jocelyn family, who traced their origins to the aristocratic French Josselins, and had seats at Hyde Hall in Hertfordshire and later Tollymore in County Down. On his father's death in 1797, Robert Jocelyn, Viscount Jocelyn, born in Dundalk in 1756, became the second earl of Roden.

A sympathetic historian wrote that the second Earl of Roden 'was a very deservedly popular nobleman, of an amiable disposition and pleasing manners, and was for many years the particular friend of the Prince of Wales, afterwards George IV'. Moreover, the second Earl 'raised a regiment of dragoons, which acquired the name of the "Roden Fox Hunters", with which he highly distinguished himself during the rebellion in 1798'.[208]

There is no evidence whatsoever that Robert Jocelyn was 'a proper blackguard' or that his path ever crossed Mrs Clarke's – although his purported intimacy with the future George IV is not a wholly positive recommendation.

Eugene Du Maurier and the Paris Commune

Six months after Ellen Du Maurier's death, her son Eugene, aged thirty-four, married Marie Rosalie Espinasse, aged twenty-two, a tradesman's daughter, in Paris. He had left the army and his profession is given as employee of the *assistance publique*. The Du Mauriers'

THINGS THEY MANAGE BETTER IN FRANCE.
SCENE—AT A PUBLISHER'S

'Parlyvoo ongly, Mossoo?' 'Yes, sare.'
'O – I see you are publishing an annual of the French *noblesse*.' 'Yes, sare.'
'Well, my name is – a – is Robinson, in point of fact; but I have some reason to believe that on my mother's side I am distantly connected with the French aristocracy, and I should like to trace –'
'Yes, sare. I ondairstand. If you shall veesh to sooscribe to my annual – thirty-six franc by year – you shall write in eet any mortal sing in ze vorld you please about yourself and your distinguished French extraction.'

seventy-five-year-old Aunt Louise died in Paris in November 1870, at her nephew's home.

Eugene and Marie Rosalie's daughter Ellen Marie Louise was born in Paris on 14 May 1871, in the last days of the Paris Commune. Eugene and his wife had recently moved to an apartment on the boulevard de la Madeleine. He gave a first-hand account of the dramatic events in a letter to his brother translated here from the French:

> Nothing in the world can convey an idea of what we have just been through and seen in Paris. I am still heartbroken and sick about it. In the rage of their defeat, the brutal insurgents set Paris on fire. Monuments, private property: they didn't spare anything. We were literally surrounded by fire, shells and projectiles of all kinds.
>
> Our new apartment is situated between the Finance Ministry and

the rue Royale, and we expected to succumb in turn. In the midst of all this, Marie was bed-ridden, recovering from childbirth. This horrible and savage struggle lasted eight full days, during which Paris was strewn with disfigured cadavers. I saw some who had been decapitated by bullets – people were gunned down in groups, men and women at every corner. The women played an even more ignoble role than the men, if that is possible. They were in charge of propagating the fire with petrol. I returned completely disheartened by all this, feeling that my power of reasoning was vacillating.

Today the cannon has stopped – what a relief!

Marie is doing very well – her milk is coming passably and young Ellen is divinely well. Marie will write to Pem [Emma] as soon as she is able. We had a very good idea in leaving our apartment on the rue Godot: it was visited by a shell that exploded on the first floor after descending from the sixth. What straits we would be in.

The London newspapers must tell you everything that has happened. This thought has prevented me from continuing a long journal that I had started for you, indicating events day by day. I have seen some very terrible things and on my next visit I will tell you all about them.

The last eight months have made a terrible breach in our poor France. One can't help envying England as we escape from such a furnace. What a people of madmen we are, and if only we had used all the blood and courage that we just expended in a fratricidal war, against the Prussians, what a drubbing we would have given them.[209]

Not long after surviving the Paris Commune, Eugene, Marie and their daughter Ellen moved from Paris to London. Ellen's brother Ralph Cecil and sister Madeleine Marie Jocelyn were born in Hendon in 1874 and 1875 respectively, and the Du Maurier cousins grew up together.

When the cat's away

In 1874 George and Emma Du Maurier and their five children moved to New Grove House.

The family spent the summer holiday of 1875 in the fashionable resort of Dieppe; the cartoonist recorded the event in fourteen drawings published from 17 July to 16 October. 'When the cat's away' – Du Maurier adopted the frequent *Punch* rubric for what was becoming a recurring theme of his cartoons – shows Wilkins and Tomkins dining at one of the best hotels, in pursuit of cheap and suitable lodgings for their families (24 July 1875).

New Grove House,
Hampstead

The following year the cartoon 'Moral pluck' offered a variation on the 'Cat's away' joke. 'Paterfamilias' returns from 'a delightful three weeks' trip on the French coast with a congenial bachelor' only to inform his disappointed family that after trying Trouville, Dieppe, Étretat, Tréport, Boulogne and all, he has concluded that 'there's no place like home' (12 August 1876). It is not known whether Du Maurier did in fact travel to France in 1876 or, if he did, whether a 'congenial bachelor' had accompanied him.

In the summer of 1877 the Du Mauriers spent six weeks in Sainte Adresse (Le Havre), and then another six weeks in Paris. They and the Scotts rented two houses in the Villa Montmorency in Auteuil, adjoining the Bois de Boulogne with the Mare d'Auteuil and the new Hippodrome d'Auteuil, and also Passy where 'Paterfamilias' had spent his formative years.

The long holiday was memorialised in eighteen *Punch* cartoons, and again almost twenty years later at the opening of Part Tenth of *The Martian*. 'The Laureate Illustrated', a full-page drawing on the 'Cat's away' theme, was the first to appear (4 August 1877). As French maids, soldiers and even children look askance, Brown, Jones and Robinson are pictured on the beach, having crossed over to 'look out for suitable lodging for their respective families. After dining succulently, they lit their cigars, and then (happy thought)' – an only slightly modified stanza of Tennyson's 'Lotos-Eaters' completes the legend.

In *The Martian*, the narrator's account of the holiday focuses first on his and Barty's return to Vibraye, where they had stayed with the Lafertés – based on Du Maurier's father's cousins, the Duvals – in 1848. Extrapolating from the partially fictionalised account, it seems that the relatives the novelist knew had either died or moved away. His second cousin, Ernest Duval, had become a barrister in Angers, 'prosperous and married', and he decided not to look him up. The friends find Vibraye has changed for the worse: 'Altogether we were uncommonly glad to get back to the Villa Montmorency....'

On a visit to Passy, Barty and Robert look for the Pension Froussard. They discover that '[n]othing remained of our old school – not even the outer walls; nothing but the big trees and the absolute ground they grew

THE LAUREATE ILLUSTRATED.

'They sat them down upon the yellow sand,/ Between the sun and moon upon the shore:/ And sweet it was to dream of fatherland,/ Of child and wife and slave; but evermore/ Most weary seemed the sea, weary the roar,/ Weary the wandering fields of barren foam./ Then some one said, "We will return no more."/ And all at once they sang, "Our island home/ Is far beyond the wave; we will no longer roam."' *The Lotos eaters*

out of. Beautiful lawns, flower-beds, conservatories, summer-houses, ferns, and evergreen shrubs made the place seem even larger than it had once been – the very reverse of what usually happens – and softened for us the disenchantment of the change.'[210]

It is not known whether Du Maurier took a holiday in France in 1881 but he published 'Public Spirit', yet another variation on his 'Cat's away' joke, on 14 May. Previous cartoons had hinged on problems with drains, both in Hampstead and abroad. Here the middle-aged Smith, Jones, Brown and Robinson join their wives for coffee after dinner. Mrs Smith asks her husband, 'What have you gentlemen been plotting downstairs, that you look so guilty?' As his friends busy themselves by examining a sculpture of a female nude, looking at a book and using a handkerchief, respectively, Smith somewhat haltingly explains that the *disgraceful* way in which foreign hotels are drained has compelled the men, in the interest of their families and other English families, to elect themselves into a kind of sanitary inspection committee. They therefore have to make a quick visit to the best-known French watering places – including Paris.

In 1886 Du Maurier made two trips to Paris with his *Punch* colleagues Burnand and Furniss. On 1 May 1886 he published another variant on the 'Cat's Away' theme. 'Compensation' depicts a dialogue between two English acquaintances meeting by chance in front of a Parisian estaminet-restaurant, whose windows advertise beer and oysters. Jones informs his compatriot that he has come over without his wife: she 'had to stop at home because of the baby'. His friend comments that 'your holiday will be half spoiled!', to which Jones replies, 'Yes. Mean to stay twice as long, to make up!'

In May 1889 Du Maurier and *Punch* travelled to Paris for the Universal Exhibition. On his return he published a final variation on the 'Cat's away' theme. '*L'Embarras des richesses* [An embarrassment of riches]. At the *Café des ambassadeurs*' (29 June 1889) depicts 'Jones and Brown, from Clapham', seated at a table at the famous Parisian café-concert. The waiter is obliged to remind them to eat before their food gets cold: their gazes and attention are focused instead on the scantily clad dancer on stage.

George and Emma's children learned French from infancy and if they were somewhat less fluent than their father, they clearly surpassed their mother. 'Sancta Simplicitas!' published in *Punch* on 14 November 1885, represents four children and their parents in a drawing room scene. Mamma admonishes one of her sons to 'read *French* sometimes'. She adds, 'Look at dear Papa, *he* hasn't much time for reading but whenever

L'EMBARRAS DES RICHESSES. AT THE CAFÉ DES AMBASSADEURS.

The garsong (To Jones and Brown, from Clapham). 'But your dinner, gentlemans! He go to make 'imself cold, if you eat 'im not!'

he's got a spare moment or two, he takes a French book out of his pocket and reads it – *just to keep up his French, you know!*' The caption specifies: '[*Dear Papa is much tickled, but keeps his amusement to himself*]'. The cover on his book reads 'Œuvres de Zola' (Zola's Works). Here 'Mamma' is unaware of the subversiveness of French books, but in another cartoon, 'The Child of the Period' (24 November 1888), the daughters portrayed are not. 'Aunt Betsy' wonders that her brother has 'so many French books in [his] library ... with all [his] daughters growing up!' One daughter – Eva – has overheard and replies facetiously: 'French books, indeed! The idea! Why, we should *never* think of reading a French book, if we could help it – *not even if Papa were to forbid us to!*'

Grandchildren and genealogy

The Du Mauriers' oldest child Beatrice became engaged to Charles Hoyer Millar, a mechanical engineer, in 1883, which may have suggested the 16 February 1884 cartoon 'An Ollendorff wanted'. Mistranslating the word 'engaged', 'Miss Mary' informs the 'fascinating Parisian' who invites her to dance that she is '*fiancée*' (betrothed) for all the rest of the evening

In April 1884 Emma Du Maurier's father, 'thought to be very well-off', died, leaving a personal estate of £270. Charles Millar recalls that Mr Wightwick's death was the only occasion on which he observed any real trouble between the Du Mauriers:

When it transpired that his business had been losing money for years and that finally he had invested what was left in an annuity for himself, leaving Mummie [Emma] to inherit only a few years of a leasehold, it was a bitter disappointment. Du Maurier must have expressed himself with considerable warmth, for on coming to the studio that afternoon I found Trixy and Sylvia looking very unhappy on the settee, my father-in-law walking up and down and evidently very angry, and poor Mummie shedding torrents of tears. Trixy and Sylvia at once bolted to the door, taking me out with them, and we all escaped for an hour or two on the Heath to allow things to settle down.[211]

The disappointing state of Mr Wightwick's finances may have been linked to his remarriage after the death of Emma's mother.

In July of the same year, twenty-year-old Beatrice married twenty-four-year-old Charles. A journalist provided an anonymous account of the ceremony in the 'Ladies' Column':

You know what Miss Du Maurier is like from the pretty girls in *Punch*, and I thought I recognised another of her father's favourite subjects in one of the bridesmaids. It was the prettiest wedding possible, but really the parents and guardians ought to have stopped in to put it off for a little. So, apparently, thought some dear old ladies near me, one of whom was crying bitterly ... and wondering whether they would like each other 'when they grew up'. The aisle was filled with the friends of the bride and bridegroom, and all the artistic world was there – Mr Millais, the Alma-Tademas, the Boughtons, young Mr Burne-Jones, Mr Val Prinsep, and a host of others. The crowd was too great to allow me to see much of the dresses, but most of the ladies' costumes were terribly 'intense', and their wearers seemed to have stepped straight out of Mr Du Maurier's drawings. The six bridesmaids wore white sprigged muslin and lace, with hats to match, and they carried large bouquets of pink and white roses.[212]

In short, for this observer the wedding ceremony and its participants were straight out of the pages of *Punch*. Geoffrey and Guy, the Millars' first two sons, were born in 1886 and 1887.

In October 1884, Du Maurier received replies from the four French departmental archivists – in Angers, Le Mans, Nantes and Rennes – to whom he had written to request information about his Busson ancestors. The letters all informed him that, at the time, parish registers were kept

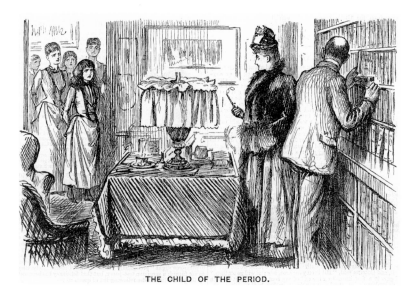

THE CHILD OF THE PERIOD.

'The Child of the Period'

at town halls and not in departmental archives. The Englishman knew that his émigré grandfather had been born in Chenu in the province of Anjou (since the Revolution, in the Department of Sarthe). The Sarthe archivist added a postscript in which he wondered whether his correspondent might have some connection to the château Du Maurier in La Fontaine-Saint-Martin, less than 30 km from Chenu, and the once-prominent Aubéry Du Maurier family.

The archivist's reply led to another exchange of letters; his second letter informed Du Maurier that Sarthe had many places named *La Bussonnière*, the most remarkable one being a château in the village of Maresché, to the north of Le Mans in the direction of Alençon. However, the archivist thought parishes in northern Sarthe less likely to have a connection to the Du Mauriers than those in southern Sarthe, near the town of La Flèche and the village of La Fontaine-Saint-Martin. Nonetheless, George wrote to the owner of the château de la Bussonnière in Maresché, who directed him to the châtelain of La Pierre in Coudrecieux: a very useful lead.

Sophie Duval had omitted her father's birthplace in her letter on family history, and neither George nor Daphne Du Maurier ever managed to discover that not only had Mathurin Busson directed the La Pierre glass-factory in Coudrecieux for many years, he had in fact been born there. His Busson ancestry can be traced back to the first parish registers in Coudrecieux, which definitively lays to rest any notions of the Bussons' aristocratic origins.

Instead, in an April 1885 letter to his daughter Beatrice, George mentioned that 'I have had a host of 14 new Bussons from La Sarthe, one of them ... connected with Louis [in reality Benjamin] Aubéry, Seigneur du Maurier, *le célèbre* diplomat in the 17th century. Perhaps the key of the mystery lies there.'[213]

On a brief trip to Paris in May 1886, Du Maurier and his *Punch* colleagues Burnand and Furniss tried to visit the *Salon des indépendants* (Independent Artists' Salon). On learning the Salon did not open until noon, they drove on to Notre Dame cathedral: 'In a beautiful recess in Notre-Dame [I] found the tomb of the Guébriants, with the little black Busson lion in the quarterings quite well preserved.'[214] The tomb mentioned was that of Jean-Baptiste Budes, maréchal de Guébriant and his wife. Guébriant was indeed related to the aristocratic Bussons of Brittany, but not to the English artist.

George Du Maurier's German-born cousin 'Eliza de Busson' died in Marylebone in the spring of 1890, followed in November by his sister Isabel, aged fifty-one, who died in Cornwall, and their brother Eugene, aged fifty-four, who died in Torquay the following month. In a letter of condolence after Isabel's death, Henry James wrote that 'I had seen your sister but once, but I had gathered from you that she was long out of health and was not positively happy.'[215] Eliza's brother Pedro, who died in Hamburg in 1900, lived the longest of the third generation of Du Mauriers.

Three books with an *air de famille*

Discussing Du Maurier's three novels in his 1897 essay, Henry James made the point that his friend's 'early childhood is specifically in the first of the trio, his later boyhood in the third, and in the second his *Wanderjahre*, his free apprenticeship, the initiations of his prime....' James adds that 'no three books proceeding from three separate germs can ever had had, on the whole, more of the *air de famille*'.[216] *Air de famille* means 'family resemblance', but it could also be translated as 'family air' or 'family refrain', which is exactly what *Ibbetson* enciphers, and what Chapter Six will decipher. *Trilby* and *The Martian*, to an extent, may be said to 'sing the same tune'.

In early 1892, as Du Maurier informed Henry James, *Trilby* was underway:

> I have begun another novel – the one about the hypnotised singer – it
> amuses me enormously. If the muse is propitious it will make a volume
> of about 50,000 words. In this novel love will be burning hot! It takes
> place in Paris in the Quartier Latin of thirty-five years ago – This is the
> life I led. *Nourri dans le sérail, j'en connais les détours* [Raised in the
> seraglio, I know its hidden ways].

The citation is from Racine's *Bajazet* and in a postscript to the letter, par-
aphrasing Gautier, Du Maurier added: 'My new novel is not for little girls
whose toast is cut up for them.'[217] *Ibbetson* is not for the overly prudish
reader either – although the extent to which James or the author's friends
generally 'deciphered' the novel is unclear.

Paul Meredith Potter was the pen name of Walter MacLean, a British
journalist based in America who adapted *Trilby* for the stage. In a brief
newspaper article published after Du Maurier's death, an anonymous
former guest recalled an anecdote the novelist told about Potter's Sven-
gali-like quality:

> That man Potter used to come here … and from the moment he entered
> the house Mrs Du Maurier was deaf to everyone else. At the dinner
> table he would lead her into obtuse discussions, in the drawing room
> he would involve her in the most complicated arguments on music and
> Buddhism. At last I demurred, but all my wife could say was 'I can't
> help it, George. He is so agreeable. I never met a man whose conver-
> sation so enthralled me.' And then little by little it began to dawn on
> the girls and me that mother was being Svengalised. I was hoist by my
> own petard, in fact, and if Potter hadn't gone away when he did I really
> believe that Trilby's fate would been duplicated not only in real life, but
> right in the bosom of my own family.[218]

The actor and theatre manager Herbert Beerbohm Tree bought the
English rights to produce *Trilby* and played the part of Svengali. A friend
recommended a young actress called Dorothea Baird to Du Maurier for
the title role; as it happened the novelist had already met Dorothea when
she lived in Hampstead as a child. Tree and Du Maurier went to see her;
Lady Tree recalled:

> Mr Du Maurier used to tell me that when Herbert and he broke in
> upon her, they found her lying all her lovely length upon a sofa, sur-
> rounded by books, and engaged in studying Desdemona. They asked

her if she would like to act Trilby, and in their hearts decided then and there that none other should. By the end of the week she was rehearsing, and her success is, of course, historic.[219]

Du Maurier wrote to his friend John Millais that

Tree took an immediate fancy to such a lovely Trilby. You would love her – 5 ft. 9 ins. – and made like a slender Venus; the little Billee … sat for my illustrations of him in the book – the first portrait, that is, the front face. They neither of them have much experience of the stage, but Tree believes in them both, and he and I have been doing our little best to coach them.[220]

The play's London premiere took place at the Haymarket on 30 October 1895 and reviews were almost wholly favourable. However, Clement Scott from the *Daily Telegraph* had not attended the opening (ostensibly because Tree, 'too often riled by the critic's disparagements of his performances', had moved him from the box to the stalls).[221] Scott attended a later performance and then wrote that Du Maurier 'must have wept tears of blood when he found the delicacy of his romance ruined alike by dramatist and artists'. Scott found Dorothea Baird amateurish but conceded 'she, doubtless, one day will be a clever actress'.[222]

Readers of the *Telegraph* may have assumed that Scott was speaking for his former brother-in-law; to make his true feelings clear the novelist wrote to the paper himself:

Will you permit me in justice to Mr P. Potter who dramatized my story and to the Haymarket Company generally to state that far from shedding 'tears of blood' on Wednesday night, I was much delighted both with the play and with the performance of it. In justice to Miss Dorothea Baird the critic might have been invited to correct his extraordinary misrepresentation contained in the following line: 'is coolly announced as making her first appearance'. When was the 'cool announcement' made? It is a matter of common knowledge that Miss Baird has been on the stage a couple of years and has played an extensive range of parts with Mr Ben Greet.[223]

When Dorothea married Henry B. Irving in July 1896, her attire included a diamond pendant, a gift from the author of *Trilby*.

While in Whitby that summer, George Du Maurier became seriously

LE MONDE OU L'ON S'AMUSE.

Du Maurier's last *Punch* cartoon, 'Le Monde où l'on s'amuse'

ill and died at home in London on 7 October 1896, two months after
John Millais and four days after William Morris. According to Du Maurier's wishes, his body was cremated and his funeral was held in Hampstead on 13 October, in the presence of his widow, his children, and his
surviving friends and *Punch* colleagues. Canon Ainger and the vicar of
Hampstead read the service and the organist played Schubert's 'Sere-
nade' and 'Adieu', Schumann's '*Nussbaum*', Wagner's '*Parsifal* Overture'
and Chopin's '*Marche Funèbre*'.

The editor and novelist James Payn wrote in the *Illustrated London
News* that

> Every Englishman with eyes in his head and a taste for humour with-
> out coarseness will miss [Du Maurier] every week. Nothing here, nor,
> indeed, anywhere, can be said to enhance his claims upon us, for we
> all admit them. Let it suffice for one who knew him to say that he was
> lovable as a friend as he was admirable as an artist – whether with pen
> or pencil – a tender-hearted, generous-minded gentleman, on whose
> tomb may be inscribed with a sincerity very rare in epitaphs, 'He left
> the world brighter than he found it, and not one enemy behind him.'[224]

Du Maurier's last *Punch* cartoon appeared in the almanac for 1897.

A newspaper item described the drawing, published under the recurring *Punch* title *Le monde où l'on s'amuse* (The world in which one amuses oneself):

> A melancholy interest attaches to the Christmas number of *Punch* this week, inasmuch as it contains the last work done by Du Maurier for the paper with which his name has been associated for more than a generation. It is a full-page drawing, a bicycling subject, introducing a group of the stately ladies whom Du Maurier delighted to draw. In the text is quoted a snatch of one of those Quartier Latin choruses dear to readers of *Trilby*.[225]

The Quartier Latin chorus refers to dancing the cancan 'night and day'. But the cartoon itself expresses a certain weariness. The cycling ladies are unsmiling and the dialogue between 'Ethel' and 'Maud' goes as follows: 'I hope bicycling will go out of fashion before next season, I *do* hate bicycling so!' 'So do I! But one *must*, you know!'

CHAPTER FOUR

GERALD AND COMPANY

[The Du Mauriers] die before middle age, often rather
painfully, and are soon forgotten. But they leave behind them
a dim fragrance of their presence, like a whisper in the air.
Daphne Du Maurier, *The Du Mauriers*

Gerald Du Maurier remarked to an interviewer that 'The guv'nor frequently took us children as models for his weekly pictures. I often say that I can trace all my childhood's doings and happenings through the pages of *Punch*!'[226] Gerald's most famous appearance in *Punch* was probably his first one: he was cast as a third-class carriage – but 'really only a *truck*' – and portrayed along with his mother and siblings in 'Delicate Consideration' (14 June 1873).

The Du Mauriers spent the summer holiday of 1877 in France, and in 'An Epicure' Gerald was the model for a small boy (called 'George'), pictured rubbing his lips after being kissed by a little French girl. When his mother says she is ashamed of him for rubbing out the kiss, the boy replies, 'I'm not rubbing it *out*, Mummy – I'm rubbing it *in*!' (25 August 1877).

In 'Cherubic' (31 August 1878), a little boy and his aunt observe a plaster bust. The boy asks three questions, and each one receives an affirmative answer from 'Auntie dear': 'Is *that* great-grandpapa?'; 'And was great-grandpapa clever?'; 'And was great-grandpapa very *good*?'. However, the child's fourth question is left unanswered: 'And is that all there *was* of great-grandpapa?'

Assuming the boy was Gerald and the aunt was George Du Maurier's sister Isabel, the relevant great-grandfather would be either

'Cherubic'

Mathurin-Robert Busson, who abandoned his young English family to return definitively to France, or Joseph Clarke, the long lost husband of the flamboyant Mary Anne. Given the relative obscurity of both men, it seems unlikely that a plaster bust would have been made of either one, although there are of course an abundance of portraits and busts of Mary Anne Clarke's paramour Frederick, Duke of York.

A few years later Gerald and 'Madeline' – possibly based on Gerald's young cousin Madeleine Du Maurier – appeared in 'Juvenile Parties (What they are getting to)' (14 February 1880). Madeline exclaims 'What *do* you think Gerald! We're to be fetched from the Browns' *at half-past nine*! It says so on the card!' Gerald answers 'No! – What a shame! I votes [sic] we don't go!' His motion is 'seconded and carried unanimously'.

The Du Mauriers in the 1880s and 1890s

Charles Millar's memoir provides a valuable account of the family from 1879. Millar recalls that

> At this time [George] Du Maurier's sister Isabel – who had married Clement Scott, for many years the leading theatrical critic on the staff of the *Daily Telegraph* – lived at Hampstead a little lower down the hill. She was naturally a frequent visitor. She was an extremely witty woman with rather a sharp tongue, whereas her husband was of a very sentimental nature, on account of which he was subjected by her to a great amount of chaff. This difference in temperament led to their estrangement, so a friendly separation was arranged, she keeping charge of the four children, two boys and two girls.[227]

Isabel's elder daughter Sybil wrote that 'my mother and her four children lived at Keats Cottage, and I remember my mother telling us that [this] was the tree [where] Keats wrote his poem to the nightingale. The year was 1880.'[228]

George and Isabel's brother Eugene, who had served many years in the French army, was described in the 1881 census as an 'agent for foreign mill of roll paper'; he and his wife and their three children lived in nearby Kilburn.

Gerald's brother Guy was a scholar at Marlborough and was then at Sandhurst; Gerald attended Heath Mount School and later Harrow.

During their summer stays in Whitby the Du Mauriers became acquainted with Henry James's friend James Russell Lowell, the United States Minister at the Court of St James from 1880 to 1885. In September 1887 Lowell read at an amateur concert and entertainment in Whitby that also included performances by May and Gerald, the two youngest Du Mauriers. May sang a Tyrolese song, accompanying herself on the banjo and with her father at the piano, as well as 'Swanee River', while Gerald performed 'The Whistling Coon'.[229]

In January 1892, Guy, May and Gerald performed at the Royal Fusilier Theatre in a burlesque written by Guy called *Morgiana*, based on *Ali Baba and the Forty Thieves*. According to a reviewer:

> Cogia, the wife of Ali, is capitally represented by Mr Gerald Du Maurier, and makes some humorous hits in describing the hard lot of the family through being pressed by creditors and dunned on all hands. Mr Gerald Du Maurier sang several funny songs and danced with much

ability. Ali Baba is played by Mr Guy Du Maurier with conspicuous success. He was 'got up' in the most grotesque style, and in his rendering of the part made a decided hit. Morgiana was played by Miss May Du Maurier, the only lady in the piece. Her impersonation was considerably marred by nervousness, but in appearance and make-up she was well suited to the part of a handsome Eastern slave-girl.[230]

A year later Guy, May and Gerald joined the 'Missing Word' burlesque company and performed Rhodes's *Bombastes Furioso* in aid of a church in Rugby. A newspaper review noted that 'Some topical songs of Mr Gerald Du Maurier's composition were introduced, and they were well received. Miss Du Maurier was very successful as Distaffina.'[231]

Sylvia, the Du Mauriers' second daughter, married Arthur Llewelyn Davies, a barrister, in August 1892. Arthur's father was the vicar of Kirkby Lonsdale; he and the Du Mauriers' friend, Canon Ainger, performed the ceremony. George Du Maurier's companions from his Paris year, Tom Lamont and Tom Armstrong, signed the register, along with his more recent friend Henry James. In a diary entry, the couple's friend, Dolly Parry, described Sylvia during her engagement:

Without being strictly speaking pretty, she has got one of the most delightful, brilliantly sparkling faces I have ever seen. Her nose turns round the corner – also turns right up. Her mouth is quite crooked.... Her eyes are very pretty – hazel and very mischievous. She has pretty black fluffy hair: but her expression is what gives her that wonderful charm, and her low voice.[232]

By 1894, Beatrice had two sons and Sylvia had one.

Twenty-year-old Gerald was now an uncle and also the subject of the cartoon 'An enigmatic grandmotherly utterance', in the 13 January 1894 issue of *Punch*. It depicts a conversation between a young boy and his grandmother: 'Angels have wings – *haven't* they grandmamma!' 'I've always heard so.' 'I heard Uncle Gerald tell Mademoiselle *she* was an angel – in the shrubbery this morning – and *she* hasn't got wings!' 'No; but *she'll have to fly!*' The legend explains that 'Uncle Gerald is the son and heir.'

Within a year of George Du Maurier's death, his youngest daughter May, 'who had taken [it] very hardly and who was thought never likely to marry', married Edward Horsman Coles, a barrister. Once again, her father's friend Alfred Ainger officiated. Charles Millar described May as follows:

She was the real wit of the family and in that respect took very much after her aunt Isabel, Clement Scott's wife. As a young girl she was very athletic and a good player both at tennis and cricket, at which she bowled round arm, but her health was never really good, and this accounted for the temperamental outbursts from which she suffered from time to time. She had no children, but she and Coley [Coles] were always a most devoted couple and happy in their life together.

He added that of all the family May was most like her mother 'in appearance, though in character she was entirely different'.[233]

The two oldest Scotts, the Du Mauriers' cousins, also married in this period. Like his cousins, Philip acted and directed, and while stationed at Curragh Camp with the Army Service Corps he met Florence Kate Carrol at a Military Amateur Dramatic Performance in Dublin; they married in late 1896. The following year Sybil Scott married John Ley Kempthorne Martyn, a solicitor, in London. Philip and Florence's son, Anthony Gerald O'Carrol Scott, born at his mother's family home Lissenhall, County Tipperary in 1899, grew up to become a major general in the British army.

Drama in 'the last hours of the nineteenth century'

Gerald explained to an interviewer that

> I had always been keen on acting and dressing up – when I was a boy I used to disguise myself as a tramp, stick a beard on my chin, and tap at the door of the guv'nor's studio. Invariably I managed to take him in, pitching him some miserable hard-up story. Finally he'd give me half a crown to get rid of me. Then I'd pull off the beard – and he'd let fly at me in his choicest French for having wasted his time! Those were my first successful attempts at acting for money![234]

Speaking to another interviewer, Gerald gave a comical summary of the beginning of his professional career:

> On leaving Harrow at eighteen, I went to University College to try to pass the 'Matric' – then I was sent to a solicitor's office – which I believe I nearly wrecked, owing to incapacity! – then joined a firm of ship-brokers – which failed! – before finally launching on a theatrical career ... through the kindness of Sir John Hare, who gave me my first part in a play called *The Old Jew*, in which I played Fritz, a German waiter.[235]

The Old Jew premiered at the Garrick Theatre on 6 January 1894, with 'a large number of theatrical people' in the audience, according to the *St James's Gazette*:

> Mr and Mrs Bancroft occupied one box, while Mrs Hare was to be seen in another. In a third could be discerned Sir Arthur Sullivan, who had composed special music for the ballad sung in the first act. From the stalls Mr Du Maurier watched his son's excellent personification of a small character; while elsewhere might be remarked Mr W.S. Gilbert, Mr Pinero, Mr Comyns Carr, Mr Forbes Robertson, Mr and Mrs d'Oyly Carte, Mr Edmund Routledge, Dr Lennox Browne, Miss Marion Terry, Miss Julia Neilson, with her husband Mr Fred Terry, Mr Ogilvie (author of *Hypatia*), and Miss Evelyn Millard.

The play had a short run but Gerald went on to act in six other plays at the Garrick that season, including a revival of Thomas William Robertson's *Caste*, and the premiere of Pinero's 'new woman' play, *The Notorious Mrs Ebbsmith*.

After Gerald had worked a year with Sir John Hare, the prominent actor Johnston Forbes-Robertson, who had acted with Gerald at the Garrick, hired him to go on tour. When Gerald returned to London at the end of the tour, Beerbohm Tree, a popular actor who had recently begun managing the Haymarket Theatre, was mounting the first British production of George Du Maurier's *Trilby*, and he offered Gerald the part of Little Billee. As he explained to his interviewer, Gerald felt he lacked the experience for the role. Instead he requested and received the small part of Dodor 'for which I modelled myself as closely as I could on my uncle, Eugene Du Maurier, from whom I knew my father had drawn the part, and who was in a French cavalry regiment'.[236]

Gerald then went to America with Beerbohm Tree's company 'and played [the actor] Fred Kerr's parts in a variety of plays'.[237] He became briefly engaged on two occasions, first to a part-Belgian singer and actress called Marguerite Sylva, and then, on returning to England, to Ethel Daphne Barrymore. In her *Memories*, Barrymore relates that she had been previously engaged to Henry Irving's son Laurence: Gerald 'was so entirely different from … Irving that I found him enchanting. He was tall and slight, not good-looking, but with great charm, gay, amusing, witty. He *swept* me and I thought, "*This is it*!" So Gerald and I were engaged.'

Ethel, whom Gerald called 'Daphne', met his family and she gave the following description:

Gerald's mother was divine to me and so were his sisters. One of them, Sylvia, was very beautiful. Her father, George Du Maurier, had often drawn her to illustrate his books; she looked exactly like the picture of the Duchess of Towers in *Peter Ibbetson*.... Another sister was Trixy, who was beautiful in a different way from Sylvia and another one was May; and they were an utterly enchanting family. But in spite of all their kindness to me, when Mrs Du Maurier began to tell me how to take care of Gerald, what to make him wear in winter and so on, it all alarmed me so that all I could think of was getting home to the four walls of my dressing room – any dressing room.[238]

Although she was still in love with Gerald, Ethel felt she could not go through with the marriage, and returned to America. Gerald eventually left Tree's company for a two-year association with Mrs Campbell's. As Angela Du Maurier put it, 'No less a person than Ethel Barrymore might have been my mother once upon a time, and also Mrs Patrick Campbell.'[239]

In early 1898 Gerald acted in *Trelawny of the Wells*, a comedy by Pinero. From late 1899 to 1901 the newspapers record performances of a comical sketch called *Charles I and Charles II*, written by Captain Guy Du Maurier and the transparently named 'S.O.N. Frère'. Eugene Du Maurier's older daughter Nell (Ellen Marie Louise) began acting in regional theatre, appearing in 1897 in another revival of Robertson's *Caste*. The Du Mauriers' cousin Eric Scott also acted and in October 1898 his photograph and a paragraph about 'the younger son of Clement Scott, the well-known English dramatic critic' appeared in an American magazine:

Being debarred from the navy on account of a slight defect in eyesight, he took up the stage, starting in with small parts in *The Shop Girl* and *The Sign of the Cross*, and beginning his American career two years ago as one of the four officers in *The Geisha*. Last winter he did good work as 'Careless' in *The School for Scandal*, and played opposite to the name part in *The Circus Girl*. In *A Runaway Girl* he is disguised as 'Bobby Barclay'.[240]

The actor Henry B. Irving performed with Scott in *The Sign of the Cross*. According to Irving's son and biographer, his father found 'a kindred spirit' in Eric Scott: 'His mother and father had parted when he was a child and since then the latter had ignored him. He was a bright intelligent youth, with his quota of Du Maurier charm. They made common cause of their broken homes.'[241] In America, Eric performed with Augustin Daly's musical comedy company, but the experience was cut short by Daly's death in June 1899. Scott returned to England, where he enlisted in the Imperial Yeomanry for a year.

In late 1897, Clement Scott gave an interview that eventually led to his resignation from the *Daily Telegraph*. He was responding to Raymond Blathwayt, a former clergyman turned journalist, for the evangelical publication *Great Thoughts*, on the topic 'Does the theatre make for good?' The 'talk with Mr Clement Scott' begins: 'In one word "No".' Exempting only 'the theatrical families of the stage, those well-known people or generations of play-actors' from his critique, Scott made the controversial assertion that 'It is nearly impossible for a woman to remain pure who adopts the stage as a profession.' He added that 'Temptation surrounds her in every shape and on every side; her prospects frequently depend upon the nature and extent of her compliance....'

When asked about 'the problem play', a sort of code word at the time for issue-oriented plays such as those of Ibsen, Scott commented favourably on the recent revival of Robertson's *Caste*, which 'survives simply because it is one of those sweet, pure romances over which people love to linger'. In Scott's view, Ibsen, on the other hand, 'fails, because his plays are nasty, dirty, impure, clever if you like, but foul to the last degree, and healthy-minded English people don't like to stand and sniff over an ash-pit'. [242]

In 1900, after resigning from the *Telegraph*, Scott started a weekly journal called *The Free Lance* that he edited, and for which he wrote 'The Drama of To-Day'. In early November his column was titled 'The Drama of the Dustbin'. The opening paragraph concluded: 'Behold almost the last hours of the nineteenth century. Ladies and gentlemen, let me introduce to you Mr and Mrs Daventry.' Frank Harris, a colourful figure, wrote *Mr and Mrs Daventry* – his only play – on an idea from his friend Oscar Wilde. Harris explained in his autobiography that the play initially attracted unfavourable reviews. 'This bad press ... will make the play,' he told Mrs Campbell, who had agreed to put it on. Harris believed Scott damned the play 'out of personal dislike for me'. Reviewers gave the phrase 'the English vice' – occurring early in the play – 'astonishing notoriety'. According to Harris 'this brought all the best class of London society in streams to the theatre'; it even caused a censor to cut the phrase out of the play. Oscar Wilde died in Paris early in the play's run. Then, 'in the middle of the success ... Queen Victoria died, and the period of mourning stopped all plays in London for a fortnight;

but after the period of mourning had passed [*Mr and Mrs Daventry*] was the only play ... revived that season'.[243]

In concluding his review Scott observed that 'If such plays are to be acted the danger becomes worse when they are well acted. It is the case here.' Mrs Campbell and Fred Kerr excelled in the title roles, and 'Young [Gerald] Du Maurier is advancing rapidly. He has a most sympathetic voice, a charming appearance, and very refined style. He had to play very delicate scenes, but they were all gracefully and intelligently thought out.'[244] Gerald's collaboration with Mrs Campbell and her company continued with two Pinero plays: *The Notorious Mrs Ebbsmith* and *The Second Mrs Tanqueray*. Theatre critic Sheridan Morley briefly summarised the plot of the latter play as 'a "woman with a past" marrying into respectable society and eventually finding that her only way out is suicide'.[245] When Mrs Campbell and her company went to America, Gerald stayed behind but she remained a close friend.

A quarter of a century later he had become 'Sir Gerald' and, following in his Uncle Clement's footsteps, took up his pen to accuse the younger generation of 'knocking at the door of the dustbin'.

A stage association with Barrie and Frohman

At a New Year's Eve party in 1897, Gerald's sister and brother-in-law Sylvia and Arthur Llewelyn Davies met the Scottish writer James Barrie, a fan of *Peter Ibbetson*, 'whose effect on various members of the Du Maurier family was to be at once eerie and beneficial'.[246]

A few years later Gerald first acted for Barrie when Sylvia and he appeared in a play Barrie had written to amuse her sons and other children. As Gerald explained in an interview,

> My first 'stage association' with J.M. Barrie was as an amateur, in the production of an impromptu play he wrote called *The Greedy Dwarf*, for which I remember I composed the incidental music – all in the key of 'C,' as being the only one I could play! We produced it in his back drawing room for the benefit of the large party of children with whom he might always be found surrounded.
>
> I was cast for the title-part, the Dwarf, with my face painted bright green, and standing behind a 'trick table' with my hands disguised as feet, and very startlingly attired, believed myself to have achieved an impenetrable disguise. An illusion, alas! which was at once completely shattered by a nephew, seated in the front row, who shouted out triumphantly 'There's Uncle Gerald!' directly the curtain rose.[247]

Sylvia played Prince Robin and Barrie himself appeared as the Cowardly Custard.

Barrie spent several summers at Black Lake Cottage in Surrey, which he acquired in 1900, and when Sylvia Llewelyn Davies and her four sons arrived at nearby Tilford in July 1901, he devoted 'all his energies to introducing [them] to a world of pirates, Indians and "wrecked islands"'. The following year these summer recreations gave rise to a novel and to *The Admirable Crichton*, a comic play about a return to nature.[248]

Gerald's first professional role in a Barrie play, and his first association with the 'Napoleonic manager' Charles Frohman, was as the Hon. Ernest Woolley, 'ducking his head in the bucket specially kept for him as a cure for sententious chatter, in *The Admirable Crichton*'.[249] A young actress called Muriel Beaumont played Lady Agatha, Woolley's fiancée, and within weeks, according to their daughters, Gerald and Muriel were engaged. Angela describes her mother's background:

> Both my mother's parents came from Cambridgeshire. My grandmother, one of sixteen children, was from Ely where her father had been agent to the then Duke of Portland. My grandfather was a solicitor who had fallen in love with her when she was twelve.... My mother was the second of five children (her eldest brother was Comyns Beaumont who became well-known in the world of journalism and editor of several national magazines). When she was still a child my grandfather lost all his money, and for the rest of their lives my grandparents lived in fairly straitened circumstances.[250]

The Admirable Crichton itself was very successful, running for over 800 performances.

Gerald's association with Barrie and Frohman continued with *Peter Pan*, which premiered in December 1904. He played both Mr Darling and Captain Hook, roles that had originally been given to the actor Seymour Hicks. But 'In Gerald's hands,' according to the author Andrew Birkin, 'the somewhat one-dimensional character of the scripted Hook began to expand in all directions, inspiring Barrie to make constant rewrites until the pirate captain came to fit the description given of him in the final version of the play.'[251] *Peter Pan* was a brilliant success, frequently reprised and for Gerald's daughters, in Angela's words, it was 'practically our birthright'.[252]

Gerald continued the story of his association with Frohman: 'Shortly afterwards *Raffles* was presented at the Comedy [Theatre], and I commenced my career as a criminal. Why, even as John Shand in [Barrie's play] *What Every Woman Knows*, you will remember I was taken for a burglar.'[253] Gerald prolonged his 'criminal' career with Frohman in *Arsène Lupin* in 1909 and *Alias Jimmy Valentine* the following year.

Returning to family history, George Du Maurier's three daughters had married, as well as Isabel Scott's two oldest children. Eugene Du Maurier's son Ralph apparently never married, although he was in all likelihood the father of a son born in Canada in 1894. The 1901 census lists Ralph as a rancher in Stand Off, Alberta, and in 1903 he entered the United States at the Blackfoot Indian Reservation in Montana. Ralph Du Maurier's son – called Eugene, presumably after his grandfather – also immigrated to the United States and founded the DuMaurier Company in Elmira, New York. In its 1936 advertising brochure called 'Magic Eyes', the DuMaurier Company characterised itself as 'America's leading binocular house'.[254] At Eugene's death in 1945, his profession was given as 'merchant seaman'; the Canadian Steamship Company employed him.

The six remaining Du Mauriers and Scotts all married between 1903 and 1909, starting with Gerald and Muriel in April 1903. Alfred Ainger officiated and the actor Henry V. Esmond and Barrie signed the register along with family members. Their daughters Angela, Daphne and Jeanne were born in 1904, 1907 and 1911 respectively. According to one source, 'Angela Du Maurier believed she owed her Christian name to Angela Mackail', one of J.M. Barrie's godchildren, who grew up to become the novelist Angela Thirkell.[255] Gerald's former fiancée, Ethel Daphne Barrymore, claimed that his second daughter was named after her. It is also the case that George Du Maurier's novel, *The Martian*, has a minor character called Daphne, whom his alter ego Barty calls his 'sister ... – "m'amour" – and who spoke both French and English equally well'.[256] The inspiration for Jeanne Du Maurier's name is not known, although in *Ibbetson* the 'small *female* child' who eventually becomes Peter's paternal grandmother and who relives in him is called Jeanne.

Clement Scott died in June 1904, only a few days after his actor friends had staged a benefit in his honour that earned several thousand pounds. In November, Scott's younger daughter Dora married Edmond Abbott Footman. Their daughter Joan Isabella, born in 1907, became an actress known professionally as Joan Clement Scott.

The last of George Du Maurier's children to marry was Guy, now a major in the Royal Fusiliers. In September 1905 he married Gwendolen Price, the daughter of a Canadian-born timber merchant, in Busbridge, Surrey. In November Eugene Du Maurier's younger daughter Marie

Madeleine Jocelyn married Valentine Edmund Browne Webber, an engineer, in Rangoon. They apparently left India not long after marrying and their daughter Marcelle Marie Jocelyn was born in 1908 in Plympton, Devon where her grandmother Marie Rosalie Du Maurier lived in 'Passy Cottage', presumably named after the place George, Eugene and Isabel had lived in as young children.[257] In June 1908 Marie Rosalie's older daughter Nell married Richard Clifford Whiteing.

Finally, in 1909 Clement Scott's younger son Eric married Josephine MacMahon. Like his father and paternal grandfather he turned to journalism; he was the drama critic for *The Bystander*, edited by Muriel Du Maurier's brother Comyns Beaumont, and from 1907 to 1909 he edited *The London Magazine*. Eric Scott also published two novels, both having to do with the stage. *The Fall of a Saint* appeared in 1910 and was turned into a silent film in 1920. In 1911 he published *Queen of All Hearts: A Stage Story*. A reviewer of *The Fall of a Saint* noted that 'it is concerned with theatricals in high places' and 'The plot centres round the death of the comte de la Merthe in a stage duel with Lord Norten, a famous amateur actor....' In addition to being a murder mystery, 'It is an illustration of the author's theory that a saint with a leaning toward priggishness is all the better for a resounding fall.'[258]

'The matinée idol of the war years'

In January 1909, in association with the impresario Frank Curzon and with help from Barrie, Gerald had produced a new play: *An Englishman's Home* by 'A Patriot'. The patriot in question was Guy Du Maurier, who was serving in South Africa at the time.[259] Gerald and his three sisters all wrote to Guy to congratulate him on the play's success.

Gerald entered into a partnership with Curzon and the first play he produced at the Wyndham Theatre was *Nobody's Daughter* by 'George Paston', the pen name of author and critic Emily Morse Symonds, who was also the niece of John Addington Symonds. According to Gerald's biographer, 'Paston' had 'a prolific record of plays' that titillated West End audiences 'without going over the edge'. The play itself was a skilful 'blend of snobbery and illegitimacy'. This was followed by *Passers By*, described by a contemporary playwright as 'respectable but a little bit naughty and with a dash of feeling'.[260]

Biographers have not mentioned Wyndham's next play, *The Perplexed Husband*, by Alfred Sutro, which dealt with women's rights. Gerald played Thomas Pelling, a tea merchant with 'a beautiful young wife, to whom he was much attached, two children, and a house in Regent's Park'

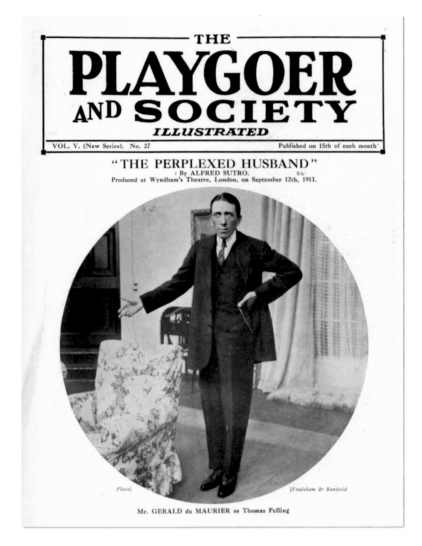

Gerald Du Maurier in 'The Perplexed Husband'

– thus far quite close to Gerald's actual circumstances. When Pelling's duties take him to Russia, his wife Sophie is influenced by a performance of *The Doll's House* and invites Mrs Elstead, 'a strong advocate for the principle of equal rights', and the head of the League of Women, known as 'the Master', to come and stay with her.

On returning home, Pelling is appalled. He hires a beautiful unemployed typist, who adores Greek sculpture and goes by the name Kalleia, to join the houseguests and feign an interest in the Cause. She reads Swinburne to Pelling and he goes so far as to kiss her once but is then overcome with shame and pays her to leave. Kalleia departs for Athens, taking 'the Master' with her to act as a guide. The disappearance of 'the Master' is a great blow to Mrs Elstead and the play ends when Sophie reappears, 'dressed in her husband's favourite frock'.[261]

In real life Muriel Du Maurier seems not to have minded leaving her acting career behind after the birth of her third child; Daphne wrote in her biography of her father that Muriel 'was Mummie [Emma Du Maurier] all over again'.[262] Angela and Daphne's writings suggest it was they who were occasionally left perplexed by their apparently placid mother (Daphne commented, 'How fully my mother was aware of [my father's] wandering eye I shall never know').[263] If Gerald was a rarely perplexed husband, from his daughters' teenage years at least he became an often-perplexed father. In Angela's words, 'Having His Daughters Kissed was the last straw to poor Daddy; I do wonder what he'd have made of sons.'[264]

In 1913 Gerald had his first great success at Wyndham's with a revival of *Diplomacy*, a thirty-five-year-old adaptation of the French dramatist Victorien Sardou's *Dora* by Clement Scott. According to a review 'The present version ... has been brought up to date. Telephones and motor-cars, even ragtime and current events, have been used in the freshening-up process....'[265]

Another success was *The Ware Case*, a new play by George Pleydell Bancroft that premiered in September 1915. A reviewer wrote that 'We were treated to a long-drawn-out dramatic thrill intensely real.' Gerald as Sir Hubert Ware was 'good natured, debonair and careless on the surface, and callous, selfish, and cruel within....'[266] Britain had entered the war and Daphne Du Maurier explained the play's appeal as follows: 'It did not send the audiences home pondering about world problems ... but it allowed them to forget that they were going back to the trenches: the murder of a brother-in-law in a lake made sense and the war did not.'[267]

The Du Mauriers had suffered a series of losses in this period. Sylvia – whose husband Arthur had died in 1907 – died in 1910, leaving five sons to be raised by J.M. Barrie. Her brother-in-law Charles Millar, who had known her since she was a child, described her as follows:

Of all the Du Maurier family Sylvia changed the most, both in appearance and in character. Of a tumultuous disposition in her girlhood, when her outbreaks at New Grove House earned her the nickname of 'the blizzard', she became greatly softened by marriage and motherhood. Her gaiety and mimicry remained unimpaired and she was as quick as ever in repartee and full of her enjoyment of life. Like Trixy, she was a devoted mother, and bore without complaint the knowledge that she had to part with her boys during the long months when she wasted to a shadow of her former self. No one who saw her in her prime was likely to forget her singular attractiveness. In a ballroom she was always a most noticeable figure, with her crooked smile and general allure. No portrait could ever do justice to her radiating charm and sweetness of disposition.[268]

Sylvia's older sister Trixy died in 1913. Her husband wrote:

Like the rest of her family she loved amusing people; her talk was always lively and vigorous, though not so witty as that of her sisters, and unlike them she did not mind being serious over serious matters. She was never flippant yet was always gay and good-humoured. Her vitality was immense and any difficulties were confronted with fortitude. It was a pleasure to see her at the local parties, surrounded by friends and the centre of all that was going on. Radiant is the best adjective to describe her, for she enjoyed life to the full and made others share in her happiness.[269]

Emma Du Maurier's death in January 1915 followed those of her two oldest daughters. According to Daphne, before leaving for the front Guy Du Maurier left his father's signet ring (ironically, engraved with the supposed Breton motto of the unrelated, aristocratic Bussons) with his brother Gerald.[270] In March Guy was killed in the war in Belgium, as was Sylvia's oldest son George. Charles Millar also sketched a brief portrait of Guy:

He was a thorough soldier and very popular in his regiment, where he was always called 'Toby' from his *Punch* association. He took his profession seriously and looked after the welfare of his men in every way. He laughed at the trivialities of barrack-square drills, and once, when his battalion was being inspected by a general, who asked him to have a certain movement made, called to his adjutant to give the necessary order. When the inspection was over the general inquired why he had not given the order himself, and his reply was, 'I forgot all that sort of thing years ago'.

Cannon Hall, Hampstead by Mary Hill

He was a great loss to the Army and also to his numerous friends. He never made an enemy. In disposition he was light-hearted and humorous, always adored by all his family.[271]

Finally, Eugene Du Maurier's widow, Marie Rosalie, died in Devon in November.

1915 was also the year attributed to two unpublished manuscripts that were illustrated by Eugene and Marie Rosalie's now-American son Ralph Du Maurier: *Customs and Legends of the Indians* and *True Stories of Indians, Wild and Civilized*. Although his official profession was 'rancher' or 'cowboy', at least one of Louis-Mathurin and Ellen Du Maurier's twelve grandchildren had found an artistic outlet other than the stage.

Barrie's producer Frohman had died on the *Lusitania* and Gerald went on to produce and act in two new Barrie plays: *A Kiss for Cinderella* and *Dear Brutus*. In Daphne's words, *Dear Brutus* was 'the last and the greatest of Gerald's wartime successes before he left Wyndham's to join the army in 1918'. Gerald played 'the part of a jaded, spoilt, successful painter, at odds with his wife and with the world'.[272] For Daphne 'something of Kicky [George Du Maurier] crept into the part, and the enchanted Dearth of the wood sang his songs in French, and used the almost forgotten Du Maurier slang, and blinked at his easel and chaffed his daughter as Kicky had once chaffed May'.[273] In 1916 Gerald and his family moved from Cumberland Terrace, where Daphne and Jeanne were born, to Hampstead, his birthplace. Their new home, Cannon Hall, was 'a large rambling Georgian house overgrown with ivy and surrounded by a high red brick wall'.[274]

Just before leaving the stage for the army in July 1918, Gerald staged three Barrie playlets at Wyndham's in aid of a hospital for wounded soldiers: *La Politesse*, *The Origin of Harlequin*, and *A Well-Remembered Voice*. *The Origin of Harlequin* was a sort of ballet 'in which the dancing was to be done by juvenile sprigs of the aristocracy'.[275] According to a newspaper article, Jeanne Du Maurier was one of these juvenile sprigs and apparently Daphne also appeared, 'dressed as a red Indian'.[276]

Gerald summed up his military experience in an interview:

> When the war broke out I was 42. For a long time the Army wouldn't have me, and it was not until 1918, when things became very tight in France, that I got a chance. I enlisted in the Irish Guards and was sent to Bushey for training. There they allowed me to scrub floors and sweep the top landing. I was just becoming proficient at my job when the war stopped![277]

Sir Gerald and 'Shingled Stage Morals'

Gerald was knighted in January 1922, during the run of *Bulldog Drummond*, a highly successful thriller discussed below. Daphne recalled, after her father's death, asking her mother why he was knighted and receiving the reply 'I don't think we ever knew.'

Daphne assumed her father received the honour 'not because of the wild popularity of *Bulldog Drummond*, a very different role from that of Will Dearth, nor for the somewhat quixotic gesture which he made in his mid-forties in 1918 by throwing up *Dear Brutus* and joining the Irish Guards as a cadet ... but plainly and simply "for services rendered to the profession".'[278] He was personally generous, and was also the president of the Actors' Orphanage and other charities.

The two most famous paintings of Gerald date from the 1920s. His Hampstead neighbour John Collier painted Sir Gerald in action in 'The Producer', and in four sittings in 1924, Augustus John painted a bust length portrait of Gerald wearing a yellow raincoat. John exhibited the painting at the Royal Academy in 1930, occasioning a short newspaper article entitled 'Distinguished Sitter's Distaste'. Stating 'I'm blessed if I like it,' Gerald explained to the journalist that he would not have the portrait hanging in his house, 'because it would shatter his illusions

Portrait of Gerald Du Maurier by John Collier

about himself every time he looked at it.' According to Gerald, 'A friend of mine said that the portrait showed all the misery of my wretched soul, and I agree with her.'[279]

The actress Gladys Cooper had begun managing in 1917 and in June 1922 at the Playhouse Theatre, she revived Pinero's *Second Mrs Tanqueray*, the play that had made Mrs Campbell famous and that Gerald had also acted in. Angela Du Maurier suggested that her father was instrumental in getting Gladys to play this and other roles originally played by Mrs Campbell. On opening night Daphne, who was fifteen at the time, wrote to Angela in Paris that 'Daddy says [Gladys] is wonderful. Beats Mrs Campbell, Mrs Kendal, etc., *hollow*.'[280]

W.A. Darlington, the dramatic critic for the *Daily Telegraph*, agreed that *The Second Mrs Tanqueray* was a personal triumph for Gladys Cooper, although with her production of the play she simultaneously 'proved herself as an actress and tumbled Pinero from his perch'. Pinero suffered because Gladys updated the play to the contemporary period, creating a ludicrous effect according to Darlington. In his view, the casting of Ellean, Mr Tanqueray's unsophisticated daughter from his first marriage, was particularly absurd. 'The part was played by Molly Kerr, daughter of that excellent actor Fred Kerr, and herself full of promise, her line being the hard-as-nails young moderns of the generation that produced the Bright Young People.' The critic added, 'I can see her now, self-confident, short-skirted, and if not shingled in fact yet having about her an aura of shingling, listening with an air of meekness to her father's decree.'[281]

At Wyndham's Theatre, revivals of *Dear Brutus* and *Bulldog Drummond* were followed in 1923 by a new melodrama by 'Hubert Parsons' (co-written by Gerald Hubert Du Maurier and Viola Tree Parsons). Angela Du Maurier, recently returned from a Parisian finishing school, recalled the production of *The Dancers*: 'two unknown-to-London young actresses flashed like comets through the night of February 15th; and from that moment London could talk of nothing but the genius of English born Audrey Carten and the American Tallulah Bankhead'.[282] Midway through the run Tallulah had her very long hair shingled – to Gerald's distress, since it played a role in a key scene.

After *The Dancers* came *Not in Our Stars* and *To Have the Honour*, which had relatively short runs, and then a revival of *Peter Pan* with Angela Du Maurier in the role of Wendy. She enjoyed the experience, although she had several unfortunate mishaps on stage and ultimately concluded 'that Wendy was far too important and big a part for a beginner'.[283]

During rehearsals for *Peter Pan*, Angela had attended a performance of *The Vortex*. Her autobiography annotates her youthful diary: 'marvellous play of a sordid nature (!!) Lillian [Braithwaite] *wonderful* and so was Noel Coward. Molly (*Kerr*) awfully good too'.[284] A reviewer described Molly Kerr as 'beautiful enough to engage in super-shingled hair'. After the run of *Peter Pan* Angela was offered a part in Lonsdale's *Spring Cleaning*, but she opted instead for a family holiday in Italy, in the summer of 1925. During their trip the Du Mauriers learned of May's illness: Gerald's only surviving sibling died at the end of July.

In April 1925 Coward's *Vortex* and Lonsdale's *Spring Cleaning* were called into question in the 'spirited controversy about the frightful decadence of the English theatre' that played out on the front pages of the *Daily Express*. It began with the judgement in the Dennistoun case – known as 'the Dustbin case' – a messy divorce that led to the passage of a law prohibiting newspapers from detailed reporting of such cases. The judge opined that these cases 'give a wholly false impression of social life and family life'. The stage was accused of being a cesspool of morbid, decadent and unsavoury plays.

The novelist and playwright Arnold Bennett gave the first opinion on 6 April. He defended the three works that had been singled out for abuse: *Spring Cleaning*, *The Vortex* and an American play called *Dancing Mothers*. Bennett argued that 'real life can show plenty of pictures worse than anything in any modern play'.

The next day the headline read 'Shingled Stage Morals. Sir G. Du Maurier's Warning. Distorted Life. Vigorous Reply to Mr Arnold Bennett.' In Sir Gerald's view,

> We are faced with the fact that what was the problem play is now the sex play; that *Lord Quex*, once scurrilous, is now, in Sir Arthur Pinero's own words, 'for the nursery'. A play that a quarter of a century ago made rakes blush and courtesans bridle.
>
> We are faced with the fact that when women shingle they shingle their morals as well; that when women got the vote they cheated the world like Willett, with his Summer Time. Who three weeks hence will be able to look a sundial in the face?
>
> The public are asking for filth; the younger generation are knocking at the door of the dustbin. Are we going to give them what they ask for?

His concluding paragraph was also noteworthy: 'Let us unwind, or evolute [sic], go to the natural opposite of things, when to be simple is thrilling – much more thrilling – when Yorkshire pudding is terribly exciting and one goes into ecstasy if it rains.'

Gerald's article was followed up by 'The Money Side of Sex Plays. Mr Knoblock Defends the Managers' and then by 'Plays that Show up Decadence. Why Mr Lonsdale Believes in Them. A New Crusade'. Taking aim at Wyndham's recently closed production of *A Man with a Heart*, Lonsdale concluded with the following remark:

> … perhaps Sir Gerald was thinking of a play which was produced a short time ago in London, in which a husband was unfaithful to his wife twice during the evening. As the play failed nobody has taken the slightest notice of that extraordinary incident. So am I to understand that if a play written of life succeeds it immediately becomes a sex play, whereas if it fails it is not?

Finally, on 11 April, a banner across the top of page 7 read 'Mr Noel Coward Defends "Strong Honest Plays"'. Coward also attacked Du Maurier: 'Sir Gerald having – if he will forgive me saying so – enthusiastically showered the English stage with second-rate drama for many years (with one exception), now rises up with incredible violence and has a nice slap all round at the earnest and perspiring young dramatists.' Bennett, Knoblock, Lonsdale and Coward were essentially all in disagreement with Gerald but he soon found someone who shared his concerns and with whom he would embark on a very successful collaboration.

That person was Edgar Wallace. At a Liverpool Press Club luncheon in 1931, Gerald told the press that 'he first got into touch with Mr Wallace by telephoning him to object to an article, "The Canker in Our Midst", which he had written for a London paper'.[285]

In Daphne's biography of her father, however, she wrote that Gerald telephoned not to object to the article, but to congratulate its author: 'Edgar had written a scathing article in a newspaper condemning a certain school of thought whose members were largely in evidence at that particular time, and Gerald, also a fanatic on the subject, telephoned to congratulate him.'[286]

Ethel Violet Wallace gave a fuller version of the story in her biography of her husband. When Gerald called after reading the offending article, Wallace mentioned that he had just sent him a letter about his new play. They agreed to meet for lunch, but

> Instead of upbraiding Edgar … Gerald adopted the infinitely wiser course of praising him for his courage in writing the article in *John Bull*. For the most part, Gerald assured Edgar, Edgar was absolutely right. But there were two glaring errors in his article. He had done irreparable damage to two women who were as innocent of that kind of wrongdoing at which Edgar hinted as an unborn babe.

Edgar maintained 'that he was quite sure of his facts', whereupon 'Gerald stooped to a bit of understandable prevarication'.

First, Gerald claimed that the husband of one of the actresses in question was at the next table and added that he would sock Wallace if he persisted. Wallace was unconvinced and then 'Gerald explained that he had known both of these women since they were little girls. There was not the faintest possibility of their being guilty of the unmentionable practices to which Edgar had stated they were addicted.' Wallace was convinced and he even 'agreed to undo the damage in so far as it was within his power to do so – by writing another article in which these two ladies would be praised for the great work they had done for their husbands, in furthering their public careers'.[287] Edgar Wallace was a notoriously prolific writer and these two interesting articles have yet to be found – in *John Bull*, in the *Daily Mail* or anywhere else, despite the efforts of bibliographers and biographers.

Whatever Edgar's motivations for attacking the 'unmentionable practices' to which certain people 'were addicted' and whatever the identity of the actresses, Gerald's stake in the issue of 'shingled stage morals' is relatively obvious. Wallace's critique may have touched on women in Gerald's 'stable', as his daughters called the revolving group of young actresses in his professional and personal entourage. Gerald's recent play, *The Dancers*, had introduced Tallulah Bankhead to the London stage; Tallulah's co-star, Audrey Carten, was said to have been Gerald's mistress. Then, too, the burgeoning love lives of Gerald's daughters seemed already to be more complicated than had been the case for his sisters or his wife.

Gerald himself seems to be responsible for some of the complications. Daphne Du Maurier's biographers have reprinted the poem he wrote for her in about 1920. Its two stanzas respectively and somewhat confusingly express a night-thought about Daphne's boyhood followed by a presentation of her girlhood as a sort of daytime option. The first stanza ends:

> And sometimes in the silence of the night
> I wake and think perhaps my darling's right
> And that she should have been,
> And, if I'd had my way,
> She would have been, a boy.

The second stanza concludes: 'And sometimes in the turmoil of the day/ I pause, and think my darling may/ Be one of those who will/ For good or ill/ Remain a girl for ever and be still/ A Girl.'[288]

Gerald's poem recalls his father's portrait of Barty's daughter, Marty, in *The Martian*. At the time Barty's wife Leah is expecting their sixth daughter and eighth child, the disembodied spirit Martia who comes to him in sleep informs him that 'I am going to be your next child.' She then considers what sex she might be, and concludes, 'Whether I'm a girl or a boy, call me Marty, that my name may rhyme with yours.' Later in the novel, as Marty grows up, 'It was her ambition to become as athletic as a boy, and she was persevering in all physical exercises – and threw stones very straight and far, with a quite easy masculine sweep of the arm; I [Barty's childhood friend Robert Maurice] taught her myself.'[289]

Gerald seems to have tolerated and even encouraged a certain amount of boyishness in his daughters (particularly Daphne and Jeanne, who each had a male alter ego as a child), yet he disapproved of lesbians. Angela recalled her parents' adamance about her 'Greek' friends 'X and Z'. In between extracts from her diary for the autumn of 1924, she commented in her memoir that

> My 'crush' on a notorious figure with supposedly ancient Greek ideas was doomed from the start. She must obviously remain nameless, but in all the weeks and months I knew her I never met anyone kinder, more generous, more amusing and so utterly uncontaminating in influencing the impressionable girl I was. She had every opportunity under the sun and never said a word on any subject that could not have been shouted from the housetops. Or more to the point, at Cannon Hall.

After the première of *Peter Pan*, Angela received 'marvellous flowers' from 'the Greek' and, when Gerald died ten years later, 'six lilies [came] to me from the sister of my dear dead X'.[290] A few years later Angela's friendship with the married American actress Mary Newcomb inspired her first novel, *The Little Less*, published in 1941 but written about a decade earlier.

Biographer Jane Dunn suggests that 'X and Z' were possibly Gwen Farrar and Norah Blaney, a couple famous for their comedy revue act.[291] Yet in 1934 when Gerald died, Gwen and Norah were still very much alive. Angela's crush on 'a notorious figure with supposedly ancient Greek ideas' may refer instead to Eva Gore-Booth, a distinguished Hampstead resident of aristocratic Anglo-Irish origin, although as her biographer puts it, she 'despised her aristocratic heritage'.[292] In addition to writing poetry, along with her companion Esther Roper, Gore-Booth espoused a variety of social reforms including trade unionism, suffragism, peace movements, Irish rebellion, prison reform, radical sexual politics and the abolition of the death penalty. In 1916 Eva, Esther and three associates founded and published a journal called *Urania*, 'which called for nothing less than the elimination of gender as a category of difference'.[293] Eva was diagnosed with cancer in 1925 and died the following year. Her last volume of poetry included an elegy to Sappho, and a line of Sappho's poetry is engraved on her tombstone in the churchyard of St John at Hampstead.

Daphne was also sent to a finishing school in Paris. There she developed a close relationship – that turned into a lifelong friendship – with Fernande Yvon, one of the teachers. In the same period Daphne had a brief fascination with the actress Molly Kerr, the younger daughter of Fred Kerr and the sister of Geoffrey Kerr, actors who had worked with Gerald. Daphne may have seen 'the hard-as-nails young modern' Molly in *The Second Mrs Tanqueray*. Angela had appreciated the 'super-shingled' Molly in Noel Coward's 'sordid' *Vortex* and, indeed, Molly went on to play 'The Shingled Lady' in Galsworthy's *Escape*.

Decades later, after marriage, children and fame, Daphne also developed what she called an 'obsessional passion' for Gertrude Lawrence, 'the last of Daddy's actress loves'.[294] She originally intended Gertrude to star in a play about George Du Maurier's maternal grandmother Mary Anne Clarke.

Inter-War Thrillers

In his autobiography, finished in 1973 but first published in 2015, the actor Alan Napier gave a glowing account of his youthful attendance at a performance of *Bulldog Drummond*:

> Instantly, I forget it is a play. It is a happening of unquestionable reality in a world populated with people of extraordinary vividness and beauty caught up in an adventure of almost unbearable excitement. And at the centre, the heartbeat and radiant source of this unmatched magic, Gerald Du Maurier.
>
> There has never been anyone like him. That is what the theatregoing public said of him during his thirty fabulous years in management. That is what every actor said of him who ever had the fun of working with him, as I was later lucky enough to have. The critics grew tired of singing the praises of his unique accomplishment and tried to earn their living by saying he should put on better plays. I shall touch on

this as I try to evoke something of his unique quality when I come to that period of my life when I met and worked with him. At the time when I saw him in *Bulldog Drummond* he was at the top of his powers and, on the stage, the man above all others you would want by your side in this tightest corner of a desperate situation. Cool-headed, quick acting, of steely courage; yet with a touch so light, a humour so non-chalant and a charm so irresistible because of its gay insolence. He was not good-looking, he was not conspicuously tall or well-built. He was Gerald. I fell under his spell that night. I worshipped him until the day of his death. I shall revere his memory to the day of mine.[295]

As the curtain fell at the première Gerald stepped out to say, 'We've given you the sex play, and we've given you the "highbrow" play. Now we want to give you a change – and here's what "Sapper" and I think is perhaps best described as a "thick-ear" play!'[296]

Gerald's remark opposed 'thick-ear' and 'highbrow', and Napier ech-oed the familiar critical reproach that Du Maurier 'should put on better plays'. But when he compared his experience of being directed by Noel Coward in one of his well-constructed plays to being directed by Gerald, Napier wrote:

> With Du Maurier the work was more creative, since he chose to build with ill-prepared lumber, often worm-eaten and shoddy, designing the house as he went along. A charming rambling, yet elegant structure would miraculously arise – apparently viable in all respects, yet owing its durability, in fact, to Gerald himself. He was the kingpin. Remove him and the entire edifice would collapse. Noel's plays can always be revived with other actors; Gerald's improvisations are unthinkable without his matchless presence.[297]

In recent years, the thrillers Gerald produced and starred in have attracted 'highbrow' attention. In *British Theatre between the Wars*, Professor John Stokes writes that 'In the history of the British stage thriller the influence and example of Gerald Du Maurier is crucial, as actor, director, entrepre-neur and collaborator.' Already in *Raffles* in 1906 Gerald's 'apparently throwaway style ... responded to changing ideas of criminality, of class, of sexuality'. After the war Gerald helped re-draft the original script of *Bulldog Drummond* to stage a kind of 'Raffles as he might have become had he been to the Front, an example of the figure of the returning soldier who figures so strongly in works of the post-war years'.[298]

Following their meeting to discuss stage morality, Edgar Wallace had his first theatrical success when he collaborated with Gerald in *The Ringer* (1926). Stokes suggests that the character called 'The Ringer' 'is a witty rebel distantly related to Raffles'. Although to some extent the play 'follows conventions established in the late nineteenth century', it seemed advanced at the time 'because the action, when it takes off, is so rapid, because it makes allusions to America, because the female characters, though still subsidiary to the male, have a greater degree of independent life, and finally, vitally, because, by all accounts, the audience found plenty of opportunities for laughter along with the excitement'.[299]

As president of the Actors' Orphanage, Gerald was the guiding spirit of 'the Grand Giggle', as the charity's annual theatrical garden party was called. In June 1926 Edgar Wallace contributed a burlesque of *The Ringer* called 'The Mystery of Room 45'. As to Gerald, according to a newspaper account,

He provided one of the sartorial sensations of the afternoon as an Eton-cropped young woman of the period. The surprise of the popular actor in a female impersonation greatly arrided the audiences, as well it might, for it was as well observed a caricature as it was deliciously droll. This egregious modernity, Lady Regula Hussey, appears in 'Dilemma,' by D.B. Whyndham [sic] Lewis, who is described as 'The English Humorist'.... Lady Regula plagues an actor-manager – very funnily played by Mr A.W. Baskcomb – to produce her play 'The Smell on the Landing.' The actor-manager demurs that it is not nearly so scandalous as 'Asleep in the Sink,' by – if one heard correctly – Miss Cynthia Daily Cesspool.[300]

Meanwhile *The Ringer* ran for over a year and Edgar Wallace was generous with the profits: the Du Mauriers used the money to buy the vacation home they called Ferryside in Bodinnick near Fowey, where Daphne's vocation blossomed. Echoing a passage in *Peter Ibbetson* that actually has to do with 'the eternal fascination of the seafaring element' in the slums at the east end of London, Daphne recalled in her memoir that she associated Fowey with her grandfather's passion for Whitby: 'Fowey was a port for the shipping of china-clay, and had no fishing fleet, yet both towns had harbours; the smell of tar and rope, mingled with sea-water, must surely be the same. So here was another bond in common with the grandfather I had never known.'[301]

In 1927 Gerald produced *Interference*, an otherwise-forgotten thriller in which he notoriously 'remained on stage in the company of a dead body for ten whole minutes, not speaking a single word'. The following year, according to Stokes, 'The modern detective story arrives on the British stage, again with Du Maurier as midwife ... with an adaptation of Agatha Christie's *The Murder of Roger Ackroyd* under the title *Alibi* starring Charles Laughton as Hercule Poirot.' Admiring Laughton's performance in the play, a contemporary reviewer wrote that 'Clearly, he has been produced by Du Maurier. No one else could have taught him how to roll that cigarette so admirably, whilst he watches sideways his victim or plays with a situation as a kitten with a ball.'[302]

Gerald had acted in a few silent films, and from 1930 financial considerations led him to return to the cinema, which he detested. In the last years of his life he appeared in *Escape*, *Lord Camber's Ladies* (co-starring Gertrude Lawrence and produced by Alfred Hitchcock), *I Was a Spy*, *The Scotland Yard Mystery*, *The Rise of Catherine the Great* and *Jew Süss*.

Twelve years after Alan Napier had been so impressed by Gerald in *Bulldog Drummond*, Gerald invited him to play a role in *The Green Pack*, a new play by Edgar Wallace. Napier later relocated to Hollywood: he obtained his first role there thanks to what he calls 'the brotherhood of Du Maurier worshippers'. He went on to work with many directors, including Hitchcock.

Long afterwards, when their paths crossed at a party, Napier 'received resounding confirmation [for his appreciation of Gerald] from an exacting and knowledgeable source':

> I have known Hitch for thirty years – I played a part for him in *Marnie* – but we've somehow never been close. Yet as soon as I said 'Gerald' his blue eyes warmed and we were drawn together. He gave his blessing to [an anecdote about a joke concerning a horse] and told me others involving Gerald and practical jokes. Then, tapping my arm he said, 'There was never anyone could touch him. He could stand on the stage and do nothing! Nothing! That's the test, you know.'
>
> I did know. Wearing this ultimate power to fascinate with such nonchalance was the gift which made Gerald unique.[303]

A word on the birds

An interviewer's account of his visit to Cannon Hall in 1932 includes a description of its aviary and Gerald's passionate interest in birds:

We went into a conservatory, which has been transformed into an aviary. Sir Gerald is passionately fond of birds; like Elizabeth Schumann [the German soprano], he can imitate any birdcall to the life. He told me that birds pleased him more than flowers, and if he had to be something lower in the scale of life than a man he would certainly choose to be a bird. In the garden he had been looking for a magpie which had lately come to nest there and his glum mood changed when he at last picked it out, perched in the top branches of an elm. In the aviary a bullfinch whistled a German folk song and, delighted with his own performance, repeated it many times. A parrot gabbled violently into the mouthpiece of an imaginary telephone. In other cages were budgerigars, shamas, cardinals and canaries with plumage of crimson, scarlet, yellow and blue, lovely-looking creatures indeed.

Sometimes Sir Gerald will suddenly disappear during the day for a few hours. No one knows where he has gone; when he returns his replies are evasive. Actually he has driven the car to some lonely country lane and sat there, listening to the birds chattering and singing, quarrelling and lovemaking.[304]

Gerald Du Maurier's brief bibliography includes the foreword to H.N. Southern's *Close-Ups of Birds*, published in 1932.

Gerald expresses his love of birds, but his foreword's overall tone is slightly melancholy. He begins, 'There is only one thing which depresses me about H.N. Southern's book, and that is that I have not written it myself.' He adds that 'jaded people like myself become wistful and discontented, regretting the time we have wasted when we might have been [writing about birds]'. He imagines that the thrill of becoming intimate with birds must be 'So much more interesting than meeting men and women'. Gerald also suggests that 'the knowledge of birds should be part of one's upbringing', an interesting statement in light of the hidden significance of certain birds in his father's works, as well as, of course, his daughter's famous story, 'The Birds'.[305]

Confirming Daphne's observation that the Du Mauriers tended to die before middle age, six of Louis-Mathurin and Ellen Du Maurier's twelve grandchildren were dead by 1932. In addition to the untimely deaths of Gerald's four siblings, Eugene Du Maurier's daughter Madeleine died in Dinard, France in 1927, and Isabel Scott's son Philip died in Montana, Switzerland in 1932. By Christmas 1933, Gerald was also ill. After undergoing an operation he died on 11 April 1934 and, like his parents, was cremated.

The Scotland Yard Mystery was playing in cinemas at the time of Gerald's death. A reviewer wrote that 'Du Maurier's debonair and polished charm dominates the picture in his own inimitable way and gives an exciting 70 minutes of thrills.'[306]

CHAPTER FIVE

DAPHNE DU MAURIER: READING AND WRITING FAMILY HISTORY

Love of family is a personal thing.
You either have it or you don't.
Daphne Du Maurier,
Preface to *The Glass-Blowers*[307]

When Gerald Du Maurier died rather suddenly in April 1934, his twenty-six year old daughter Daphne had already published three quite different novels, in 1931, 1932 and 1933.

The first one, *The Loving Spirit*, took place in Cornwall and was 'an epic novel of several generations of a shipbuilding and seafaring family dominated by the life and spirit of one woman, Janet Coombe'.[308] Janet was based on Jane Slade (1813–85), the matriarch of a Cornish shipbuilding family: their vessels included a schooner called the *Jane Slade*. By Daphne's time, the *Jane Slade* had been left to rot and when it was finally broken up the figurehead was given to her. It still adorns the Du Mauriers' Cornish home Ferryside, a former boatyard.

Before *The Loving Spirit* was even published, Daphne had written *I'll Never Be Young Again*. Dealing with relationships and set in the contemporary period, it was also the first of her five novels with a male narrator. Next came *The Progress of Julius*, centring on Julius Levy, born in Paris in the second half of the nineteenth century, who eventually ends up murdering his daughter. Daphne transposed many of her ambivalent feelings toward her own father into her portrayal of Julius, yet, as with her first two books, Gerald read it and apparently saw nothing untoward.

In May 1934, on the advice of her agent, Daphne signed a contract with a new publisher, Victor Gollancz, for a biography of her father. She finished writing *Gerald: A Portrait* in the summer following her father's death, and it came out before the end of the year.

Gerald: friend, brother and father, too

Daphne's book states clearly what her biographer Margaret Forster calls Gerald's 'refrain': 'I wish I was your brother instead of your father.'[309] However, according to Forster, Daphne 'pulled back from revealing the full extent of her own very mixed feelings about him'. For this reason 'It was a shock to [Daphne] to discover that a great deal of what she had so lovingly written was regarded on publication as, on the contrary, quite unacceptable.'[310]

In this context, family members defended Daphne's biography. Her uncle, Charles Millar, concluded his own memoir, *George Du Maurier and Others*, with an appreciation of her book:

> [Gerald's] life by Daphne … has been both applauded and attacked. It is a masterful analysis of his character, showing both its strength and its weaknesses; in fact, it seems to set a standard in biography which is unlikely to be paralleled, for biographers seldom have the courage to present more than a comparatively few of the many facets which go to make a complete picture.[311]

Daphne's older sister, Angela, wrote that Gerald himself would have approved:

> Of one thing I am most certain, he would have given highest praise and his blessing to *Gerald*, which would never have been written, I am sure, if Daphne had not discussed such an idea with him at some time. It came in for a great deal of adverse criticism from old friends who thought daughters should have old-fashioned filial ideas about parents, and who obviously 'hadn't a clue', as the saying is, to Daphne's and Daddy's relationship. And its most bitter detractors I find are people (mostly men) who never knew Gerald.[312]

Daphne's portrait of her father was a critical and financial success and in January 1935 she agreed to write a second work of non-fiction for Gollancz. From then on Gollancz became her permanent publisher and at intervals in her career she dug ever deeper into the past to produce her three family history novels: *The Du Mauriers* (1937), *Mary Anne* (1954), and *The Glass-Blowers* (1963).

The fact of being Gerald's daughter obviously affected Daphne's approach to more distant family history. It gave her a unique viewpoint that was in some ways an advantage, but in others a handicap. Among the advantages was the fact that she spoke French, less fluently than her grandfather of course but still well enough to feel comfortable with the French words and phrases sprinkled throughout his works. In addition to French, Daphne also spoke a sort of private Du Maurier language that her friend Oriel Malet described:

> Many families, it seems, adopt a private language of their own. The Du Mauriers had done this, so Daphne explained, as far back as the distant glass-blowers. They, like all closed communities such as miners, fishermen, or actors, evolved a common language of their own and in Kicky's [George's] day his children had used an Anglo-French argot among themselves.[313]

Although Daphne's childhood equipped her linguistically to interpret her grandfather's works, she was handicapped by her father's apparent lack of interest in their family's French origins. In *Gerald*, Daphne wrote that her father's decision to relocate to Hampstead, his birthplace, in 1913 made him 'very conscious of his family' and 'gave him a little sense of importance and duty'. Yet in the same paragraph we learn that 'His French ancestry did not really excite him as it did [his sister] May....' Daphne commented, 'How little he had known of Papa's [George's] inner self, his little hopes and fears, his problems never mentioned, his dreams unspoken save in his books.'[314]

In the coming years, Daphne became the primary interpreter of her grandfather's life and works. Would her reading of his first novel *Peter Ibbetson* – 'all about one's outer and one's inner self', as the narrator announces in the opening paragraphs – enable her to come closer than Gerald had done to George Du Maurier's inner self?

Missing husbands in *The Du Mauriers*

Following the publication of *Gerald*, Daphne's frequent visits to her family's vacation home in Fowey began to inspire a work of fiction, *Jamaica Inn*, published in 1936. It proved to be her greatest success to date and her new publisher was anxious for another novel. However, Daphne preferred to honour her contract and write a book about her grandfather, along the lines of *Gerald*. She accumulated enough documents on family history to begin writing but just then her husband's battalion was posted to Egypt. From the outset she intensely disliked both Egypt and her role as an officer's wife. Nonetheless, Daphne continued with her second biography, which was proving more difficult to write than the first one.

Margaret Forster explains that 'In *Gerald* [Daphne] had made up nothing, essentially, but in *The Du Mauriers*, because the characters were not known to her, she sought to bring them alive by inventing situations which were sometimes hard to marry with the facts.' When Daphne finally finished she wrote to Gollancz, 'I feel it is something of a *tour de force* to have written it in an Egyptian summer.'[315]

The invented situations that fly in the face of facts are especially apparent in the first part of the book, for which Daphne possessed the least amount of documentation. Wishing to emphasise that both of George Du Maurier's parents – Louis-Mathurin Busson Du Maurier and Ellen Clarke – had grown up in London without a father and then gone to live in France with their respective mothers, she gave them the same year of birth and had their paths cross on the same boat in March 1810. In fact, Louis-Mathurin and Ellen were born in November 1797 and August 1798 respectively. Neither the Du Mauriers nor the Clarkes could have arrived on the continent before 1815, nor is it likely they took the same boat.

Without knowing anything about the circumstances of Louise Busson Du Maurier's meeting with either Ellen Clarke or the future Duchess of Palmella, whom Daphne renamed 'Eugénie St Just', she had the three meet at a girls' school in Paris. Actually, Louise's Portuguese friend Eugenia Teles da Gama was married in Lisbon in 1810 at the age of twelve and could not have been at school in Paris at the time the Busson Du Mauriers and the Clarkes arrived.[316] Then, although Daphne possessed a copy of the parish record of Louise's unfortunate marriage – since

BY
DAPHNE DU MAURIER

THE
DU MAURIERS

THEIR LIVES FROM
the departure to France in 1810 of
MARY ANNE CLARKE, mistress of the
Duke of York and great-great-grandmother of DAPHNE DU MAURIER,

TO

the marriage in 1863 of DAPHNE
DU MAURIER's grandfather 'Kicky'–
GEORGE DU MAURIER, the famous
Punch artist and author of
Trilby and the beloved
Peter Ibbetson

Dust jacket of the Gollancz edition of
The Du Mauriers

'Godfrey' Wallace also went missing – she changed its date from 1817 to 1830, presumably to bring it closer to the period that interested her (because her protagonist, George Du Maurier, was born in 1834).

Given that Daphne was recreating events that had taken place in nineteenth-century France based on a limited number of documents, these and other inventions are understandable. What is more surprising is what Michael Holroyd's introduction calls her 'romantic comedy' approach to family history: 'The story is full of terrible events – prison, penury, a missing husband here, a court case there – all arranged as romantic comedy and marvellous entertainment (it would make a fine basis for a musical). The pain of life has been eradicated.'[317]

Daphne's first four novels had explored some dark places and her portrait of her father had also been nuanced – overly nuanced, in the opinion of some of Gerald's contemporaries. Why then should she choose to narrate an earlier period of family history – especially one that was 'full of terrible events' – in a 'romantic comedy' vein?

Gerald inevitably influenced his daughter's view of 'Kicky'. His brief preface to the 1931 Everyman edition of *Trilby* contains his only published writing on his childhood. After announcing that his father's 'output was phenomenal' for a man with only one eye, and a very frail one at that, Gerald commented

> He had the strange faculty of being able to work, that is to say write and sketch, in a studio where people wandered in and out, chatted, played and sang at the piano, where dogs barked to be taken out for a walk, and where a canary would perch on his pencil whilst he was concentrating his attention on a child's profile and at the same time planning out the next chapter of the novel he was writing.

Borrowing Michael Holroyd's terms, after mentioning what for his father was a 'terrible event' – the loss of sight in one eye – Gerald the gifted actor and director begins staging 'a romantic comedy and marvellous entertainment' set at New Grove House in Hampstead. However, Gerald was not a writer and his preface does not expand upon this version of family life. The next sentences read: 'This all happened over thirty years ago, but to me it is as if it were yesterday, and I worship the memory of it. And now about *Trilby*.'[318]

In a long passage of *The Du Mauriers* (containing faint echoes of 1 Corinthians 13), Daphne discussed *Peter Ibbetson*'s 'rose-coloured' depiction of its author's early years:[319]

When Kicky wrote *Peter Ibbetson*, fifty years later, he shut his eyes and dreamt true very much as Peter did in the book. He saw the past through the eyes of his own boyhood. He ate *soupe aux choux* [cabbage soup] and *vinaigrette de bœuf bouilli* [boiled beef in vinaigrette] and drank claret at one franc a bottle; he fished for tadpoles in the Mare d'Auteuil; he pushed his little wheelbarrow through the garden gate to the mysterious tangled avenue; he was a child again, with a child's lovely inconsequence, pottering happily from day to day. Everything was joyous and *couleur de rose* [rose-coloured], as he said to himself. But he did not see, because he had not seen as a child, that this sunny, blessed existence was precarious, toppling, and insecure, even as his own first childish steps. He did not see the anxious care with which his mother saved the poor threads of her income so that Kicky and Gyggy and Isabella should eat their *soupe à la bonne femme* [leek and potato soup] and dig their patch of garden *sans souci* [without a care]. He never knew of the debts, the harshly worded letters from creditors, that awaited his father, 'le beau Pasquier', when he climbed the stairs to wish his son good night, singing softly, as though the house of Busson had no care. He remembered his mother's smile as she sat beside her harp; the puckered frown he never saw. He heard all the melodies of those days, the singing and the playing, but the strained silence, the anxious letters that Ellen penned to Louise in Portugal, and the little sums sent to her in return, while Louis-Mathurin visited reluctant firms with his portable lamp and obtained an order here and there by luck – these he did not hear, these he did not see.[320]

Daphne had her grandfather assert that when he looked back on the past in *Ibbetson*, 'Everything was joyous and *couleur de rose*.'

However, George Du Maurier's last book, *The Martian*, gave the title *Sardonyx* to his fictional alter ego Barty Josselin's first novel. Rather than suggesting joy and the colour pink, the word names a stone – appropriate for *Peter Ibbetson* since 'Pierre' as Peter is called at birth means 'stone' and since 'Ibbetson', the surname of the adoptive father he eventually assassinates, breaks up the letters in 'stone'. *Sardonyx* also suggests 'sardonic', meaning apparently but not really proceeding from gaiety, according to its etymology. The intricate, Anglo-French cipher in which George wrote his novel causes the joyous, rose-coloured façade Daphne and readers generally have perceived to crumble, as it were, exposing something very different in its place. The 'deciphered' novel conveys a disabused, sometimes cynical view of both personal and family history (insofar as 'dreaming true' allows Peter to explore 'antenatal', as well as actual, memories). *Ibbetson* ultimately reveals its author's awareness of a series of interconnected family secrets which have shaped his 'inner self'.

Daphne's second foray into family history did not sell as well as *Gerald* but her family and friends were pleased with *The Du Mauriers*. Her next two books were novels with a Cornish setting: the tremendously successful *Rebecca* (1938), followed by *Frenchman's Creek* (1941). Still, *Peter Ibbetson* and French family history were not entirely absent from Daphne's mind, since she gave the surname 'Aubéry' to the Breton aristocrat turned pirate who seduces the heroine of *Frenchman's Creek*. Daphne took the surname from the 'authoritative and commanding' lady whose name appears at the top of Peter Ibbetson's 'pedigree': George Du Maurier borrowed it from the 'real' (but unrelated) Du Mauriers who once lived at the château Du Maurier in La Fontaine-Saint-Martin.

In 1947 Daphne wrote an introduction to *The Martian* for a joint Pilot Omnibus and Peter Davies Limited edition of her grandfather's novels, and in 1951 she edited and introduced a selection of her grandfather's youthful letters, once again for her Du Maurier cousin Peter Davies. It had been ten years since Daphne wrote *The Du Mauriers*: she was a more experienced writer and no longer living in Egypt but her reading of her grandfather's life and works remained unchanged.

Daphne's introduction to *The Martian* somewhat ahistorically extends her 'rosy' interpretation of her grandfather's view of the past from *Ibbetson* to all three of his novels:

> Kicky was a happy little boy – or so he imagined, when fifty years later he wrote about his childhood – and the scents and sounds of that pre-imperial Paris, the rumble of wheels on cobbled stones, the crack of a whip, the white dust at the corner of the rue de la Pompe, the chestnut trees in flower, even the smell of burnt bread, black coffee, and tobacco on the warm spring air, comes floating up from the pages of *Peter Ibbetson*, *Trilby* and *The Martian*, proving very possibly, as Kicky himself believed, that nothing is ever forgotten that we have known and experienced and seen, but all images are printed in our sub-conscious minds like photographs.

She concludes with an extract from *Gerald*, which she characterises as follows: 'Some fourteen years ago the writer of this introduction wrote more fully about Kicky and his days, and about Kicky's son Gerald, and risking repetition once again, will conclude with a quotation from that biography, which in a sense was but an off-shoot of *The Martian*.'[321] (Rather self-deprecatingly, Daphne suggests here that her portrait of her father – arguably the best of her family biographies – is 'but an off-shoot' of her grandfather's least successful novel.)

'The Young George Du Maurier', Daphne's introduction to her grandfather's youthful letters, ends with an even longer extract from another source. It is taken from the memoirs of Sissie Frith, a daughter of the painter William Powell Frith, who had modelled for Du Maurier as a child. She too depicted a 'rosy' scene: 'It was always a delight to me to watch Du Maurier draw, while Mrs Du Maurier sat and sewed, and the children played about the floor unchecked.'[322] The relaxed atmosphere at the Du Mauriers' must have contrasted with Frith's own childhood home: her memoirs refer discreetly to the fact that her father led a double life, fathering twelve children with his wife, and seven with his mistress.

The flamboyant Mary Anne

In the aftermath of *Rebecca*'s success, an ultimately unsuccessful plagiarism suit in an American court led Daphne to cross the Atlantic in November 1947.

On board the *Queen Mary* she met Ellen Doubleday, the wife of her American publisher, with whom she would be staying during the trial (a real-life 'echo' of the shipboard meeting between young Louis-Mathurin Busson Du Maurier and Ellen Clarke that she had imagined in *The Du Mauriers*). Daphne and Ellen Doubleday went on to develop a close friendship.

Ellen became a 'peg', according to Daphne's code word, leading her to write the play *September Tide*.[323] In the play an attractive widow – inspired by Ellen – almost has an affair with her artist son-in-law – 'secretly' based on Daphne herself. Originally entitled *Mother*, and dedicated to Daphne's mother Muriel, *September Tide* was first produced in Oxford in November 1948. The main role was given to Gertrude Lawrence, whom Daphne described as 'the last of Daddy's actress loves'.[324]

Had Muriel Du Maurier reflected on *September Tide*, its dedication might have made her uncomfortable. Already in 1941 her older daughter Angela had dedicated *The Little Less* – the novel she had written about a decade earlier, inspired by her fascination with the married American actress Mary Newcomb – 'To MUMMIE *With Dearest Love*'.

According to biographer Jane Dunn,

Years later a friend of Angela's was reading the book on the lawn at Ferryside [in Cornwall] while Muriel reclined on a steamer chair in the sun. When the friend held out the book and asked if she had read it, Muriel, with a small shudder, admitted that she never read any of her daughters' novels because she could recognise all the main characters, and it made her uneasy. She then avoided further conversation about a subject she found distasteful by pulling the fabric canopy on the chair down so that it covered her face, obscuring sight of the book affectionately dedicated to her.[325]

Presumably then Lady Du Maurier also avoided reading *September Tide*, as she did with her daughters' novels generally.

In the original production Gertrude Lawrence played 'Stella Martyn' – the character Ellen Doubleday had inspired – and Daphne apparently transferred some of her own feelings, to whose intensity Ellen never fully responded, to Gertrude. Daphne also contemplated writing another play, based on George Du Maurier's maternal grandmother, the Regency courtesan Mary Anne Clarke. According to Oriel Malet, Daphne believed 'that so flamboyant a personality would be a perfect part for Gertrude'.[326] However, Gertrude died unexpectedly in 1952 and Daphne chose to write *Mary Anne* as a novel instead, dedicated to both her ancestress, who died in 1852, and to Gertrude. In Ellen Doubleday's wake, Gertrude too had become a 'peg'.

Gerald Du Maurier seems to have been more interested in his father's English forebears than in the French ones. A portrait of Mary Anne hung in Cannon Hall, the Du Mauriers' home in Hampstead, and Gerald described her to an interviewer:

That's my great-grandmother ... the notorious Mary Anne Clarke, mistress of the Duke of York. A bad lot, I am afraid, no better than she should have been. But I think she was more wronged than wronging. The Duke of York treated her very badly. After he had deserted her came the scandal of the Duke's disposal of Army commissions. When Mary Anne Clarke was cross-examined in the House of Lords [in reality, the Court of King's Bench] by the Duke of Buckingham [Baron Ellenborough] she was asked: 'Under whose protection are you now?' 'I had hoped,' she quietly replied, 'under your Lordship's.' She was as witty as she was lovely. My father was christened at the house at Rotherfield where she once lived.[327]

Daphne relates the same anecdote in both *The Du Mauriers* and *Mary Anne*, which covers her ancestress's childhood, marriage, relationship with the Duke of York, House of Commons testimony, court cases and celebrity, and essentially ends with her release from prison in 1814.

The novelist enjoyed researching *Mary Anne* but she was dissatisfied with the final result, commenting that 'The whole thing is lacking in human interest and reads like a newspaper report.' She added that 'it is definitely not romantic – I'm done with romance forever (no pigment left)'.[328] The perspective of a family member who knew Mary Anne Clarke – someone like her grandson George Du Maurier – would certainly have added 'pigment', but Daphne firmly believed her grandfather never portrayed Mary Anne.

Daphne repeatedly underestimated her grandfather's awareness of family history. She wrote in *The Du Mauriers* that in *Ibbetson* 'Kicky painted no portrait of his comic prodigal brother, and grandmamma Clarke in Boulogne was left severely alone, as was his aunt Louise and the Palmellas....'[329] In one of his youthful letters to his mother, George Du Maurier commented, 'How you and Uncle can be brother and sister, I don't know, and give it up.' Daphne annotated the sentence, 'Kicky may have been unaware of his grandmother's reputation. George and Ellen Clarke could have had different fathers.'[330]

It is true that, in his post-*Trilby* autobiographic interview, after about a page of (largely misleading) information on his French ancestry, George Du Maurier devoted exactly five words to his English side: 'My mother was an Englishwoman....'[331] Within his family history novel *Peter Ibbetson*, the narrator states that he and his female alter ego 'have not had time to attempt the unravelling of our English ancestry....'[332]

This disingenuous claim is meant to obscure the fact that, far from leaving his notorious grandmother 'severely alone' or being 'unaware of [her] reputation', George made this 'authoritative and commanding' figure the protagonist of Peter and Mary's joint 'true dream', the composer of 'the strange melody that has had so great an influence on [their] lives'.[333] However, Du Maurier's Victorian sensibilities were such that he disguised the Regency courtesan as a provincial Frenchwoman called 'Gatienne Aubéry, Dame du Brail'.

The novelist took the surname 'Aubéry' from the 'real', aristocratic Du Maurier family. Her rather enigmatic nickname *la reine de Hongrie* (the queen of Hungary) had belonged to his émigré grandfather's mother.

Hungarian variations in *The Scapegoat* and *The Glass-Blowers*

On returning from her first visit to the region of France where her ancestors had lived, in the autumn of 1955 Daphne embarked on what she
described to a friend as 'not the story of my life, but what-might-be,
if once-upon-a-time-there-had-been, and if black had been white, and
male had been female, and the world had been different etc., etc.'.[334] The
resulting novel, *The Scapegoat*, transposed some of what Daphne knew
about her French ancestors into the present.

The narrator, John, a British historian vacationing in France, is made
to trade places with a French aristocrat, Count Jean de Gué, the owner
of a glass-foundry. Daphne had learned that although her ancestor had
emigrated, his sister Sophie's husband François Duval had actively participated in the Revolution. This led her to imagine opposing political
stances between the de Gué siblings. During the German occupation of
France, Jean de Gué had been a resistant and he accuses his sister's fiancé
– Maurice Duval – of collaboration. The surname 'de Gué' echoes Le
Gué de l'Aunay, the name of the hamlet where the Du Mauriers' Duval
relatives had lived.

The footnote at the bottom of the first page of Sophie's letter on the
Busson family captured the attention of both George and Daphne Du
Maurier. It described her mother, the former Madeleine Labbé, in two
short sentences: 'She was a superb woman, hardy, of a masculine character. She was nicknamed *la reine de Hongrie* [the queen of Hungary].'
George used the nickname for the ancestress of 'very masculine character' at the top of Peter Ibbetson's pedigree. In Daphne's transposition of
family history in *The Scapegoat*, the Hungarian queen with the masculine character is not Count Jean de Gué's mother – the widowed countess
is portrayed as a morphine addict – but rather his mistress, a Hungarian called Béla, 'the name of successive Hungarian kings', and also a
near-anagram of the surname 'Labbé'.

Daphne returned to Sarthe in the summer of 1957 during the production of Robert Hamer's film based on her novel. She had had a difficult
year because her husband had what seems to have been a nervous col-
lapse, and her mother died after a long illness. She would not actually
begin work on *The Glass-Blowers* until 1962, after writing and publishing a short story collection called *The Breaking Point* (1959) – the
title and the stories within reflected her state of mind – and *The Infernal
World of Branwell Brontë* (1960), a biography.

Where *The Scapegoat*, set in the present, incorporates scattered references to Busson family history, *The Glass-Blowers* is the product of

Daphne and Alec Guinness on location for *The Scapegoat*. A Hollywood
studio wanted Cary Grant for the lead role but Daphne insisted on
Alec Guinness: he reminded her of Gerald

sustained research into the people and events described in Sophie's letter. Part One, which tells the Bussons' story up to the Revolution, is
called *La Reyne d'Hongrie*.[335] The narrator, Sophie, gives the following
explanation of her mother's nickname: her father drew the outline of her
mother's figure as the inspiration for the shape of an apothecary's bottle.
Merchants 'filled the flask with eau-de-toilette, calling it the perfume of
la Reyne d'Hongrie after Elizabeth of Hungary, who had remained beautiful until she was past seventy'. (In *Ibbetson*, George Du Maurier had a
very different Hungarian queen in mind.)

In the first years of the Bussons' marriage they lived in the Le Maurier farmhouse on the estate of Chérigny, and their first two children,
Mathurin-Robert and Pierre, were born there. Daphne imagines that
the châtelaine – she calls her the marquise de Cherbon – 'made a great
favourite' of Mme Busson. Sophie explains the consequences:

> It has always seemed to me significant that [Mathurin-]Robert's first
> memories, whenever he spoke of them, should not be of the farmhouse
> Le Maurier, or of the lowing of cattle, the scratching of hens and other

homely sounds, or even of the roar of the furnace chimney and the bustle of the glass-house; but always of an immense salon, so he described it, filled with mirrors and satin-covered chairs, with a harpsichord standing in one corner, and a fine lady, not my mother, picking him up in her arms and kissing him, then feeding him with little sugared cakes.[336]

Sophie adds that in allowing her son 'to be fed and fondled by the marquise', Mme Busson inadvertently sowed a 'small seed of longing' into Mathurin-Robert's being that 'certainly was partly responsible for [his father's] death'. The seed of longing eventually develops into *folie des grandeurs*. (The marquise dies shortly after this scene, so no seed of *folie* is sown in the Bussons' second son Pierre.)

Several years later the Bussons have moved on to the château de La Pierre: M. Busson and his associates direct the glass-factory and their lease includes the use of the château, exacerbating his eldest son's *folie*. When Mathurin-Robert finishes his apprenticeship at the foundry, a small ceremony takes place: he walks proudly 'as though he were to be made a marquis'. He bows to the assembly, looks up at his mother, and according to Sophie,

> It seemed to me that she bowed in return, half to my brother, half to herself, and as she towered above me, magnificent in her brocade gown, the whole aspect strangely changed with the powder in her hair, I felt, child as I was, that she was more than my mother; she was some sort of deity, more powerful than the gentle statue of the Blessed Virgin standing in the church ... the equal of God himself.

When King Louis XV visits the foundry later that year, Sophie comments, 'I did not understand why she should put on a brocade gown for my brother, and wear nothing but her Sunday dress for the King.'[337]

These episodes of incipient *folie des grandeurs* were inspired partly by Sophie's footnote on her mother and partly by George Du Maurier's portrayal of *la reine de Hongrie* in *Peter Ibbetson*. They set the stage for Daphne's dramatisation of Sophie Duval's anecdotes concerning her oldest brother. As we saw in Chapter One, he became an officer in a regiment of arquebusiers without telling his father, who accidentally saw him in uniform in Paris when he was supposed to be at work in the provinces; he financed a masked ball for the ladies of Chartres by selling crates of glassware destined for Parisian merchants; he went through his first wife's dowry in less than a year by establishing a new glass-factory at the château de Rougemont; he took young Sophie to the première of Beaumarchais' *Marriage of Figaro* and managed to get them invited to watch the play from the box of duke of Chartres, his fellow Freemason. Mathurin-Robert's *folie des grandeurs* reached its peak in 1789, when he immigrated to London with his second wife and began adding 'Du Maurier' to his original surname.

Sophie had addressed her letter to her 'English' nephew Louis-Mathurin. Sometime before his death (in 1856), believing some of the details reflected badly on the family, Louis-Mathurin scored through them. Researching French family history over a century after this bowdlerisation had occurred, Daphne wanted to ensure that Sophie's letter reached its intended audience – the émigré's descendants, and beyond them, her own readers generally – in particular by restoring and elaborating on the scored-through passages, which could be read with a magnifying glass.

When George Du Maurier created the pedigree of his fictional heroes Peter and Mary by combining a few authentic family names with a host of aristocratic names and titles, he appeared to have further enhanced the 'adjustments' to family history that had already been made: his grandfather's addition of a suffix, his father's bowdlerisation of Sophie's letter. In organising the family papers she inherited from her grandfather, Daphne carefully 'undid' any possible ambiguity about the facts. She conscientiously separated authentic documents pertaining to 'her' Bussons from those that concerned unrelated aristocratic families.

Daphne placed Sophie Duval's letter and copies of various acts of baptism, marriage and death in 'The Busson Research File No 1'. The parchment one of Daphne's ancestors had acquired tracing the descent of the aristocratic Bussons of Brittany, as well as documents concerning the château belonging to the 'real' (aristocratic) Du Mauriers, went into another file headed 'Busson Research No 2 (Less Important)'. So that no mistake could be made, Daphne annotated the family tree of the aristocratic Bussons 'not our Bussons'. A typescript of a handwritten note by her grandfather is annotated 'wrong Château Maurier!', as is a postcard of the château with the additional information 'Believed by George Du Maurier to have been his ancestral home. Quite a different family.'

In sorting through the papers she inherited to determine which ones were more or less important, Daphne wished to establish that any notion of the Bussons' aristocratic origins was factually inaccurate and that her grandfather never knew this. In so doing, she completely neglected the use he had made of these 'real' and 'fake' family papers: the factually false version of family history *Peter Ibbetson* presents is in fact an

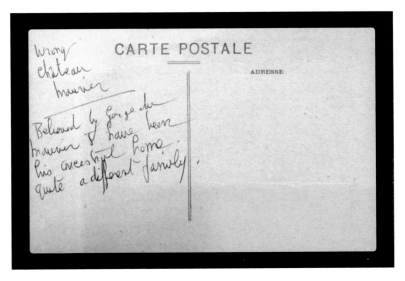

Daphne's annotation on the back of a postcard of the château du Maurier

interpretation of the aristocratic fantasy. The pedigree allows the heroes Peter and Mary to discover their 'common ancestress': the 'very masculine' *reine de Hongrie*. In retrospect, it seems hardly credible that Daphne never made any connection between Peter and Mary's 'true dream', and the bisexual fantasy that affected her personally and that was the motor of many of her works, such as *September Tide*.

Associating her childhood alter ego 'Eric Avon' with the masculine narrators of several of her novels, Daphne puzzled over this aspect of herself in her memoir:

> [W]hy did I pick on Eric Avon as an alter ego and not an imaginary Peggy Avon ...? Whatever the reason, he remained in my unconscious, to emerge in later years – though in quite a different guise – as the narrator of the five novels I was to write, at long intervals, in the first person singular, masculine gender, *I'll Never be Young Again*, *My Cousin Rachel*, *The Scapegoat*, *The Flight of the Falcon*, *The House on the Strand*.... [E]ach of my five narrators depended, for reassurance, on a male friend older than himself.[338]

In *The Scapegoat*, the narrator John states 'why [Count Jean de Gué's Hungarian mistress] should bear a man's name was more than I could guess'.[339]

In the swearing-in scene of *The Glass-Blowers*, the narrator Sophie associates her brother's temptation to see himself as a marquis with the resemblance of their mother – *la Reyne d'Hongrie* – to 'some sort of deity ... the equal of God himself'. Yet within the novel the nickname is said only to refer to Mme Busson's beauty.

An undeciphered novel

When George Du Maurier gave the nickname *la reine de Hongrie* to Peter and Mary's 'very masculine' ancestress, he inserted it into a complex web of aristocratic names and titles that, as discussed in the next chapter, clearly plays upon a French connotation of the phrase: 'the queen of eunuchs'. Instead of revealing his émigré grandfather's aristocratic imposture, as Daphne did in *The Glass-Blowers*, George's novel explored the fantasy of sexual indifferentiation that, in his view, underlies *folie des grandeurs*.

Daphne Du Maurier's narrator, Sophie, suggests her brother's *folie des grandeurs* was partly responsible for their father's death. In *Ibbetson*, George had gone much further: his heroes only discover their pedigree – and their kinship – once Peter is sentenced to death for parricide. Where Daphne acknowledged that the male alter ego she invented as a child 'remained in my unconscious' and emerged in several of her works, her grandfather's hero, the inmate of a Criminal Lunatic Asylum, declares: 'My hope, my certainty to be one with Mary some day – that is my haven, my heaven – a consummation of completeness beyond which there is nothing to wish for or imagine.'[340]

How curious then that where family history was concerned, Daphne could conclude that 'my poor *Trilby* grandfather [was] on the wrong track'.[341] Having researched and written *The Du Mauriers*, *Mary Anne* and *The Glass-Blowers*, Daphne Du Maurier possessed both the curiosity and the grasp of family history that ought to have enabled her to decipher *Peter Ibbetson*. Yet despite her self-proclaimed terrible desire to get at the *truth*, where George Du Maurier's 'inner self' was concerned, she never did. Instead, it was almost as if Daphne unintentionally performed a gesture comparable to Louis-Mathurin's censorship of some of the most interesting details of his aunt Sophie's letter. Daphne's lifelong misreading of *Ibbetson* in effect bowdlerised her Victorian grandfather's profoundly personal and decidedly 'blue' excursion into the past. The entire situation was rather 'queer', as Daphne had commented to her friend Oriel.

CHAPTER SIX

A VERY
TRANSPARENT CIPHER

[George] Du Maurier ... does not take the subject of descent
too seriously. 'One is never quite sure,' he says, with the
shadow of a smile, 'about one's descent. So many accidents
occur. I made use of many of the names which occur in the
papers concerning my family history, in Peter Ibbetson.'
Robert H. Sherard, 'The Author of *Trilby*. An Autobiographic
Interview with Mr George Du Maurier'

Du Maurier gave his most detailed account of his French ancestry in his
1895 interview with Sherard. Although his statements are largely misleading, they must be read very closely:

My full name is George Louis Palmella Busson Du Maurier, but we
were of very small nobility. My name Palmella was given to me in
remembrance of the great friendship between my father's sister and the
duchesse de Palmella, who was the wife of the Portuguese ambassador
to France. Our real family name is Busson; the 'Du Maurier' comes
from the château le Maurier, built some time in the fifteenth century,
and still standing in Anjou or Maine, but a brewery today. It belonged
to our cousins the Aubérys, and in the seventeenth century it was the
Aubérys who wore the title of Du Maurier; and an Aubéry Du Maurier
who distinguished himself in that century was Louis [in reality, Benja-
min] of that name, who was French ambassador to Holland, and was
well liked of the great king. The Aubérys and the Bussons married and
intermarried, and I cannot quite say without referring to family papers
– at present at my bank – when the Bussons assumed the territorial
name of Du Maurier; but my grandfather's name was Robert Mathurin
Busson Du Maurier, and his name is always followed, in the papers

which refer to him, by the title *gentilhomme verrier* – gentleman glass-blower. For until the Revolution glass-blowing was a monopoly of the *gentilshommes*; that is to say, no commoner might engage in this industry, at that time considered an art. You know the old French saying:

'*Pour souffler un verre* [To blow a glass]

Il faut être gentilhomme.' [One must be a gentleman.]

A year or two ago ... I was over in Paris with Burnand and Furniss, and we went into Notre Dame, and as we were examining some of the gravestones with which one of the aisles is in places laid, I came upon a Busson who had been buried there, and on the stone was carved our coat-of-arms, but it was almost all effaced, and there only remained, clearly distinguishable, the black lion, my black lion.

In fact, as discussed in Chapter Two, the Du Mauriers' 'very small' claim to nobility was the somewhat dubious papal title George's father had acquired in 1821. It had nothing to do with the French aristocracy of the *ancien régime*.

The novelist's statement mixes a few facts with intentional misinformation. Among the facts are that his aunt was employed by the duchesse de Palmella, and the château le Maurier does still exist. It once belonged to the Aubéry Du Maurier family and Benjamin Aubéry Du Maurier was Louis XIII's ambassador to Holland. However, the castle has never been a brewery and, more importantly, there is no connection between the Aubérys and the Busson ancestors of the English Du Mauriers, whose 'territorial name' actually refers to a very modest farmhouse and which they only assumed after the French revolution and in London.

As to the 'old French saying' the novelist cites, it comes from 'Le Verre' ('The Glass'), an 'old French' drinking song by the chansonnier Armand Gouffé (1775–1845). Punning on the fact that *souffler* (to blow) also had the slang meaning of 'to drink in one go', one verse of the song 'proves' the nobility of the glass by the fact that to blow a glass – or, according to the pun, to drink a glass in one go – one had to be a gentleman.

Finally, it is true that the military hero Jean-Baptiste Budes de Guébriant was related to the aristocratic Busson family from Brittany, had a black lion on his coat of arms, and is buried in Notre Dame. But the Du Mauriers' Busson ancestors were not from Brittany, were not aristocrats, had no coat of arms and had no connection to this family.

The sentences that immediately follow, in which Du Maurier refers his interviewer to his novel, are extracted above as epigraph. If we now turn to the aristocratic pedigree the author's fictional alter egos Peter and

LA BELLE VERRIÈRE.

From left to right: Jeanne de Boismorinel (who relives in Peter); her father the Comte de Boismorinel; her mother Anne Budes, Dame de Verny le Moustier; and her grandmother Gatienne Aubéry, Dame du Brail

Mary discover in the climax of their joint 'true dream', it has very few elements in common with the letter of the author's family history.

Where George Du Maurier was the great-grandson of the glass-blower Mathurin Busson and his wife Madeleine Labbé, nicknamed *la reine de Hongrie*, Peter and Mary are 'the great-great-grandchildren and only possible living descendants' of a short-lived gentleman glass-blower called 'Mathurin Budes, Seigneur de Verny le Moustier' and his wife 'Gatienne Aubéry, Dame du Brail', called *la belle Verrière* and also nicknamed *la reine de Hongrie*.

Besides replacing his ancestors' surnames Busson and Labbé with the aristocratic surnames Budes and Aubéry, and adding 'territorial names', the novelist inserted an additional generation between his fictional alter egos and their forefather the glass-blower. He also, in effect, eliminated his great-grandfather Mathurin and his grandfather Mathurin-Robert, since Peter and Mary's ancestor dies during his wife's pregnancy and she then gives birth to the twin daughters from whom they descend (that is, she does not have a son).[342]

It may seem that the novelist was quite confused about his French origins and mingled a few authentic family names with aristocratic names to create a pedigree that had no relevance to his own family. In fact, as Du Maurier obliquely hinted in his interview, he cleverly combined authentic and inauthentic names in order to encipher a penetrating analysis of family history.

La Belle Verrière, 'the fair glassmaker'?

In addition to the family nickname *la reine de Hongrie*, George also bestowed the epithet *la belle Verrière* on Peter and Mary's ancestress Gatienne. Within the novel he intentionally mistranslates the phrase as 'the fair glassmaker'. In reality the word *verrière* designates a large glass window rather than a female glassmaker.

Peter describes the light in his 'true dream' as 'more beautiful than that which streams through old church windows of stained glass': *Notre Dame de la Belle Verrière* is the name of a renowned stained glass window in Chartres cathedral.[343] Currently known in English as the Blue Virgin window, it represents the Virgin Mary crowned, seated on the throne of wisdom and holding her infant son, with her feet on a footstool and surrounded by angels carrying candles and swinging thuribles, beneath a descending dove representing the Holy Spirit.[344]

In pre-revolutionary France the possession of a dovecote was an aristocratic privilege and, as mentioned in Chapter One, Knights of the Holy Spirit wore a badge in the form of a Maltese cross with fleur-de-lys between the arms of the cross and a descending dove in the centre. Additionally, on the estate of Chérigny where the Du Mauriers' forefather was born, the glass-foundry looked out on the dovecote. Whether or not George Du Maurier ever visited Chérigny or was familiar with a description of the estate, he seems somehow to have associated an aristocratic origin (in which one's father is a lord) with an immaculate conception (one's father is the Lord).

I will return to the key term *la belle Verrière* below, to suggest its ciphered English meaning within *Ibbetson*.

'Our cousins the Aubérys'

Where the farmhouse le Maurier on the estate of Chérigny is located in the village of Saint-Martin-de-Chenu, the otherwise unconnected

*Notre Dame de
la Belle Verrière,*
a stained glass
window in Chartres
cathedral

château Du Maurier, 30 km away, is in La Fontaine-Saint-Martin (Saint Martin's Fountain). The name of the village derives from a local legend.

Martin, a Hungarian soldier-saint who later became Bishop of Tours, is said to have struck a rock with his staff, discovering a miraculous source near the village with which he baptised thousands of heathens. A weeping willow tree overhangs St Martin's fountain, behind the church. The locally famous stained glass artist François Fialeix (1818–86) commemorated the legend in a stained glass window in the church.

George Du Maurier had learned from his correspondence with the departmental archivist in Sarthe that the château du Maurier once belonged to the Aubéry Du Maurier family. At some point he acquired a biography of Benjamin Aubéry Du Maurier, the French ambassador to Holland in the reign of Louis XIII (and eventually, his granddaughter Daphne inherited the book).[345]

The biography opens with an extract from the ambassador's memoirs in which he relates an anecdote told to him by his Protestant mother Madeleine, Jean Aubéry's second wife:

> I often heard my mother say that when she was expecting me, several times she had great difficulty in escaping from being drowned, like several others of all ages and both sexes, by a lord of the country, a great persecutor of the religion she professed, who had them thrown into a river near his house, saying that he made them drink in his big glass.

It is a matter of historical record that Jean V de Champagne persecuted Protestants by throwing them into his fishpond. Pescheseul, Jean de Champagne's château, is located on the banks of the Sarthe River: its name is said to derive from its fishing rights (the verb *pêcher* means 'to fish'). The 'gentle craft' of angling was a recurring subject of humour in *Punch*, and in George Du Maurier's mind the anecdote appears to have triggered a series of associations.

The Aubéry Du Mauriers were nobles of the robe – a term mentioned in passing in *Ibbetson*. The surname 'Aubéry' suggests the homophones *aubère* and *haubert*. *Haubert* means 'hauberk' or 'coat of mail' and a *fief de haubert* is a knight's fee, defined as 'the amount of land the holding of which imposed the obligation of knight service'. The word apparently also suggested the archaic erotic metaphor *fourbir le haubert d'une femme*, 'to polish a woman's coat of mail'. When Peter was a child his family papers were kept 'in a horse-hair trunk'. A horse's coat is known as a *robe* in French and *aubère* designates a colour of horse's coat also known as *fleur de pêcher* or 'peachblow', but which could be misinterpreted as 'flower of fishing'. *Fleur de pêcher* in the sense of peachblow or fishing also suggests *fleur de péché*, 'flower of sin'.

'Gatienne Aubéry, Dame Du Brail' – the name Du Maurier invented for Peter and Mary's 'common ancestress' – reflects these associations. Within the novel 'le Brail' names a stream. Meanwhile *Gatienne* is the title of a French novel published in 1882 by Du Maurier's contemporary Georges de Peyrebrune (1841–1917). The eponymous heroine is a young woman from the working classes who is victimised by an unscrupulous nobleman; in the wake of her seduction she composes a sad tune. Ominously, her composition is played at her wedding to another man. When Gatienne's persecutor returns to torment her after her marriage, she drowns him in the Seine River and later drowns herself there. Georges de Peyrebrune was the *nom de plume* of a popular woman writer who was herself the natural daughter of a wealthy Englishman and his French mistress.

By coincidence both Benjamin Aubéry's mother and Mathurin-Robert's mother, who lived two centuries later, were called 'Madeleine'. Aubéry related his pregnant mother's story in his memoir as an example of the persecution of Protestants, without any suggestion that he questioned his paternity. Outside of any religious context, George Du Maurier apparently interpreted the anecdote as emblematic of the *droit du seigneur*, and understood it as a possible explanation of the conscious or unconscious motives for his grandfather's adoption of the suffix 'Du Maurier'.

The *droit du seigneur* was already obliquely present in the very first narrative of Busson family history, written by Sophie Duval. It was thematised in Beaumarchais's play *The Marriage of Figaro*, whose premiere Mathurin-Robert attended with his young sister Sophie, in the box of the future Duke of Orleans, as mentioned in Chapter One.

The aristocratic surname Budes

Where Mathurin-Robert's father was named Mathurin Busson, in *Peter Ibbetson* the short-lived gentleman glass-blower from whom the heroes descend is called 'Mathurin Budes'.

George Du Maurier took the surname from the historical figure Jean-Baptiste Budes de Guébriant, the Marshal of France whose tomb he had come across in Notre Dame. Although Budes was from Brittany, he attended a Jesuit college in La Flèche, within 15 km of La Fontaine-Saint-Martin; however there is no known connection between the Budes family and the Aubérys. The Marshal's wife, known as the Maréchale de Guébriant, had the reputation of an ambitious woman, who had her first marriage dissolved in order to marry him.

After Budes's death in battle, King Louis XIV named the Maréchale as his ambassadress extraordinary to Poland. The Maréchale's precise mission consisted in accompanying the French princess Louise-Marie de Gonzague, whom the Polish king had married by proxy, to Poland, and then persuading the king to consummate his union with the princess, although she was said to have been the mistress of the Marquis of Cinq-Mars.

A widely circulated manual of historical costumes with which Du Maurier was probably familiar portrays the Maréchale in her elegant widow's weeds, her niece Anne Budes and the suite of 'red-heeled gentlemen' who accompanied them on their mission to Poland.[346] The novelist

The Maréchale de Guébriant, her niece Anne Budes, and their suite of red-heeled gentlemen (from Auguste Racinet's manual of historical costumes)

'borrowed' the name 'Anne Budes' for the mother of the 'small *female child*' who relives in Peter: in Peter's recurring 'childish dream' she takes her child by the hand to feed pigeons in their *pigeonnier* (in erotic slang, 'any resort devoted to venery'). Her husband, the child's father, is described as a 'red-heeled gentleman'.

Rather than giving the character Mathurin Budes any of the Breton estates of the Budes de Guébriant family, Du Maurier makes him a gentleman glass-blower and locates his glass factory at Verny le Moustier – once a magnificent estate in Maine that belonged to another Marshal of France.

Verny le Moustier, a most interesting old manor

In the course of his research in Sarthe, Du Maurier came across one 'Jehan Busson', Lord of Verny le Moustier and Monhoudéard in the fifteenth century. There is no reason to believe that this figure had any relation to the novelist's ancestors, nor was glass ever made at Verny; nonetheless he chose to locate the gentleman glass-blower's factory there.

Within twenty-four hours of discovering her kinship with Peter, Mary leaves for France to visit the houses where his ancestors had lived. He learns that 'Verny le Moustier was not the least interesting of these old manors'; 'It had been built three hundred years ago, on the site of a still older monastery (whence its name)....'.[347] *Moustier* is indeed an old word for monastery or church; it survives in place names and in a small number of expressions.

The novelist was apparently aware of a nineteenth-century controversy that involved the catchphrase *mener la mariée au moustier* (to lead the bride to the monastery). An apocryphal story associated the phrase with monks at the Abbey of Saint-Théodard in Montauriol in southern France, who supposedly subjected their serfs to the *droit du seigneur*. The serfs' rebellion against this practice was (erroneously) said to have led to the founding of the Protestant stronghold of Montauban.[348]

In the era of King Louis XIV, the Lord of Verny was René III de Froulay. At the revocation of the Edict of Nantes he led the dragoons in expeditions against Protestants in the principality of Orange. He went on to receive the titles Knight of the Holy Spirit, Marshal of France and General of the Galleys of France. Marshal of France is a military distinction and the Marshal's emblem is his baton, adorned with fleur-de-lys, symbolising the French monarchy (and in other contexts, the Virgin Mary and the city of Florence).[349] At the same time *maréchalerie* is the French term for the profession of horse-breaking or farriery.

The estate of Verny was sold and largely destroyed at the Revolution but, along with the dovecote, the Marshal's painting collection survives, in particular a series of thirty portraits of royal mistresses on horseback: what a Victorian might call 'pretty horse-breakers'.[350]

Although the trade of horse-breaking or farriery is unrelated to glass-blowing, the words 'farriery' and *verrerie* are phonetically close. When considered in the light of the Marshal's paintings, the epithet Du Maurier invented for Peter and Mary's ancestress – *la belle Verrière de Verny le Moustier* – suggests 'the pretty horse-breaker of Verny le Moustier'. The phrase gives an unexpected and unorthodox meaning to the Blue Virgin window at Chartres.

In late nineteenth-century slang a 'soiled dove' was a high-flying harlot. In the vocabulary of horsemanship, *un coup d'encensoir* (a swing of the thurible) describes the up-and-down movement of a horse's head, while *couronné* (crowned) means 'broken-kneed': a slang expression for a girl or woman who has been seduced. When linked to the military career of Verny's châtelain, the throne of wisdom suggests a ducking stool and a dragonnade or forced conversion.[351]

Mary, Queen of Hungary

In addition to the epithet *la belle Verrière*, the novelist gives Gatienne the nickname *la reine de Hongrie* (the Queen of Hungary). As previously

One in a series of thirty portraits of royal mistresses on horseback, from the collection of René III de Froulay, Marshal of France

discussed, this was the actual nickname of the novelist's great-grand-mother Madeleine Busson, who was also described by her daughter Sophie as 'a superb woman, hardy, of a masculine character'. Du Maurier's novel expands upon this brief description: in their 'true dream' Peter and Mary learn that their ancestress 'was said to have been the tallest and handsomest woman in Anjou, of an imperious will and very masculine character'.[352]

It is not known which Hungarian queen Mme Busson's nickname referred to, but to her great-grandson it apparently suggested Queen Mary of Hungary, named Governor-General of the Netherlands after her husband died in battle. In *The Lives of Gallant Ladies* the chronicler Brantôme characterised Mary of Hungary as 'mannish' and also described the Triumphs of Binche, a ten-day festival of chivalry she organised at Mariemont, her palace of pleasure. The Triumphs culminated in a fake siege in which several of the queen's ladies in waiting were 'abducted' by 'wild men' on horseback. Mary of Hungary is also said to have composed the Protestant hymn 'Let me not oppose misfortune'.

The French *hongre* means 'gelding', the practise of castrating horses having supposedly originated in Hungary. Du Maurier emphasises the 'Hungarian' dimension of Peter and Mary's pedigree by making the twin from whom Mary descends marry an officer in the Hungarian army.

The ciphered trade of farriery gives new meaning to other expressions as well. As noted above, the twin from whom Peter descends marries a 'red-heeled gentleman'. 'Red heels' denote a French aristocrat but in this context the phrase suggests a horse with wounded heels. The French word *encloué* describes a horse's foot that has been wounded by a nail: it is also a slang term for a passive homosexual.

Peter and Mary are related through their musical fathers, 'those two born nightingales of our race'.[353] In describing Peter's father's musical serenades, Du Maurier pastiches the opening verses of Wordsworth's 'O Nightingale!' and Alexander Pope's 'Universal Prayer':

> O Nightingale! whether thou singest thyself, or, better still, if thy voice be not in thy throat, but in thy fiery heart and subtle brain, and thou makest songs for the singing of many others, blessed be thy name! The very sound of it is sweet in every clime and tongue: Nightingale, Rossignol, Usignuolo, Bulbul! Even Nachtigall does not sound amiss in the mouth of a fair English girl who has had a Hanoverian for a governess![354]

A slang meaning of *rossignol* is 'pass-key', and in French farriery, a *rossignol* is a hole pierced at the base of the horse's tail, in the erroneous belief that it cured them of broken wind.

The Song of the Sad Commensal

When Peter Ibbetson was a child, his parents' music inspired a recurring dream in which he heard his favourite song. However, on awaking he could not recall the tune, only the words *triste – comment – sale* (sad – what – dirty).

After killing his adoptive father and being sentenced to death, Peter is able to meet his childhood friend Mary – now the Duchess of Towers – in his dreams each night. One night she lulls him awake, as she puts it, with 'a song that was as familiar to [him] as "God Save the Queen"'. Mary informs Peter that the true title of their joint favourite tune is *Le Chant du Triste Commensal* (The Song of the Sad Commensal). *Triste – comment – sale* and *Triste Commensal* are phonetically close to a third phrase that does not appear in the novel: *triste comme un saule* (sad like a willow).

Du Maurier borrowed the motif of acoustic distortion from the second chapter of A. de Pontmartin's novel *Entre chien et loup* (1866). In the following chapter the aristocratic hero, in a sort of delirium on returning to Paris after a long absence, confuses a contemporary music-hall rendition of *Nothing is sacred to a sapper* with Maria Malibran's performance of the Willow Song, which he had heard in his youth.[355]

Ibbetson contains several broad hints that *Le Chant du Triste Commensal* – from which Peter and Mary evolve the secret of their kinship – and the Willow Song are one and the same. 'Desdemona's song from [Rossini's] *Otello*' is performed immediately after Peter and Mary's first adult meeting, at a musical soirée. When Mary joins Peter in a 'true dream', she reminds him his mother used to play the aria *Assisa al Pie d'un' Salice* (Seated at the foot of a willow) on the harp. *Magna sed Apta* – the name Peter and Mary give to the palace of art where they meet nightly in their dream – contains an opera box in which Peter can hear the Willow Song again and again. In Rossini's opera, Desdemona sings 'Seated at the foot of a willow,/ Immersed in grief,/ Complained the hapless Isaura,/ A prey to relentless love.'

When Mary visits France in the flesh, Peter learns from her that the winding stream of his childish dreams 'was called "Le Brail", and had given its name to [his] great-great-grandmother's property'. It has become little more than a ditch, 'with a fringe of gnarled and twisted willows and alders'.

Ibbetson's cipher posits the Willow Song as a kind of national anthem of 'horse-breaking'. Du Maurier was almost certainly familiar with Théophile Gautier's famous poem 'Contralto' (1849), which equates a number of Rossini arias including the Willow Song with the Louvre statue of the sleeping hermaphrodite.

Why should 'a provincial French woman who lived a hundred years [before Peter and Mary]' be said to have composed the Willow Song? What does Peter and Mary's joint 'favourite tune' have to do with the trade of glassmaking, or with the Du Mauriers in particular?

The Du Mauriers' connection 'with the past history of England'

In creating Peter Ibbetson's pedigree, Du Maurier took a handful of historically accurate references to the parents of his émigré grandfather and mingled them with elements borrowed from unrelated aristocratic families. In so doing he covertly referenced not only another 'trade' but also another branch of his family tree.

Peter states explicitly that Mary and he 'have not had time to attempt

Caricature of Mary Anne Clarke by Charles Williams

the unravelling of our English ancestry as well – the Crays and the Des-
monds, the Ibbetsons and the Biddulphs, etc. – which connect us with
the past history of England'.[356] In fact, the ciphered trade of farriery or
horse-breaking points directly to the Du Mauriers' connection to 'the past
history of England', via George Du Maurier's maternal grandmother, the

'Hanoverian' 'horse-breaker' Mary Anne Clarke.

As discussed in Chapter Two, it was she who left her husband, passed for a widow and then 'made lots of money for her two daughters' not by managing a glass factory but by blackmailing her former lover Frederick, Duke of York, Bishop of Osnabrück, and Commander-in-Chief of the Horse Guards during the Napoleonic wars. In addition to the caricatures discussed in Chapter Two, 'The Female Agent' depicts Mrs Clarke wearing the Duke's cocked hat and bearing his sword, beneath the British flag adorned with the white horse of Hanover. She was also frequently pictured in the blue gown and the veil she wore for her testimony at the House of Commons. Her costume bears a passing resemblance to Mary's in the Blue Virgin window at Chartres.

If *la belle Verrière* is read as Mary Anne Clarke in disguise, then her two daughters would represent Ellen Du Maurier and Mary Anne Bowles. The red-heeled gentleman M. de Boismorinel and Ulric Seraskier, an officer in the Hungarian army, become the fictional counterparts of her daughters' respective husbands, Louis-Mathurin Busson Du Maurier and Captain Bowles.

In composing the Pasquier pedigree, the novelist grafted three generations of his *maternal* family tree – Mary Anne Clarke, her daughter Ellen and himself as a small *girl* – above three generations of his paternal family tree – namely the engimatic Marie-Françoise Bruaire, her son Louis-Mathurin and himself. This allows both George and his parents to appear twice: he is his mother's *daughter* (and bizarrely, his paternal grandfather's *wife*), as well as his father's son.

Inspired by Keats's 'magic casements, opening on the foam/ Of perilous seas', *Magna sed Apta* where Peter and Mary meet in their dream contains a 'magic window' by a divan, where they 'can sit and gaze on whatever [they] like'. It allows them to see their common ancestress's glass factory in both the past and the present; they are eventually even able to enter their dream and mix with her.

In 'Our great-great-grandmother' Du Maurier illustrated the scene in which his male and female alter egos appear in the company of 'Gatienne, with her lovely twin-daughters Jeanne and Anne, and her gardeners round her, all training young peach and apricot trees against what still remained of the ancient buttresses and walls of the Abbaye de Verny le Moustier'.[357]

The illustration must be deciphered like a rebus. Gatienne's gardeners hold watering cans: *arroser* (to water) has a sexual meaning in French erotic slang. Wearing a widow's veil like the Maréchale in the costume

OUR GREAT-GREAT-GRANDMOTHER.

Peter and Mary are able to enter their 'true dream' and mix with their
great-great-grandmother

manual, Gatienne stands beside the Abbaye wall training fruit trees:
foutre en espalier describes what is euphemistically called a 'standing
embrace'. In this case 'great-great-' in the illustration's title must be
taken ironically and it can be understood to represent George Du Maurier's *English* grandmother (note that one of her daughters holds a pruning
knife to her mother's back). In modern terms we could say that *Ibbetson*
portrays the author's male and female 'selves' as a consequence of the
fascination/repulsion that his once-notorious grandmother inspired.

The rather explicit cipher in which Du Maurier composed his first
novel has apparently gone undetected, allowing his contemporaries to
assure that his humour was never coarse. In a sense, the readers best
equipped to perceive the cipher were his five children who knew French,
knew something of family history and knew their father's turn of mind.

As a child Daphne Du Maurier met all four of her father's siblings,
but by her eighth birthday only her father and his youngest sister May

survived. What Daphne perceived as Gerald's relative lack of interest in French family history may have masked a reluctance to confront some of what he knew.

When Daphne approached family history after her father's death, she sensed the importance of both *Peter Ibbetson* on the one hand and Mary Anne Clarke on the other, yet never recognised her ancestress's deeply disguised presence in the novel. One can only wonder whether if Daphne had deciphered her grandfather's novel, it might have alleviated some of her angst over what she called her 'No. 2 self' or 'the boy in the box'.

The Mare d'Auteuil, Loch Ness and Mars

Peter Ibbetson's central motif is the Mare d'Auteuil in the Bois de Boulogne. In Du Maurier's illustration Peter and Mary's mothers – *la belle Madame Pasquier* and *la divine Madame Seraskier* – are seated on the bench by the old willow as their children and friends fish in the pond. Peter comments 'La Mare d'Auteuil! the very name has a magic, from all the associations that gathered round it during that time, to cling for ever.'

One obvious association with the French *mare* is the English 'mare', particularly in the context of the ciphered trade of farriery. The English 'mare' is a homophone of *mère* (mother), and Peter adds that 'In after years, and far away among the cold fogs of Clerkenwell, when the frequent longing would come over me to revisit "the pretty place of my birth", it was for the Mare d'Auteuil I longed the most'.[358]

Shelley's 'Ode to the West Wind' is pastiched in *Ibbetson*, and Du Maurier was apparently aware that in many ancient sources such as Virgil's *Georgics*, mares were said to conceive by the west wind. This myth underlies the chronicler Brantôme's facetious comparison of certain promiscuous married ladies to mares on the borders of Andalusia, who 'set their natural opening against the wind blowing in these plains, which doth so enter in and assuageth their heat and getteth them with foal'.[359]

George Du Maurier's last two novels are not intricately ciphered as the first; there does not appear to be any hidden equine imagery, for example. Water imagery, however, is central to all three novels.

Trilby's 'pedigree' bears comparison to that of the 'small *female* child' who relives in Peter. The small girl's father, 'the red-heeled gentleman', makes her believe she can manufacture little cocked hats in coloured glass, and his 'never-still small voice' sings unremittingly in Peter's head. Similarly, Trilby tells Little Billee that 'My father sang like a bird. He was a gentleman and a scholar, my father was. His name was Patrick Michael O'Ferrall, Fellow of Trinity, Cambridge. He used to sing "Ben Bolt".'[360]

Trilby's mother was a barmaid at the *Montagnards Écossais* (Scottish Highlanders) bar in Paris, and

> *Her* parents weren't married at all. Her mother was the daughter of a boatman on Loch Ness, near a place called Drumnadrochit; but her father was the Honourable Colonel Desmond. He was related to all sorts of great people in England and Ireland. He behaved very badly to my grandmother and to poor mamma – his own daughter! deserted them both! Not very *honourable* of him, *was* it? And that's all I know about him.

Where the maternal grandfather of the 'small *female* child' is a *gentilhomme verrier* who dies of a wolf bite during his wife's pregnancy, here, similarly but less dramatically, 'the Honourable Colonel Desmond' deserts his mistress and their daughter. Trilby turns out 'to be a kind of cousin (though on the wrong side of the blanket) to no less a person than the famous Duchess of Towers'.[361] Indeed, Peter's female alter ego Mary's mother's maiden name was Laura Desmond, containing a near-anagram of 'Desdemona'.

Turning from *Trilby* to *The Martian*, Barty himself wonders about Martia:

> Who and what could Martia be?
>
> The reminiscence of some antenatal incarnation of his own soul? the soul of some ancestor or ancestress – of his mother, perhaps? or, perhaps, some occult portion of himself – of his own brain in unconscious cerebration during sleep?
>
> As a child and a small boy, and even as a very young man, he had often dreamt at night of a strange, dim land by the sea, a land unlike any land he had ever beheld with the waking eye, where beautiful aquatic people, mermen and mermaids and charming little merchildren (of which he was one) lived an amphibious life by day, diving and sporting in the waves.[362]

The reader learns that Martia has successively inhabited Barty's father Lord Runswick (the son of the Marquis of Whitby, of distant Breton origin), his mistress Antoinette Josselin (the daughter of toilers of the sea near Dieppe), their son Barty, Barty's wife Leah and, finally, Barty and Leah's daughter, Marty.

Although it is Du Maurier's least successful novel, *The Martian* is of interest for family history, in part because unlike the author's previous heroes Peter and Little Billee, Barty marries and becomes a father and grandfather. Barty and Leah have nine children to George and Emma Du Maurier's actual five: some of them play small roles in the novel, where they are collectively described as 'festive and frolicsome young Bartys of either sex'.[363]

Du Maurier drew both Beatrice and Sylvia as 'nightingales' seated at the piano: Beatrice in 'The Two Thrones' (published in *Punch* on 7 June 1879), and Sylvia as *la rossignolle* Mary Trevor in the illustration '*Quand on perd, par triste occurrence*' in *The Martian*. At the time of his death, the novelist also had five grandchildren, all boys, the oldest of whom was ten. Young Geoffrey Millar had modelled for the illustration 'O Nightingale', showing Peter Ibbetson in his crib, enthralled by his father's voice. A few years later young Jack Davies was depicted in the identical position, in a *Punch* cartoon on a different theme ('A Fortiori', 8 June 1895).

The text of *The Martian* includes a letter 'From George Du Maurier, Esqre., A.R.W.S., Hampstead Heath, to the Right Honble. Sir Robert Maurice, Bart., M.P.', the narrator. The end of the letter mentions Barty's children briefly, and the writer adds that 'I'm told the grandchildren are splendid – chips of the old block too.'[364]

END NOTES

1 D. Du Maurier, Preface to *The Glass-Blowers*, *TLS* 5447/8 (24/31 August 2007), p. 18

2 R. de Linière and P. Cordonnier, 'Les Origines sarthoises de l'auteur de *Les Du Maurier*, roman anglais, et les maîtres-verriers sarthois', *Revue du Maine*, 26 (1956), pp. 204–12

3 O. Malet, ed. *Letters from Menabilly* (London: Weidenfeld & Nicolson, 1993), p. 58

4 D. Du Maurier, *The Glass-Blowers* (London: Gollancz, 1963), p. 15

5 Malet, p. 133

6 Malet, p. 131

7 Daphne uses the accepted expression *folie de grandeur*. Throughout I have reverted to the original French expression *folie des grandeurs*

8 Mary first explains to Peter that 'my dear father had learned a strange secret of the brain – how in sleep to recall past things and people and places as they had once been seen or known by him – even unremembered things. He called it "dreaming true"….' G. Du Maurier, *Peter Ibbetson* (London: Gollancz, 1969), p. 224.

9 *Ibbetson*, p. 314

10 Sophie's letter is reproduced in my book *Sur les pas de Daphné Du Maurier* (Vendôme: Cherche-Lune, 2010), pp. 170–2. In this and other references, unless otherwise indicated, all translations are my own.

11 For the Labbé genealogy, see P. Robert, *L'Ascendance française de Daphné Du Maurier (Maine-Touraine)* (Tours: Centre Généalogique de Touraine, 1993), p. 37

12 See *Sur les pas de Daphné Du Maurier*, p. 170

13 *The Glass-Blowers*, p. 21

14 *L'Ascendance française*, p. 12

15 *The Glass-Blowers*, p. 33

16 See C. Léger, 'La Verrerie de la Brûlonnerie à Busloup', *Éclats de verre*, 18 (November 2011), pp. 18–28

17 At the time of the premiere, Louis-Philippe was Duke of Chartres; he received the title Duke of Orleans on the death of his father in 1785

18 The blue ribbon signified that the duke was a Knight of the Order of the Holy Spirit. The badge of the order, a Maltese cross with four gold fleur-de-lys between its arms and a descending dove in the centre, hangs from the blue ribbon.

19 *Sur les pas de Daphné Du Maurier*, pp. 170–71

20 The legend is reprinted in P. Vallerange, *Curiosités percheronnes et beauceronnes* (Paris: Passard, 1861)

21 From a typed transcript of Mathurin-Robert Busson's letter, dated 9 May 1787, held by the Du Maurier Manuscripts Collection (hereafter DMM), Heritage Collections, University of Exeter, ref. EUL MS 144/1/9/3

22 DMM, ref. EUL MS 144/1/9/3

23 National Archives T 93/29

24 M. Weiner, *The French Exiles, 1789–1815* (London: John Murray, 1960), p. 124

25 DMM

26 National Archives T 93/28

27 National Archives PRIS 10/51

28 National Archives PRIS 4/16

29 National Archives T 93/16

30 *The French Exiles*, pp. 102–03

31 National Archives T 93/17 and T 93/19

32 National Archives T 93/20

33 On Pierre Busson's career as a notary, see also M. Mémin, 'De la famille des verriers, Pierre Busson, un curieux notaire', *Revue historique et archéologique du Maine* (1968), pp. 192–204

34 See C. Léger, 'La Verrerie de Rougemont à Saint-Jean-Froidmentel', *Éclats de verre*, 15, (May 2010), pp. 7–15

35 *Sur les pas de Daphné Du Maurier*, p. 132

36 A. Rousselin, 'Le Clergé français pendant la persécution révolutionnaire', *Études*, 68, 4e série, t. 1, p. 557

37 The autobiographical fragment is found in a notebook at DMM, ref. EUL MS 207/2/3/2

38 *Ibbetson*, p. 35

39 *The Universal Magazine of Knowledge and Pleasure*, Vol. LXXXIII (October 1788), p. 219

40 *Ibbetson*, p. 238

41 Louise Wallace's copy of her husband's baptism is included in her great-niece Sybil Martyn's scrapbook held in the O'Carrol Papers, Glucksman Library, University of Limerick

42 This record is held by the India Office, British Library, L/MIL/9/111 f.190

43 See 'Richardson v. Wallace' in *The Globe*, 14 December 1808

44 J. Grant, 'Story of a Hussar of the Regency', *The Ross-shire Buffs* (London: George Routledge, 1878), p. 203

45 W. Wallace, *Memoirs of William Wallace, Esq.* (London: W. Simpkin, 1821), pp. 8–9

46 *Memoirs*, p. 11

47 *Memoirs*, pp. 18–19

48 *Memoirs*, p. 19

49 The British Library has a copy of an anonymous pamphlet entitled *Life of Mary Kent, alias Mrs Bertram, well known in the fashionable circles as Mother Bang* (London: Duncombe, s.d.)

50 *Memoirs*, pp. 27–30

51 *Memoirs*, p. 58

52 'Story of a Hussar', p. 210

53 'Story of a Hussar', pp. 210–11

54 *Memoirs*, p. 22

55 *Memoirs*, p. 156

56 11 March 1823, *Morning Post*

57 P. Berry, *By Royal Appointment* (London: Femina, 1970), pp. 216–17

58 A. Milman, *Henry Hart Milman DD Dean of St Paul's: A Biographical Sketch* (London: John Murray, 1900), pp. 45–46

59 11 October 1815, *Bury and Norwich Post*

60 23 October 1815, *Hampshire Chronicle*

61 11 December 1816, *Bury and Norwich Post*

62 29 July 1817, *Manchester Mercury*

63 13 November 1817, *Cheltenham Chronicle*

64 See Chapter I, 'L'Affaire Burke/ Clarke', in W.L. McLendon, *Une ténébreuse carrière sous l'Empire et la Restauration: Le comte de Courchamps* (Paris: Minard, 1980), pp. 25–53

65 N. Tolstoy, *The Half-Mad Lord. Thomas Pitt, 2ⁿᵈ Baron Camelford (1775–1804)* (New York: Holt, Rinehart and Winston, 1979)

66 M. Anne-Élie-Pierre-Jean Commaille was a wealthy lawyer who had begun buying the property in 1813. In 1816 he leased part of it to the Prince of Belmonte-Pignatelli, a Sicilian aristocrat who was a counsellor to the tsar. See B. de Andia and D. Fernandès, *Rue du Faubourg-Saint-Honoré* (Paris: s.d.), pp. 128–30.

67 12 August 1824, *Devizes and Wiltshire Gazette*

68 29 September 1826, *Stamford Mercury*

69 Archives Nationales AJ/37/322,3

70 Unpublished autobiographical fragment, DMM, ref. EUL MS 207/2/3/2

71 G. de Stacpoole, *Irish and Other Memories* (London: A.M. Philpot, 1822), p. 8.

72 *Ibbetson*, p. 263

73 R.H. Sherard, 'The Author of *Trilby*. An Autobiographic Interview with Mr. George Du Maurier', *McClure's Magazine*, IV:5 (April 1895), p. 393

74 Archives Nationales MC/ET/ XXX/761

75 M. Serval, *A l'ombre de Sophie Arnould. François-Joseph Bélanger, architecte des Menus-Plaisirs. Premier architecte du comte d'Artois*, II (Paris: Plon, 1930), pp. 17–37

76 Letter from J.-L. Busson Du Maurier to M. von Struve, 29 December 1845

77 The summary is found in H. Schroeder, ed., *Lexikon der hamburgischen Schriftsteller bis zur Gegenwart*, Vol. 1 (Hamburg: Perthes-Besser and Mauke, 1851). Jacques-Louis's name is erroneously listed as 'Jean Louis'.

78 DMM, ref. EUL MS 207/2/3/2

79 M. Telles da Gama, *Le Comte-Amiral Vasco da Gama* (Paris: A. Roger and F. Chernoviz, 1902), Appendix B, pp. 176–88

80 The reference of the letters is DMM,

EUL MS 207/1/1

81 *Description des machines et procédés consignés dans les brevets d'invention, de perfectionnement et d'importation tombés dans le domaine public, II* (Brussels: Montagne de Dion, 1839), p. 103

82 Letter from L.-M. Du Maurier to Louise Wallace, 19 October 1835, DMM

83 On the breach of promise court case, see *The London and Paris Observer*, Vol. II (1826), pp. 840–42

84 14 November 1829, *Dublin Morning Register*

85 5 December 1829, *Dublin Morning Register*

86 V. Chambers, ed. *Old Men Remember Life on Victoria's Smaller Island: Memories of the Isle of Wight* (Ventnor: Ventnor & District Local History Society, 1988), p. 18

87 See C. Gogarty, *From Village to Suburb: The Building of Clontarf since 1760* (Dublin: Clontarf Books, 2013), pp. 9–11

88 Letter from L.-M. Du Maurier to Louise Wallace, 11 July 1854, DMM

89 Letter from L.-M. Du Maurier to Louise Wallace, 3 December 1854, DMM

90 J. Holdsworth, *Geology, Minerals, Mines & Soils of Ireland* (London: Houlston & Wright, 1857), p. 198

91 Sherard, p. 396

92 Sherard, p. 393

93 J. de Campos e Sousa, 'Palmela e os Du Maurier – Reparos a uma obra de Daphne Du Maurier', *Arqueologia e Historia*, Vol. 12 (1966), p. 171

94 Sherard, p. 393

95 Sherard, p. 394

96 Letter from G. Du Maurier to Henry James, 18 September 1884, Houghton Library, Harvard University

97 'New Music', *The Ladies' Companion*, Vol. XIII, 2nd series (1858), p. 330

98 Sherard, p. 394

99 Letter from L.-M. Du Maurier to Louise Wallace, 10 October 1841, DMM

100 D. Du Maurier, ed. *The Young George Du Maurier: A Selection of his Letters, 1860–67* (London: Peter Davis, 1951), p. 192

101 Sherard, p. 394

102 Letter from L.-M. Du Maurier to Louise Wallace, 6 March 1842, DMM

103 *The Young Du Maurier*, 272. *Déménager* is 'to move house'; 'déménagéd' is an Anglo-French neologism

104 *Ibbetson*, p. 30

105 M.W. Oborne, *A History of the Château de la Muette* (Paris: OECD, 1998), p. 94

106 W. Gibson, *Rambles in Europe in 1839* (Philadelphia, PA: Lea and Blanchard, 1841), p. 86

107 Unpublished autobiographical fragment, DMM, ref. EUL MS 207/2/3/2

108 *Ibbetson*, p. 34

109 Unpublished autobiographical fragment, DMM, ref. EUL MS 207/2/3/2

110 A version of this episode with

a priest and with '*Stabat Mater dolorosa*' appears in *The Martian* (London: Harper & Brothers, 1898), pp. 105–06

111 *The Young Du Maurier*, p. 272

112 *Ibbetson*, p. 29

113 Unpublished autobiographical fragment, DMM, ref. EUL MS 207/2/3/2

114 See Y. Armand, 'Jean-Baptiste Froussard (1792–1848), fondateur de l'École Latine à Montfleury', *Bulletin de l'Académie delphinale* (March–April 1992), pp. 49–54

115 *The Martian*, p. 22

116 This extract and the one that follows are from *The Martian*, p. 67

117 *The Martian*, pp. 75–6

118 *The Martian*, p. 69

119 *The Martian*, pp. 82–3

120 Sherard, p. 394

121 L.M. Lamont, *Thomas Armstrong, C.B.: A Memoir 1832–1911* (London: Martin Secker, 1912), p. 148

122 'Mr Du Maurier at New Grove House, Hampstead', *The Western Daily Press*, 20 August 1884

123 *The Martian*, pp. 141–2

124 *The Martian*, p. 144

125 *The Young Du Maurier*, p. 56

126 *The Martian*, p. 145

127 Sherard, p. 396

128 'Recollections of an English Gold Mine', *Once A Week*, V (21 September 1861), p. 364

129 *Thomas Armstrong, C.B.*, p. 161

130 Letter from L.-M. Du Maurier to Louise Wallace, 5 November 1843, DMM

131 Letter from E. Du Maurier to George Du Maurier, 12 July 1856, DMM

132 Sherard, p. 397

133 E. Marshall, 'Author of *Trilby*', *Galveston Daily News*, 6 May 1895

134 *Thomas Armstrong, C.B.*, p. 149

135 L. Ionides, *Memories* (Ludlow: Dog Rose Press, 1996), pp. 63–4

136 V. Prinsep, 'A Student's Life in Paris in 1859', *The Magazine of Art* (1904), Second Series, p. 340

137 *Trilby*, p. 52

138 J.D. Barry, 'All About *Trilby*', *Galveston Daily News*, 3 December 1894

139 E.R. and J. Pennell, *The Life of James McNeill Whistler* (Philadelphia, PA: J.B. Lippincott, 1908), Vol. 1, p. 56

140 Ionides, *Memories*, p. 8

141 See *Thomas Armstrong, C.B.*, pp. 191–3. The song, '*Les Amours du siècle*', is published in *Nouvelle Lyre canadienne: Recueil de chansons canadiennes et françaises* (Montreal?: s.n., 1882), pp. 256–9.

142 See the entries for 'tart' and 'double-barrelled' in J.S. Farmer and W.E. Henley, *Slang and its Analogues past and present* (s.l.: s.n., 1903)

143 *Trilby*, p. 52

144 *Trilby*, p. 198

145 *Trilby*, p. 205

146 *Thomas Armstrong, C.B.*, p. 116

147 *The Martian*, p. 189

148 D. Du Maurier, *The Du Mauriers* (London: Gollancz, 1937), p. 264

149 L. Ormond, *George Du Maurier* (London: Routledge and Kegan Paul, 1969), p. 63

150 *The Martian*, p. 190

151 F. Moscheles, *In Bohemia with Du Maurier* (New York: Harper & Brothers, 1897), pp. 83–4

152 *The Martian*, p. 194

153 *The Martian*, pp. 196–7

154 *The Martian*, p. 214

155 *The Martian*, p. 217

156 Moscheles pp. 34–5 and 45

157 *The Martian*, p. 226

158 G. Du Maurier, *Social Pictorial Satire* (London: Harper & Brothers, 1898), pp. 15–16

159 *The Martian*, p. 252

160 Moscheles, p. 45

161 Moscheles, pp. 47–8

162 Moscheles, p. 59

163 *The Martian*, pp. 264–5

164 Sherard, p. 398

165 *The Martian*, p. 277

166 *The Martian*, pp. 281–2

167 *The Martian*, p. 286

168 M. Raine, 'All the Year Round at Graefrath' (1859), MS Stadtarchiv Solingen, Germany

169 'All the Year Round at Graefrath', p. 13

170 Letter from G. Du Maurier to Mrs Fortescue, May 1860, Morgan

171 *The Martian*, p. 317

172 See *Thomas Armstrong, C.B.*, p. 147

173 Letter from E. Du Maurier to Louise Wallace, 14 July 1859, DMM

174 'Mr George Du Maurier at New Grove House, Hampstead', *Whitby Gazette*, 21 August 1891

175 *The Young Du Maurier*, p. 14

176 *Thomas Armstrong, C.B.*, p. 151

177 *The Young Du Maurier*, p. 16

178 *The Young Du Maurier*, p. 27

179 5 April 1896, Glasgow University Library

180 *Ibbetson*, p. 99

181 *Trilby*, pp. 227–8

182 *Thomas Armstrong, C.B.*, p. 148

183 *The Young Du Maurier*, p. 44

184 *The Young Du Maurier*, p. 101

185 *The Young Du Maurier*, pp. 117 and 124

186 *The Young Du Maurier*, p. 134

187 *The Young Du Maurier*, p. 136 and 143–4

188 *The Young Du Maurier*, facing p. 177

189 *The Young Du Maurier*, p. 161. For more information on George's early years in London, see also Chapter 4 of Leonee Ormond's biography.

190 *The Martian*, pp. 335–7

191 *The Young Du Maurier*, p. 182

192 *The Young Du Maurier*, p. 232

193 C.C. Hoyer Millar, *George Du Maurier and Others* (London: Cassell, 1937), p. 8

194 *The Young Du Maurier*, pp. 237 and 241

195 *The Young Du Maurier*, p. 246

196 *The Young Du Maurier*, pp. 251 and 252

197 *The Young Du Maurier*, p. 258

198 *Punch*, 6 January 1866

199 *Punch*, 20 January 1866

200 Millar, pp. 33–4 and 235

201 *Punch*, 15 September 1866

202 *The Young Du Maurier*, p. 271

203 *The Young Du Maurier*, p. 274

204 *The Martian*, p. 30

205 A character in Henry James's novel *The Princess Casamassima* who was partly based on Du Maurier is called Hyacinth Robinson

206 *The Martian*, p. 28

207 *The Martian*, 18, 149, 243 and 386–7

208 E.G.S. Reilly, *Historical Anecdotes of the Boleynes, Careys, Mordaunts, Hamiltons and Jocelyns* (Newry: J. Henderson, 1839), p. 112

209 Letter from E. Du Maurier to George Du Maurier, 29 May 1871, DMM

210 *The Martian*, pp. 433–5

211 Millar, p. 34

212 'Girls' Gossip', *Dundee Evening Telegraph*, 4 August 1884

213 Millar, p. 45

214 Letter from G. Du Maurier to Emma Du Maurier, 12 May 1886, jmbarrie.co.uk

215 Letter from H. James to George Du Maurier, 27 November 1890, Houghton Library, Harvard University

216 H. James, 'George Du Maurier' in *Harper's New Monthly Magazine* (September 1897), pp. 604–05

217 Letter from G. Du Maurier to Henry James, 5 February 1892, Houghton Library, Harvard University

218 'Du Maurier's Joke on His Wife', *Salt Lake Tribune*, 25 October 1896

219 M. Tree, 'Herbert and I', *Herbert Beerbohm Tree: Some Memories* (London: Hutchinson, 1920), p. 99

220 L. Irving, *The Successors* (London: Rupert-Hart Davis, 1967), p. 209

221 *The Successors*, p. 231

222 *The Daily Telegraph*, 1 November 1895

223 *The Successors*, p. 232; a slightly abridged version of this letter appeared in *The Daily Telegraph*

224 The paragraph is taken from J. Payn, 'Our Note Book' in *The Illustrated London News*, 17 October 1896

225 'Du Maurier's Last Work', *Dundee Advertiser*, 1 December 1896

226 W.S. Meadmore, 'A morning with Sir Gerald Du Maurier', *The Windsor Magazine*, Vol. 76, p. 694

227 *Millar*, p. 82

228 Sybil Martyn's scrapbook is held with the O'Carrol Papers, Glucksman Library, University of Limerick

229 'Fashionable Amateur Concert at the Congress Hall,' *The Whitby Gazette*, 10 September 1887

230 'Morgiana', *The Era*, 16 January 1892

231 'Provincial Theatricals', *The Era*, 15 April 1893

232 A. Birkin, *J.M. Barrie and the Lost Boys* (New Haven, CT: Yale University Press, 2003), p. 51

233 *Millar*, p. 235

234 'A morning with Sir Gerald Du Maurier', p. 699

235 G.B. Crozier, 'A Dressing-Room Chat with Mr Gerald Du Maurier', *Strand Magazine*, Vol. 60, p. 379

236 'A Dressing-Room Chat', p. 380

237 'A morning with Sir Gerald Du Maurier', p. 699

238 E. Barrymore, *Memories, An Autobiography* (New York: Harper, 1955), pp. 88–91. Actually the Duchess of Towers was an exact portrait of Du Maurier's oldest daughter Beatrice, according to her husband's memoir.

239 A. Du Maurier, *It's Only the Sister* (Truro: Truran, 2003), p. 9

240 'The Stage', *Munsey's Magazine* (October 1898), pp. 144–5

241 L. Irving, *The Successors* (London: Rupert-Hart Davis, 1967), p. 260

242 R. Blathwayt, *Does the Theatre make for Good?* (London: A.W. Hall, 1898), pp. 3–7

243 Citations from Harris's *My Life and Loves*, Volume 4

244 C. Scott, 'The Drama of the Dustbin', *The Free Lance* (3 November 1900), pp. 10–11

245 S. Morley, *Gladys Cooper: A Biography* (London: Heinemann, 1979), p. 92

246 J. Harding, *Gerald Du Maurier* (London: Hodder & Stoughton, 1989), p. 48

247 'A Dressing-Room Chat', p. 381

248 Birkin, pp. 83–4

249 'A Dressing-Room Chat', p. 381

250 A. Du Maurier, *Old Maids Remember* (London: Peter Davies, 1966), pp. 140–41

251 Birkin, p. 109

252 *Only the Sister*, 14

253 J. Wightman, 'Mr Gerald Du Maurier', *The Playgoer and Society Illustrated*, Vol. 2, p. 31

254 DuMaurier Company, advertisement, *Magic Eyes*, 1936

255 M. Strickland, *Angela Thirkell: Portrait of a Lady Novelist* (London: Duckworth, 1977), p. 12

256 *The Martian*, p. 89

257 The family tree in the front pages of *The Du Mauriers* shows one grandchild for Eugene and Marie Rosalie Du Maurier. In fact, Marie Madeleine's daughter Marcelle was their second grandchild, since Marie Madeleine's brother Ralph is the presumed father of Eugene Du Maurier, born in Canada in 1894.

258 'From the Bookshelves', *The Playgoer and Society Illustrated*, Vol. 2, p. 176

259 On Guy Du Maurier's military career see S. Cooper, *The Final Whistle: The Great War in Fifteen*

Players (Stroud: Spellmount, 2012), pp. 36–53

260 Harding, pp. 76–7

261 'The Story of *The Perplexed Husband*', *The Playgoer and Society Illustrated*, Vol. 5, pp. 74–76

262 D. Du Maurier, *Gerald: A Portrait* (London: Gollancz, 1934), p. 230

263 D. Du Maurier, 'The Matinée Idol', *The Rebecca Notebook and Other Memories* (London: Gollancz, 1981), p. 72

264 *Only the Sister*, p. 64

265 'Diplomacy at Her Majesty's Theatre', *Dundee Evening Telegraph*, 21 October 1913

266 'Our London Letter', *The Manchester Courier*, 6 September 1915

267 'Matinée Idol', p. 67

268 Millar, pp. 219–20

269 Millar, p. 225

270 *Gerald: A Portrait*, p. 165

271 Millar, pp. 235–6

272 'Matinée Idol', p. 73

273 *Gerald: A Portrait*, pp. 178 and 180

274 'A morning with Sir Gerald Du Maurier', p. 690

275 D. Mackail, *The Story of J.M.B.* (London: Peter Davies, 1941), p. 521

276 'Young actresses in a children's play at Wyndham's Theatre', 26 June 1918, *The Daily Mirror*; J. Dunn, *Daphne Du Maurier and Her Sisters* (London: HarperPress, 2013), p. 23

277 'A morning with Sir Gerald Du Maurier', p. 701

278 'Matinée Idol', pp. 75–76

279 *The Scotsman*, 30 September 1930

280 *Only the Sister*, p. 25

281 W.A. Darlington, *Six Thousand and One Nights* (London: Harrap, 1960), p. 102

282 *Only the Sister*, p. 60

283 *Only the Sister*, p. 86

284 *Only the Sister*, p. 78

285 'Edgar Wallace's Way', *The Yorkshire Evening Post*, 16 October 1931

286 *Gerald: A Portrait*, p. 263

287 E.V. Wallace, *Edgar Wallace by His Wife* (London: Hutchinson, 1932), pp. 203–06

288 M. Forster, *Daphne Du Maurier* (London: Chatto & Windus, 1993), p. 13

289 *The Martian*, pp. 413–5 and 444

290 *Only the Sister*, pp. 75–6, 80 and 177

291 Dunn, p. 77

292 S. Tiernan, *Eva Gore-Booth: An Image of Such Politics* (Manchester: Manchester University Press, 2012), p. 1

293 Tiernan, p. 224

294 From a letter cited in Forster, p. 421

295 A. Napier, *Not Just Batman's Butler* (Jefferson, NC: McFarland, 2015), p. 61

296 'Bull-Dog Drummond', *The Era*, 30 March 1921

297 Napier, p. 138

298 J. Stokes, 'Body parts: the success of the thriller in the inter-war years' in

British Theatre between the Wars, 1918–1939 (Cambridge: Cambridge University Press, 2000), pp. 41 and 46

299 'Body parts', pp. 48–9

300 'The Garden Party', *The Stage*, 24 June 1926

301 D. Du Maurier, *Growing Pains: The Shaping of a Writer* (London: Gollancz, 1977), p. 98

302 'Body parts', p. 53

303 Napier, p. 124

304 'A morning with Sir Gerald Du Maurier', pp. 692–3

305 H.N. Southern, *Close-Ups of Birds* (London: Hutchinson, 1932), pp. 7–9. Thanks to Xavier Lachazette for bringing this book to my attention.

306 *The Surrey Mirror*, 8 June 1834

307 Preface to *The Glass-Blowers*, p. 18

308 H. Doe, *Jane Slade of Polruan* (Truro: Truran, 2002), p. 8

309 *Gerald: A Portrait*, 272. Angela's two memoirs confirm this refrain.

310 Forster, p. 115

311 Millar, p. 240

312 *Only the Sister*, p. 170

313 Malet, 'Prologue: A Loving Spirit' in *Letters from Menabilly*, pp. 16–17

314 *Gerald: A Portrait*, pp. 187–91

315 Forster, pp. 125–6

316 Genealogical and historical details concerning the Palmella family are corrected in J. de Campos e Sousa, 'Palmela e os Du Maurier – Reparos a uma obra de Daphne Du Maurier', *Arqueologia e História*, vol. 12, 1966, pp. 151–80

317 M. Holroyd, Introduction to *The Du Mauriers* (London: Virago, 2004), p. x

318 G. Du Maurier, Preface to *Trilby* (London: J.M. Dent, 1931), p. vii

319 *Ibbetson* make extensive use of literary pastiche and the Biblical phrase 'as in a glass darkly' appears twice, both times in relation to 'dreaming true', pp. 75 and 281.

320 *The Du Mauriers*, pp. 145–6

321 D. Du Maurier, Introduction to *The Martian*, *The Novels of George Du Maurier* (London: The Pilot Press, 1947), p. xvii

322 *The Young Du Maurier*, p. xx

323 A 'peg' is 'Someone whom one momentarily invests with romantic glamour, but more particularly as the inspiration for a fictional character' according to O. Malet's glossary in *Letters from Menabilly*, p. x

324 Forster, 421

325 Dunn, p. 157

326 Malet, p. 37

327 W.S. Meadmore, 'A morning with Sir Gerald Du Maurier', *Windsor Magazine*, 76 (1932), 695

328 Forster, p. 274

329 *Du Mauriers*, p. 145

330 *The Young Du Maurier*, pp. 14–15

331 Sherard, p. 393

332 *Ibbetson*, p. 278

333 *Ibbetson*, pp. 266; 271; 274

334 Malet, p. 56

335 Daphne chose to use an archaic form of the French expression for 'the queen of Hungary'

336 *The Glass-Blowers*, pp. 30–33

337 *The Glass-Blowers*, pp. 39–41

338 *Growing Pains*, p. 59

339 D. Du Maurier, *The Scapegoat* (London: Gollancz, 1957), p. 208

340 *Ibbetson*, p. 306

341 Malet, p. 85

342 Mathurin-Robert is not shown on Peter's pedigree, but he is nonetheless discreetly present in the novel, via 'The Chime', the last poem Peter composes before committing parricide. Its theme is 'a medieval prisoner who cannot sleep' and who sets words to the tune of a chime. Peter 'tried to fancy that his name was Pasquier de la Marière, and that he was my ancestor.' Peter's poem ends with the lines 'I know that he,/ My luckless lone forefather, dust so long,/ Relives his life in me!'

343 *Ibbetson*, p. 174

344 The implied meaning of this image in *Ibbetson* is in many points comparable to E. Jones's interpretation of 'The Madonna's Conception through the Ear', *Essays in Applied Psychoanalysis II* (London: Hogarth Press, 1951), pp. 266–357

345 H. Ouvré, *Aubéry Du Maurier. Ministre de France à La Haye* (Paris: Auguste Durand, 1855)

346 See A. Racinet, *Le Costume historique V* (Paris: Firmin-Didot, 1888)

347 *Ibbetson*, pp. 266–9

348 See A. Bourreau, *The Lord's First Night: The Myth of the Droit de Cuissage* (Chicago: University of Chicago Press, 1998), pp. 59–66

349 The French equivalent of the catchphrase 'a blot on one's escutcheon' refers to *de la merde au bout du bâton*

350 With the addition of the horses, Vernie's series of portraits of royal mistresses is comparable to the Hampton Court and Windsor Beauties, discreetly alluded to in *Ibbetson*, p. 102

351 Du Maurier's interest in dragonnades and conversion plays on the fact that in French slang *changer de religion* has a sexual meaning

352 *Ibbetson*, p. 269

353 *Ibbetson*, p. 269

354 *Ibbetson*, p. 38

355 A. de Pontmartin, *Entre chien et loup* (Paris: Michel Lévy, 1866)

356 *Ibbetson*, p. 278

357 *Ibbetson*, p. 270

358 *Ibbetson*, pp. 32-33

359 From Alfred Richard Allison's translation of *The Lives of Fair and Gallant Ladies*

360 *Trilby*, p. 20

361 *Trilby*, pp. 401–02

362 *The Martian*, p. 267

363 *The Martian*, p. 404

364 *The Martian*, pp. 348–52

SELECTED
BIBLIOGRAPHY

Unpublished Sources

George Du Maurier, autobiographical fragment, Du Maurier Family Papers, Heritage Collections, University of Exeter Library

Letter from Mathurin-Robert Busson to M. de Montaran, Du Maurier Family Papers

Letters from Louis-Mathurin Busson Du Maurier to Louise Wallace, Du Maurier Family Papers

Letters from Eugene Du Maurier to George Du Maurier, Du Maurier Family Papers

Letters from Eugene Du Maurier to Louise Wallace, Du Maurier Family Papers

Letter from George Du Maurier to Louisa Margaret Fortescue, Morgan Library and Museum, New York

Letters from George Du Maurier to Henry James, Houghton Library, Harvard University

Letter from Madeleine Fargeaud to Daphne Du Maurier, Du Maurier Family Papers

Letters from Henry James to George Du Maurier, Houghton Library, Harvard University

Margaret Raine, 'All the Year Round at Graefrath', MS Stadtarchiv Solingen, Germany

Scrapbook of Sybil Martyn, O'Carrol Papers, Glucksman Library, University of Limerick Special Collections

Published Sources

Anon., 'Historical Chronicle', *The Universal Magazine of Knowledge and Pleasure*, Vol. LXXXIII (October 1788)

Paul Berry, *By Royal Appointment: A Biography of Mary Ann Clarke, Mistress of the Duke of York* (Femina, 1970)

Andrew Birkin, *J.M. Barrie and the Lost Boys* (Yale, 2003)

Pierre de Bourdeille, Seigneur de Brantôme, *The Lives of Gallant Ladies* (Panther, 1965)

Alain Bourreau, *The Lord's First Night: The Myth of the Droit de Cuissage* (Chicago, 1998)

Kirsty Carpenter, *Refugees of the French Revolution: Émigrés in London, 1789-1802* (Palgrave, 1999)

Simon Cooke and Paul Goldman (eds.), *George Du Maurier: Illustrator, Author, Critic* (Routledge, 2016)

Stephen Cooper, *The Final Whistle: The Great War in Fifteen Players* (Spellmount, 2012)

Helen Doe, *Jane Slade of Polruan* (Truran, 2002)

Angela Du Maurier, *It's Only the Sister: An Autobiography* (Peter Davies, 1951)

— *Old Maids Remember* (Peter Davies, 1966)

Daphne Du Maurier, *The Du Mauriers* (Gollancz, 1937)

— *Gerald: A Portrait* (Gollancz, 1934)

— *The Glass-Blowers* (Gollancz, 1963)

— *Growing Pains: The Shaping of a Writer* (Gollancz, 1977)

— 'Introduction to *The Martian*', in *Novels of George Du Maurier* (Pilot, 1947)

— *Mary Anne: A Novel* (Gollancz, 1954)

— 'Preface to *The Glass-Blowers*', TLS 5447/8, 24/31 August 2007

— *The Rebecca Notebook and Other Memories* (Gollancz, 1981)

— *The Scapegoat* (Gollancz, 1957)

— (ed.), *The Young George Du Maurier: A Selection of His Letters, 1860-67* (Peter Davies, 1951)

George Du Maurier, 'The Illustration of Books from the Serious Artist's Point of View' II, *Magazine of Art* (September 1890)

— *The Martian (Harper, 1898)*

— *Peter Ibbetson (Gollancz, 1969)*

— 'Recollections of an English Goldmine', *Once A Week* V (21 September 1861)

— *Social Pictorial Satire (Harper, 1898)*

— Trilby (Osgood, McIlvaine, 1895)

Gerald Du Maurier, 'Foreword', in H.N. Southern, *Close-Ups of Birds* (Hutchinson, 1932)

— 'Preface', in George Du Maurier, *Trilby* (J.M. Dent, 1931)

Jane Dunn, *Daphne Du Maurier and Her Sisters: The Hidden Lives of Piffy, Bird and Bing* (HarperPress, 2013)

Margaret Forster, *Daphne Du Maurier* (Chatto & Windus, 1993)

James Grant, 'Story of a Hussar of the Regency', *The Ross-Shire Buffs* (Routledge, 1878)

Anne Hall, *Sur les pas de Daphné Du Maurier: Au pays des souffleurs de verre* (Cherche-Lune, 2010)

James Harding, *Gerald Du Maurier: The Last Actor-Manager* (Hodder & Stoughton, 1989)

Michael Holroyd, 'Introduction', in Daphne Du Maurier, *The Du Mauriers* (Virago, 2004)

Luke Ionides, *Memories* (Dog Rose, 1996)

Laurence Irving, *The Successors* (Rupert-Hart Davis, 1967)

Henry James, 'George Du Maurier', *Harper's New Monthly Magazine* (September 1897)

L.M. Lamont (ed.), *Thomas Armstrong C.B.: A Memoir 1832-1911* (Martin Secker, 1912)

Christian Léger, 'La verrerie de la Brûlonnerie à Busloup', *Éclats de verre* 18 (November 2011)

— 'La verrerie de Rougemont à Saint-Jean-Froidmentel', *Éclats de verre* 15

(May 2010)

Raoul de Linère and P. Cordonnier, 'Les origines sarthoises de l'auteur de *Les Du Maurier*', *Revue du Maine* 26 (1956)

Oriel Malet (ed.), *Letters from Menabilly: Portrait of a Friendship* (Weidenfeld & Nicolson, 1993)

Will L. McLendon, *Une Ténébreuse Carrière sous l'Empire et la Restauration. Le Comte de Courchamps* (Minard, 1980)

Marcel Mémin, 'De la famille des verriers, Pierre Busson, un curieux notaire', *Revue du Maine* (1968)

Charles Christian Hoyer Millar, *George Du Maurier and Others* (Cassell, 1937)

Arthur Milman, *Henry Hart Milman DD Dean of St Paul's: A Biographical Sketch* (John Murray, 1900)

Felix Moscheles, *In Bohemia with Du Maurier* (Harper, 1897)

Alan Napier, *Not Just Batman's Butler: The Autobiography of Alan Napier* (McFarland, 2015)

Michael W. Oborne, *A History of the Château de la Muette* (OECD, 1998)

Leonee Ormond, *George Du Maurier* (Routledge, 1969)

Henri Ouvré, *Aubéry Du Maurier Ministre de France à La Haye* (Auguste Durand, 1853)

Jane Ellen Panton, *Leaves from a Life* (Eveleigh Nash, 1908)

Georges [Mathilde Georgina Elisabeth] de Peyrebrune, *Gatienne* (Calmann Levy, 1882)

Armand de Pontmartin, *Entre chien et loup* (Michel Lévy, 1866)

Valentine C. Prinsep, 'A Student's Life in Paris in 1859', *Magazine of Art* (February 1904)

Pierre Robert, *L'Ascendance française de Daphné Du Maurier (Maine-Touraine)* (Centre Généalogique de Touraine, 1993)

A. Rousselin, 'Le Clergé français pendant la persécution révolutionnaire', *Études*, 68, 4e série, t. 1

Robert H. Sherard, 'The Author of *Trilby*: An Autobiographic Interview with Mr George Du Maurier', *McClure's Magazine* IV:5

George de Stacpoole, *Irish and Other Memories* (A.M. Philpot, 1822)

John Stokes, 'Body parts: the success of the thriller in the inter-war years', in Clive Barker and Maggie B. Gale, *British Theatre between the Wars* (Cambridge, 2000)

Prosper Vallerange, *Curiosités percheronnes et beauceronnes* (Passard, 1861)

Ethel Violet Wallace, *Edgar Wallace by His Wife* (Hutchinson, 1932)

William Wallace, *Memoirs of William Wallace, Esq.* (W. Simpkin, 1821)

Margery Weiner, *The French Exiles 1789-1815* (John Murray, 1960)

Derek Winterbottom, *The Grand Old Duke of York: A Life of Prince Frederick, Duke of York and Albany, 1763-1827* (Pen & Sword, 2016)

ACKNOWLEDGEMENTS

Thank you to Dr. Christine Faunch and the staff at Heritage Collections, University of Exeter Library, where I began my research.

Thank you also to Jean-Jacques Loisel and the Éditions du Cherche-Lune, for introducing me to Christian Léger, Percheron historian, and to Colette Vion, translator, and for publishing my research into the Du Mauriers' French ancestors; thanks to Tessa Montgomery for her Preface.

And thanks to James and Kate O'Mara, for accompanying me to French 'Du Maurier country', and to James for his photographs. Thanks to Élisabeth de Montmagner, and Frédéric and Sophie de Montalembert, for welcoming us to their respective estates. Thanks to Christian Browning for his photograph of the glass.

Thanks to the following institutions: the Archives Nationales; the British Museum; the Camden Local History and Archives Centre; Departmental archives of Indre-et-Loire, Loir-et-Cher and Sarthe; Musées du Mans; the National Archives; and the National Portrait Gallery.

For their comments on drafts, thanks to Elaine Briggs and Xavier Lachazette. And especially, thanks to Ian Strathcarron, Lucy Duckworth and everyone at Unicorn Publishing Group; to Leonee Ormond, who edited this book, and to Ocky Murray, who designed it.

LIST OF ILLUSTRATIONS

Endpapers

Front Crest used by the Du Mauriers

Back Seal of Mary Anne Clarke

Back cover (clockwise from top left)

Mary Anne Clarke (née Thompson), by Adam Buck, watercolour on ivory (1803)

George du Maurier, by Sir John Everett Millais

Daphne Du Maurier, by Dorothy Wilding (1931)

Gerald Du Maurier, by Claude Harris, vintage bromide print (c. 1910s–1920s)

Picture Credits

© Chichester Partnership (pp. 2, 90, 159)

© James O'Mara (pp. 11, 12, 165)

© Domaine de la Pierre (p. 14)

© British Museum (pp. 21, 33, 40, 173)

© The National Archives (p. 23)

© Victoria and Albert Museum, London (p. 76)

© Heidelberg University Library (pp. 93, 94, 97, 103, 106, 108, 110, 114, 117)

© National Portrait Gallery (p.101 and back cover)

Courtesy of Camden Local Studies and Archives Centre (p.133)

© Musées du Mans (p. 170)

© Everett Collection Inc / Alamy Stock Photo (back cover)

© Aberdeen Art Gallery (back cover)

INDEX

Page numbers in *italics* denote photographs, those with the suffix 'n.' refer to information in the end notes section. Characters from novels are qualified by the suffix '(fictional)'.